MX 0320886 9

D0321423

This bc

Beyond Madness

Therapeutic Communites

Series editors: Rex Haigh and Jan Lees

The Therapeutic Community movement holds a multidisciplinary view of health which is based on ideas of collective responsibility, citizenship and empowerment. The tradition has a long and distinguished history and is experiencing a revival of interest in contemporary theory and practice. It draws from many different principles – including analytic, behavioural, creative, educational and humanistic – in the framework of a group-based view of the social origins and maintenance of much overwhelming distress, mental ill-health and deviant behaviour. Therapeutic Community principles are applicable in a wide variety of settings, and this series will reflect that.

Thinking About Institutions
Milieux and Madness
R.D. Hinshelwood
ISBN 1 85302 954 8
Therapeutic Communities 8

An Introduction to Therapeutic Communities
David Kennard
ISBN 1 85302 603 4
Therapeutic Communities 1

Therapeutic Communities
Past, Present and Future
Edited by Penelope Campling and Rex Haigh
ISBN 1 85302 626 3
Therapeutic Communities 2

Therapeutic Communities for the Treatment of Drug Users
Edited by Barbara Rawlings and Rowdy Yates
ISBN 1 85302 817 7
Therapeutic Communities 4

A Therapeutic Community Approach to Care in the Community
Dialogue and Dwelling
Edited by Sarah Tucker
ISBN 1 85302 751 0
Therapeutic Communities 3

Beyond Madness

PsychoSocial Interventions in Psychosis

Edited by Joseph H. Berke, Margaret Fagan,
George Mak-Pearce and Stella Pierides-Müller

Foreword by R.D. Hinshelwood

Jessica Kingsley Publishers
London and Philadelphia

A version of Chapter 6, 'The Wednesday Meeting,' previously appeared as Pierides, S. (2000) 'Working Together: Aspects of a therepeutic container ar work.' In S. Brooks and P. Hodson (eds) *The Invisible Matrix*. London: Rebus Press.
The publishers gratefully acknowledge permission to reproduce this material.

All rights reserved. No paragraph of this publication may be reproduced, copied or transmitted save with written permission of the Copyright Act 1956 (as amended), or under the terms of any licence permitting limited copying issued by the Copyright Licensing Agency, 33–34 Alfred Place, London WC1E 7DP. Any person who does any unauthorised act in relation to this publication may be liable to prosecution and civil claims for damages.

The right of the contributors to be identified as authors of this work has been asserted by them in accordance with the Copyright, Designs and Patents Act 1988.

First published in the United Kingdom in 2002 by
Jessica Kingsley Publishers Ltd,
116 Pentonville Road, London
N1 9JB, England
and
325 Chestnut Street,
Philadelphia, PA 19106, USA.

www.jkp.com

Site WH	MIDDLESEX UNIVERSITY LIBRARY	
Accession No.	0320886	
Class No.	WM 62 BEY	
Special Collection	✓	

© Copyright 2002 Jessica Kingsley Publishers

Library of Congress Cataloging in Publication Data
A CIP catalog record for this book is available from the Library of Congress

British Library Cataloguing in Publication Data
A CIP catalogue record for this book is available from the British Library

ISBN 1 85302 889 4

Printed and Bound in Great Britain by
Athenaeum Press, Gateshead, Tyne and Wear

Contents

Section 3: Narratives

Section 4: Authority and Money

Foreword

R.D. Hinshelwood

The Arbours is a self-conscious institution, aware of its history – emerging from R.D. Laing's experiments in the 1950s and 1960s – and of its continual renewal in the present. But the Arbours has taken an inward turn. It has moved on from Laing's adversarial posture towards society and the family, and, with Joe Berke's leadership, it has absorbed the psychoanalysis of the inner world into the existential philosophy of the authentic person. Authenticity is hampered by internal obstacles, internal to each person, as well as external ones from the family and society. This is R.D. Laing with balance.

In these pages there is a whole community of guests wandering in from the Arbours Crisis Centre. They are, as it were, invited here, and indeed encouraged to inform us of their stay. With them is a community of authors, those working at the Crisis Centre or longstanding friends and colleagues of the Centre. There is a sense of being amongst an in-group – an Arbours group – but a welcoming and hospitable group.

That quest for authenticity emerges all the time. Every description of a guest seems to bring to life in a personal way the whole institutional structure of persons, procedures and teams. And that is the Arbours *raison d'être*. It self-consciously stands beside, but also distinct from, mainstream psychiatry. It is about persons and their relationships; symptoms and diagnoses are secondary. Therefore a degree of opposition exists between their emphasis on relations and inner states of mind, and the general psychiatrist's focus on an ever-more mechanical conception of the suffering subject.

At the same time, there is a powerful awareness of the need to integrate these contrasting perceptions – the relational and the mechanical. Such integration is not impossible – as has been shown by the many services in Scandinavia – but there is professional and personal resistance to too much integration. And the Arbours knows where it stands. It is firm about supporting the person of the psychotic patient, and this is what brings the place to life on these pages. The guests are persons to relate to. That often means heroic battles between hope and despair within the resident therapeutic teams caring under stress with the most difficult of people. The presence of relationships, suffering and emotions is the nature of the Arbours institution.

The intense focus on conflict and struggle, for guests and for therapists, marks this as a psychoanalytic text. The idea of containing all that within an encompassing human structure is the motivating impulse for the work and for the book. It is a containing in words – à la psychoanalysis – that is paramount. Crises in the Crisis Centre are outbursts of acting-out, and the methods for containing crises are in words. Elsewhere (Hinshelwood 2000) I have speculated on a different Arbours – one where a community of guests and therapists paid attention to action as simply a part of community life, not as an extraneous intrusion, as it is in a psychoanalytic session.

It has occurred to me that if the mode of expression of neurotic patients is words and we use free associations, and the mode of expression of children is play and we use a play therapy, then the mode of expression of a psychotic is a non-symbolic communication in the form of action, whereby we must consider at least engaging with psychotics in some active mode (Hinshelwood 2001). This must lead us to some idea of therapeutic action. I would argue, too, that this is the unique opportunity of a therapy conducted as a living-together community, unlike psychoanalytic sessions. A community can only survive if a great deal of physical action is performed in maintaining the physical survival of the members (and the accommodation). If we act together in a community we are not necessarily acting-out – we are mostly surviving and flourishing. We need to have some idea of the difference between a therapeutic form of action with psychotic people in the daily living together, and a therapeutic form of action with us as therapists in the therapy room. It is distinct from an untherapeutic acting-out; and is indeed distinct from the expressive forms of therapy (art, music etc.). The key to this is that actions are not symbolic, as words are, and thus they are crucial for those people whose symbolic functions are destroyed or maimed. We have to understand that non-symbolic actions can be effective containers as well as words. Perhaps they are not as good as words, but for so many disturbed minds, symbols are beyond them: actions are their medium; and a community is an active enterprise.

The Arbours Crisis Centre is the one place where such ideas could be embarked upon. It is the one service I know that has begun to develop a psychoanalytically informed practice of containing in the living-together routines. The Crisis Centre is a thoughtful place, and a self-reflective place. This book is testimony to these attributes. Its reputation as pioneering an advanced and humane form of psychiatry is attested and confirmed by this book. Its future is to advance new ideas and try them out. Good luck to this unique enterprise as it continues to renew itself in the future.

References

Hinshelwood, R.D. (2000) 'Response to the Arbours Crisis Centre 25th Celebration.' *British Journal of Psychotherapy 17*, 215–232.

Hinshelwood, R.D. (2001) *Thinking about Institutions: Milieux and Madness.* London: Jessica Kingsley Publishers.

Contributors

Joseph H. Berke is an individual and family psychoanalytic psychotherapist. He is Founder and Director of the Arbours Crisis Centre, London, and a lecturer and teacher. He is the author of many articles and books on psychological, social, political and religious themes, including *Mary Barnes: Two Accounts of a Journey Through Madness* (1971) (with Mary Barnes); *The Cannabis Experience* (1974) (with Calvin Hernton); *I Haven't Had To Go Mad Here* (1974); *The Tyranny of Malice: Exploring the Dark Side of Character and Culture* (1988); *Sanctuary: The Arbours Experience of Alternative Community Care* (1995) (co-editor); and *Even Paranoids Have Enemies: New Perspectives on Paranoia and Persecution* (1998) (co-editor). He is currently working on *Psychoanalysis and Kabbalah* (with Stanley Schneider).

Rena Bina MSW is a social worker working in Israel. She is Supervisor of the Half Way House and Transitional Group Apartments for Emotionally Disturbed Adolescents and Young Adults, Miltam, B'nai Brak, Israel.

Edith David was Financial Administrator of the Arbours Crisis Centre for several years.

Lois Elliott is a psychoanalytic psychotherapist in private practice and Associate Director of the Arbours Crisis Centre in London, where she works as a team leader. She is a facilitator of the Arbours Crisis Centre Support Programme and works as a consultant at the Arbours Psychotherapy Service.

Margaret Fagan is a psychoanalytic psychotherapist. She was a team leader at the Crisis Centre for several years and is now training as a child psychotherapist at the Tavistock Clinic. She is Senior Psychotherapist at Brookside Young People's Unit, Goodmayes Hospital, Essex.

Laura Forti was born in Florence and studied philosophy and psychology at Milan University. She lives in London, where she has been working with the Arbours Association from its beginnings. She is a Team Leader at the Arbours Crisis Centre and is Co-ordinator of one of the Arbours Therapeutic Communities. She also works as a psychotherapist in private practice. She has published a collection of papers on alternative psychiatry, *L'Altra Pazzia* (Feltrinelli: Milan).

Kate Hardwicke is a psychoanalytic psychotherapist in training with the Arbours Association. She has worked as a resident therapist at the Arbours Crisis Centre since June 1996. Previously she was involved in the Place to Be, a project working psychodynamically with children, parents and teachers in South London schools. Her interests are in psychotic and borderline phenomena.

R.D. Hinshelwood is a psychoanalyst, former Clinical Director of the Cassel Hospital, Richmond, Surrey, and Professor of Psychoanalysis at the University of Essex. He has sustained a longstanding interest in therapeutic communities and has worked to apply psychoanalytic ideas to groups and social systems. He is the author of many papers and books, including *What Happens in Groups* (1987) and *A Dictionary of Kleinian Thought* (1989).

Martin Jenkins, who died in 1996, was a psychoanalytic psychotherapist in private practice and for a number of years Associate Director of the Arbours Crisis Centre, where he worked as a team leader and supervisor. He taught on the Arbours Training Programme on crisis intervention, psychosis, and bereavement. His main area of expertise was psychotic and borderline phenomena. Martin was a co-founder member of the Association of Arbours Psychotherapists' Borderline Workshop, and Arts and Psychoanalytic Thought Workshop.

Richard Lucas is Consultant Psychiatrist at St. Ann's Hospital, London N15. He is a member of the British Psycho-Analytical Society. Dr Lucas received his psychiatric training at the Maudsley Hospital, London, and for eighteen years was Consultant Psychiatrist at Claybury Hospital, a large mental asylum, until its closure. Dr Lucas has a particular interest in adapting contributions from psychoanalytic thinking in the understanding and management of psychosis within general psychiatric practice. He has written papers on the differentiation of the psychotic from the non-psychotic part of the personality; the psychotic wavelength; puerperal psychosis; the role of the psychotic workshop; and the dynamics of recurrent manic-depressive psychosis. He is Chairman of the General Psychiatry section of the Association for Analytic Psychotherapy in the NHS; he is also a member of the Professional Advisory Committee of the Arbours Crisis Centre.

George Mak-Pearce is a psychoanalytic psychotherapist in private practice in Norwich. He also works at the Brandon Centre, a community-based psychotherapy service for young people aged 12 to 25 years, and has written on engaging young adolescents in psychodynamic therapy. He has worked as a resident therapist and then Team Leader at the Arbours Crisis Centre, and as a psychotherapist at the Health and Counselling Section, Kingston University, Kingston-upon-Thames.

Brian Martindale FRCPsych is a member of the Board of ISPS (the International Society for the Psychological Treatments of the Schizophrenias and Other Psychoses) and Chairman of the UK Network of ISPS. Together with colleagues Dr Martindale organized the 12th International Symposium of ISPS in 1997 in London. He was a founding member and first Chairman (1991–97) of the European Federation of Psychoanalytic Psychotherapy in the Public Sector, and is now Honorary President. He is currently Western European Zone Representative for Psychiatry to the World Psychiatric Association. He is a psychoanalyst and Consultant Psychiatrist in Psychotherapy in the Ealing, Hammersmith and Fulham Mental Health NHS Trust in West London. He has published on a range of topics and edited two books: *Supervision and its Vicissitudes* (1997) (with Margareta Morner); and *Psychosis: Psychological Approaches and their Effectiveness.*

Mats Mogren is Co-founder and Director of the Gothenburg Psychotherapy Institute. He is a psychologist and psychoanalytic clinician, supervisor, lecturer and teacher in a variety of settings: university, psychiatry, social welfare, criminal jurisdiction. His main areas of interest include psychotic phenomena in their various manifestations, and the relation between culture, society and the individual. He has written articles on Oedipus, the Berlinklinic and the cinema, and the Carnival in Rio.

Lizzi Payne originally trained as a General Nurse and went on to specialize in Mental Health. She holds a certificate in clinical supervision and has completed post-graduate training in drama therapy. Her varied clinical experience includes hospital and community work in the National Health Service and the voluntary sector. Miss Payne spent three years living and working at the Arbours Crisis Centre as a resident therapist while training with the Arbours Association in psychoanalytic psychotherapy.

Stella Pierides-Müller is a psychoanalytic psychotherapist in private practice, Team Leader at the Arbours Crisis Centre, a teacher and supervisor. Co-founder and member of the Association of Arbours Psychotherapists' Arts and Psychoanalytic Thought Workshop, her main area of work involves borderline psychotic conditions, and her areas of interest include artistic creativity in the visual arts and in literature. She is the co-editor of *Even Paranoids Have Enemies: New Perspectives on Paranoia and Persecution* (1998).

Julia Saltiel is a psychoanalytic art psychotherapist in private practice. She has been working at the Arbours Crisis Centre and its Support Programme, as well the Arbours therapeutic communities, for a number of years. She has set up and run art therapy programmes in a Richmond Fellowship community for adolescents. She is currently setting up and running art therapy programmes in the new Tulip therapeutic community.

Stanley Schneider is a psychoanalyst; Professor and Chairman of the Program for Advanced Studies in Integrative Psychotherapy, the Hebrew University, Jerusalem; Professor and Chairman of the Department of Guidance and Counselling, Michlalah, Jerusalem; Adjunct Professor, Wurzweiler School of Social Work, Yeshiva University, New York; and Co-founder and former Director of the Summit Institute, Jerusalem. He is the author of many books and articles on psychological and social themes, and is currently working on *Psychoanalysis and Kabbalah* (with Joseph Berke).

Tamar Schonfield is an Associate Member of the British Psycho-Analytical Society. She is an Israeli-trained clinical psychologist and psychotherapist and Member of the Association of Arbours Psychotherapists since 1989, and an Arbours Crisis Centre Team Leader since 1994. She also works in private practice.

Catherine Sunderland trained as a nurse and is completing her training as a psychoanalytic psychotherapist with the Arbours Association. She has worked as a resident therapist at the Arbours Crisis Centre.

General Introduction

*Joseph H. Berke, Margaret Fagan, George Mak-Pearce
and Stella Pierides-Müller*

In everyday language psychosis is associated with wild frenzies, crazed deliriums, and frightening activities. It conveys confused and confusing states of mind and behaviour, and a wide array of seemingly inexplicable experiences. Psychotic individuals appear to be living a waking nightmare, to inhabit a frightful world, which they seek to assuage by pulling friends and family into it, or by erecting barriers around themselves and others.

In psychiatry the description 'psychosis' is often used synonymously with the diagnosis 'schizophrenia'. The latter denotes signs and symptoms which include a wide variety of perceptual, cognitive, emotional and behavioural disturbances. These have been defined and refined over the past century, in particular, by the Swiss psychiatrists Eugen Bleuler and his son Manfred, and others. Major diagnostic manuals, such as the DSM IV, continue to objectify, and try to gain consensual agreement about, the nature of 'schizophrenic' symptomatology. Interestingly the manuals pay little attention to the interpersonal implications of the condition, although the 19th century psychiatrist Emil Kraepelin described what he called 'the praecox feeling', an eerie, uncomfortable experience he felt in the presence of a schizophrenic.

There remain considerable differences between the two terms which are worth noting. Schizophrenia is a medical-psychiatric entity with specific diagnostic and prognostic (outcome) features. Psychosis is a state of being which may be considered aberrant in some cultures, but socially syntonic in others. A 'schizophrenic' may or may not be psychotic, and a psychotic person may or may not have been diagnosed as schizophrenic.

Both tend to arouse intense, usually negative, feelings in others, as well as the epithet 'mad'.

Some people are not mad all the time. Sometimes they identify with the psychotic, and other times with the non-psychotic sides of themselves. In recent decades 'borderline' or 'borderline condition' has been widely used to describe people who seem to fall in and out of madness. These terms have become especially prominent in psychoanalysis as a way of describing people who rely on the mental mechanism of splitting to protect their states of mind as well as their fragile sense of self.

While there exists some agreement about the definition of psychosis, there is much less consensus about how to intervene with people who suffer a psychotic condition and how to work within their immediate social network. We think that 'intervention' is a much more useful concept than 'treatment', because an intervention is something done on *behalf of* another, while 'treatment' is something done *to* another. Moreover, treatments, like medication, ECT and involuntary hospitalizations, are often restrictive and punitive. They are certainly not 'treats'.

This polyphony of activity evolved directly from the historically diverse roots of the concept of psychosis. Moreover, it originated from diverse efforts to understand and define the difficulties faced by those who suffer aberrant states of mind and being. The word 'suffer' is important. Psychosis is not a fantasy, and we sympathize deeply with all those who are tormented by the splitting and fragmentation of their inner worlds and outer relationships.

This book aims to explore ways and means of intervening on behalf of people who are or have been considered by others psychotic, schizophrenic or borderline. The editors and authors of this book have all been involved with the Arbours Crisis Centre in various capacities. The Centre is a unique facility, established in 1973, where therapists and patients (called 'guests') live together in order to establish a space where extremes of distress can be tolerated, understood and ameliorated. It is the only facility of its kind in Britain and, sadly, one of the very few facilities in Britain where psychotic individuals can receive a predominantly psychological (as opposed to physical) treatment intervention.

The Centre consists of three separate but interrelated and interrelating systems: the milieu, the group and the team. The milieu is the whole Centre as an active interpersonal environment. The group refers to the group of people resident at any one time: the three resident therapists and the six people staying at the Centre as their guests. House meetings take place four times during the week and consist of meetings with all those resident in the Centre. The team includes the 'guest', a 'team leader', who is an experienced psychotherapist co-ordinating the intervention, a 'resident therapist', and, whenever appropriate, a trainee. The continuity of care provided in the Crisis Centre is vital to the containment of these guests. The different professional spaces, a multiplicity of supervision meetings, and thoughtful ongoing interactions weave an interpersonal matrix that holds and contains periods of intense disturbance that can arise not only in the guests but in therapists who work with them as well.

By means of this book the contributors and ourselves wish to demonstrate that integrated psychological and social interventions (PsychoSocial) with individuals with sudden or long-standing psychoses are an effective means of helping people in psychotic or quasi-psychotic states. Moreover, we believe that such interventions are an effective alternative to traditional physically based, psychiatric treatments.

We would also point out that for us PsychoSocial differs from other interventions which are called by the same name. Thus the term 'psychosocial' is often used synonymously with a treatment regime that integrates medical, psychological and physical intervention, and which may utilize psychotherapy, medication and hospitalization. For us, PsychoSocial means an approach which is essentially psychodynamic (intrapsychically-oriented) and socially-dynamic (interpersonally-oriented). Or, as we point out to guests at the Arbours Centre, the healing 'magic' is in 'relations'.

Closeness, need, attachment, I–Thou as opposed to I–It connections, are what our 'guests' find exceptionally difficult and persecuting. Therefore, they try to avoid contact with others. Significantly, medical-psychiatric and early psychoanalytic definitions of psychosis serve a similar function. They tend to erect a nosological barrier to keep the disturbing person at a distance. In his 1917 *Introductory Lectures* Freud wrote:

> Observation shows that sufferers from narcissistic neuroses have no capacity for transference or only insufficient residues of it... Consequently the mechanism of cure which we carry through with other people – the revival of the pathogenic conflict and the overcoming of the resistance due to repression – cannot be operated with them. They remain as they are... They manifest no transference and for that reason

are inaccessible to our efforts and cannot be cured by us. (Freud 1917, p.447)

Despite this gloomy prediction, many thinkers have made considerable headway in reversing both the general psychiatric and Freud's early psychoanalytic perspectives. Carl Jung, Melanie Klein, R.D. Laing, Gregory Bateson, Wilfred Bion, Herbert Rosenfeld, Leslie Sohn, Loren Mosher and others have shown that aberrant behaviour has intelligible antecedents in the psychotic individual's experience. Far from being *in*sensitive to external relationships, they are *over*-sensitive. That is part of the problem. Their psychosis can be seen as a defensive screen against external and internal worlds, which are experienced as overwhelmingly threatening.

Klein, in particular, laid the groundwork for understanding the psychotic experience by defining the psychic mechanisms that contribute to it. These include splitting, dissociation, projection, projective identification and denial. The development of the concept of projective identification, in particular, allowed Rosenfeld, Donald Meltzer, Hanna Segal and others to develop and clarify Klein's conceptualizations. Thus, by understanding projective processes, and, in particular, the operation of projective identification, the therapists at the Centre are able to tolerate the daily occurrence of becoming the focus of the guests' projections and of getting caught up in them.

In the 1960s Laing and his colleagues refined these perceptions against a background of what he called 'social phenomenology', which was an attempt to create a science of subjectivity. He argued that only by considering the psychotic person in his own terms can we come to grips with psychotic experience, begin to understand it and find ways of coping with it. This work extended in many directions, from understanding the metaphorical content of psychotic thought, to demystifying 'schizogenic' transactions.

On a practical level, these 1960s pioneers and their successors created communities (Kingsley Hall, the Philadelphia Association and the Arbours in London; Soteria, Boyer Martin Lodge and Diabasis in California; Burch House in New Hampshire; and other communities in Switzerland, France, Italy and Israel) where 'disturbed' people could live. These served as sanctuaries where the nightmares they feared, and the nightmares they created through their defensive postures, could be mitigated. These places were themselves influenced by an earlier generation of social psychiatrists, such as Maxwell Jones and Tom Main, who had pioneered therapeutic communities at Dingleton Hospital in Scotland (where men and women patients were allowed to mix for the first time in decades); the Henderson Hospital, Sutton, Surrey; and the Cassel Hospital, Richmond, Surrey.

Many family therapists, such as Murray Bowen, Ross Speck, Lyman Wynne and Margaret Singer, have emphasized the importance of the social field around a psychotic person. They point out that this field includes all the family members, relatives, friends, helpers, strangers and professionals in the immediate vicinity of a psychosis, all those who are affected by a particular person, and who, in turn, try to affect him. They realized that by effecting a change in the field one can change the mental, emotional or behavioural conditions of each and every member of the field. This is what we have been able to demonstrate at the Arbours Centre. Even the most disturbed and disturbing guest can calm down and become communicative in a social setting which is itself calm, containing and non-aggressive.

By integrating field theory with modern psychoanalytic thought, our aim is to effect a transformation of chaotic inner rhythms, what Bion (1984) called the transforming of 'beta elements', into 'alpha functions' – that is, a mind state that allows for conscious awareness and for the metabolism of emotional impressions that misread and distort reality.

Significantly these chaotic rhythms can be intrapsychic, as Bion discusses, or interpersonal, as family therapists aver. In either case a state of calm helps to overcome the bizarre manipulation of the internal and external worlds that we see in severe mental disorder. It follows that any intervention with psychotic individuals needs to take into account this particular problem. Our PsychoSocial interventions have been relatively successful primarily because they address this issue by providing whole environments, where a day-to-day, hour-to-hour metabolizing of new experience can take place through the mindful presence and facilitation of the therapists who live at the Centre, as well as by those who support them (*see* Pierides-Müller, Section One below).

Obviously our interventions rightly oppose acting upon psychotic regressions and concrete thinking by imposing degrees of concrete holding or intrusion. We refer to brutalizing regimes of hospitalization, drugs and ECT. This being said, we recognize that many hospitals are caring and that some medication may be necessary (although ECT is best reserved for the slaughterhouse).

By 'concrete' we mean hard, solid, heavy, non-thinking. This refers to a mind-less or mind-incapacitated action, something imposed on someone, *in spite of* and *out of tune with* their wishes and needs. 'Good medications' are those which calm, and promote reflection and communication. 'Bad medications' are those which act as a biochemical straightjacket, which inhibit feeling, and interfere with thinking. For a short period this may be necessary. But for more than a few weeks it is unhelpful and inevitably done for the sake of others. Moreover, it may be maintained indefinitely, that is without thinking, without proper review. Thus, the treatment of 'narcissistic personality disorders', to quote Freud, via the transformation of carers into 'brick-walled mothers', to quote Bion, can be devastating. It perpetuates a baleful power structure, which leads to inevitable withdrawal on the part of those so treated, itself inevitably seen as part of the illness.

We have also seen that any enthusiastic intervention, even by inexperienced practitioners, may be of some help, and clinical studies have shown that psychotherapy in specialist units by experienced practitioners has proved exceptionally helpful with schizophrenic patients (Karon and Vandenbos 1981). Likewise, PsychoSocial treatment programmes have been shown to be remarkably effective in the healing of psychotic conditions. For example, Loren Mosher and his colleagues have demonstrated that first- and second-episode persons labelled as schizophrenic could be successfully treated in a special milieu without the use of neuroleptic drugs (Mosher and Bola 2000).

In a separate development, the psychological effects of institutionalization on staff perceptions of patients, in particular, have been noted by Tom Main (Main 1957). Patients were seen as good or bad depending on whether they were behaving obediently, compliantly and were being grateful to the staff. In other words, psychotic patients were expected to behave in ways that would please the staff and which, from the perspective of a psychodynamic understanding, were incompatible with their condition. As Herbert Rosenfeld noted (Rosenfeld 1987), these ups and downs of staff reactions are particularly related to the ebb and flow of the transference and counter-transference among the staff to their patients, and vice versa. When these processes are unexplored and unresolved, the emotional difficulties of the staff are directly passed on to their patients. Where these can be understood and worked through in therapeutic communities like the Arbours Centre, the designated patients are more able to step out of their 'roles' and become human. Moreover, they elicit more humane responses to themselves, and can even become, as Harold Searles has noted, therapists to their therapists, an important act of reparation.

Therefore, for both conceptual and practical reasons this study has been entitled *Beyond Madness*. This means that we have tried to get past rigid medical metaphors and social stigmas in order to understand the personal and interpersonal implications of the phenomena called 'madness'. Similarly the interventions described here extend far beyond bottling people up or 'treating' an illness. They are directed to a multiplicity of worlds, across generations, and extend through intra- and inter-psychic time and space. There may be no 'cure'. But if the men and women on whose behalf we have intervened feel less disordered and more empowered, and are able to navigate their way through their various social fields with their dignity and self-respect intact, then it should be considered a job well done. In this respect it is important to note that in order to preserve confidentiality we have changed the names and identifying details of the guests discussed. But we have done so without altering their essential stories.

The book is divided into four main sections, each preceded by a brief introductory discussion written by ourselves. Section One considers theoretical and historical issues. Section Two focuses on PsychoSocial methodology, in particular the very special organization of the Arbours Centre. Section Three provides detailed narratives. Finally Section Four explores the fundamental issues of money and power: what costs are involved and how, and from where, authority flows. The Conclusion, that follows, is our attempt to summarize the overall effectiveness (as measured by the resulting diminution of suffering, success in social re-integration, personal growth, and decreased costs) of the PsychoSocial approach.

We are very pleased that Professor Robert Hinshelwood has written a foreword to the book. Through his work at the Cassel Hospital, the Association of Therapeutic Communities, the journals *Therapeutic Communities* and the *British Journal of Psychotherapy*, the Planned Environment Therapy Trust, and a host of other ventures, he has established himself as a seminal figure in the application of psychoanalysis and social therapies to interventions with psychotic and borderline individuals.

We are also very pleased that Dr Brian Martindale has written the Epilogue. Working within the National Health Service, he has developed kindred models for PsychoSocial interventions and is actively pursuing these ideas through his writings and in his position as chairman of the International Society for the Psychological Treatment of the Schizophrenias and Other Psychoses.

References

Bion, W.R. (1984) *Learning from Experience*. London: Karnac Books.

Freud, S. (1917) *Introductory Lectures on Psycho-Analysis* (*General Theory of the Neuroses, Part III*). *Vol 16: The Standard Edition of the Complete Psychological Works of Sigmund Freud*. London: Hogarth Press.

Karon, B.P. and Vandenbos, G.R. (1981) *The Psychotherapy of Schizophrenia*. New York: Jason Aronson.

Main, T. (1957) 'The Ailment.' *British Journal of Medical Psychology 30, 3, 129–145*.

Mosher, L. and Bola, J. (2000) 'The Soteria Project: Twenty-Five Years of Swimming Upriver.' *Complexity and Change 9*, 1, 68–74.

Pierides-Müller, S. (2002) 'The Power of the Play.' Section one, this volume.

Rosenfeld, H. (1987) *Impasse and Interpretation*. London: Tavistock Publications.

Section One

Historical and Theoretical Perspectives

Introduction

Joseph H. Berke, Margaret Fagan, George Mak-Pearce
and Stella Pierides-Müller

The Crisis Centre began with the idea that a personal crisis can be a pivotal moment, either for a mental and social breakdown or for a breakthrough into a new and vital dimension of living. Subsequently we tried to embody this idea with a physical and interpersonal environment – the Arbours Crisis Centre – where such positive transitions can take place.

For George Mak-Pearce the Centre was his home, a place to live and learn. Along with outlining the containing function of the Centre, his chapter begins the book by describing the essential tasks of the resident therapists: to bear despair when others can not cope, and to convey hope when everything seems lost. To do so George had to serve in many capacities from role model to transference object, the screen for a myriad projections. He asks the question of what kind of figure he will become: loved, hated, intimate, useless? In reply he offers the notion of a 'temporal transference'. To help the psychotic and quasi-psychotic residents in the way they truly need help, he has to hold their future in his 'I', and be the bearer of their expectations. At the same time, he needs to keep an eye open towards his own future, and struggle to make sure that it is not 'dead', as some guests would have it, but full of possibility.

Richard Lucas situates the work of the Centre within the past history of attempts to define 'madness' and respond to it, often brutally and sometimes humanely. After reviewing the medical model, he summarizes the psychoanalytic approach to psychosis beginning with Freud and leading to the ideas of Klein, Bion, and others. His personal challenge is to bring the insights of psychoanalytic thinking into the domain of tradi-

27

tional psychiatric practice. Lucas shows that 'asylum' can be given, both by reading the inner realities of psychotic persons and by developing integrated interpersonal interventions within a community setting. For him medication is an adjunct to communication, not a means of shutting people up and keeping them out of mental or emotional sight.

Mats Mogren, who is director of the Gothenburg Institute of Psychotherapy, concurs that the 'healing power' lies in relationships, not drugs *per se*. His chapter introduces the work being done at Varpen and Gyllenkroken in Sweden, kindred facilities to the Crisis Centre. Moreover, Mogren illustrates the ways by which the people at these centres change from a position of dependency to active participation in the life and culture of Swedish society. Interestingly his inspiration emerged from the psychosocial philosophy developed in Argentina by Enrique Pichon-Rivière and his colleagues. So if Richard Lucas focuses on the temporal ramifications of the Crisis Centre, Mats Mogren looks at the spatial matrix, from South America to Northern Europe. Moreover, Mogren places the concept of psychosis within a cultural context. He notes how 'madness' or 'insanity' fascinates the theatre and cinema, art and literature, science and religion – in other words, all the major areas of human experience.

Stella Pierides-Müller concludes the first section by expanding the cultural context or, as she would put it, the mythic dimension of madness. She distinguishes between personal myths concretized by the psychotic mind, and universal myths dramatized by playwrights such as Euripides, who express the shock of primordial emotions through the form of an unfolding story. Pierides-Müller points out that in psychosis these base feelings cannot be tolerated. They threaten the imagination from every angle – an imagination which cannot symbolize feelings as in drama or literature, but which takes every impulse as a kernel of hate, an indigestible solid to be spat out or wiped out. When these activities take place within a family or larger societal setting unwilling to see meaning in and learn from 'the shadow side' of existence, horror ensues. The psychotic individual becomes doubly estranged – from his own experience, as well as from his cultural context. The result is a person trapped within the nightmare of his mind, knocking hopelessly against the brick wall of social and medical convention. Pierides-Müller argues that residence at the Centre enhances the opportunity for guests to alter inner tragedies and elaborate therapeutic imaginative narratives.

CHAPTER I

Working with the Dread of the Future

George Mak-Pearce

One of the first things that strongly impressed me about the philosophy of the Arbours Crisis Centre was the conviction that no-one would be prejudged or condemned by his or her past. Repeatedly there would be individuals looking for help and arriving with referral letters depicting a horrific childhood, abuse, self-harm and destruction and a long adult psychiatric history. Repeatedly there would be discussions as to whether it was appropriate to accept this or that person – they may disrupt things, upset others and not be able to use the kind of help we offer. In these discussions a key factor in the decision-making was whether this person had shown any sign of wanting things to work out differently. The notion that a breakdown or crisis can be a turning point, the start of something new and different for an individual, is vital in the motivation of both the individual and the helpers. While this can easily sound like idealistic dreaming when contrasted with the chronic nature of some people's suffering, it nevertheless remains central to the Arbours philosophy. This is, I believe, a strength and is a philosophy that needs articulating. However, it is a philosophy that is often under siege from the therapist's own sense of despair, which can be activated and inflamed for many reasons. One such reason is the intense projective identification with the despair of those who come looking for help. The balance between hope for the future and dread of the future, how the therapists may use their awareness to address such feelings and how this may help clinically, is what I want to investigate in this chapter.

I worked as a resident therapist (RT) for a number of years at the Arbours Crisis Centre and then went on to become a team leader. I have therefore experienced at first hand the rewards and difficulties of being a therapist with two very different roles within the Centre. One difficulty of being a RT is that as a trainee therapist you are living at the Centre with your clients. Residents at the Centre are referred to as 'guests': the idea behind this is that the three RTs live in the Centre and it is their home. The team (usually a team leader, RT, and student on placement) meets prospective residents for an initial consultation. If a stay is to be offered, the RT contacts the individual and invites them to be their guest at their home. It is the RT who welcomes the new guest to the Centre, settles them down and facilitates their immediate future in the new environment. To this extent the RT is from the outset the holder of hope, the anticipator of conflict and the container of dread of what is about to be.

Where the stay is a short one of just a few weeks therapists have to be very sensitive to working within a time-limited framework. Fear of the immediate future, both of how much and of how little may happen, would naturally be a central feature of moving into a residential community. One could say that the arrival stage produces very strong feelings about the future. It invites phantasies of abrupt and dramatic change or of inevitable failure.

A crisis responded to sensitively can be a turning point, a creative shift in the individual's sense of self. But who believes this? In my experience most new guests at the Centre do not. Moreover, they might well resent the optimistic, self-righteous tone of such a statement were it to be voiced. Understandably, a guest may reason that if the RT really was in touch with their despair, pain and dread, they would never offer platitudinous hope for the future. An expression of optimism on the part of the RT can be like a red rag to a bull – evidence to the guest that their entrenched misery is being avoided or misunderstood.

Set against this pessimism, it is at the same time crucial for most guests to be able to believe that the RT can be the holder of hope. If the RT identifies with the projected despair too intensely, they, the guests, may feel crushed and give up. It is not difficult to see how a guest could get tangled-up in this apparent 'Catch 22', resulting from their conflicting needs to both preserve and destroy optimism. For the RT, maintaining and expressing a creative attitude towards the future – working with it within the group and containing dread between sessions – can be immensely difficult.

Of course the RT is not working alone with this task. It is here that the structure of the formal meetings needs to be brought into the picture. On a weekly basis, the Centre provides between three and five team meetings, four house meetings, one art and one movement therapy meeting. Thus, most weekdays there are one or two formal meetings structured into the guest's day. The question is whether such an intense schedule helps the RT have an easier life. Does this schedule mitigate suffering, abate acting out, and nourish guests so that they quietly digest their insights between sessions? Or does something else happen?

There is, of course, no fixed answer. In my experience guests will sometimes calm down and work both in and out of sessions. This will often be during the middle phase of their stay. During this time they may well socialize with the group in a very constructive way. They may take ideas from the meetings, revisit their past with new-found ego strength, initiate a process of grieving, and try to do things differently with their fellow guests. They may acknowledge and tolerate shame at their contribution to the chaos in the past and present. This can be a very valuable time.

However, things are not always so integrated and constructive. Individual guests can fall apart between sessions, lurch into psychosis; they can be aggressive, can self-harm, and otherwise act out. They can disrupt the group and boycott meetings. They can leave the Centre, make complaints, or cut off contact entirely. Inevitably, it is the RT group that is immediately faced with the task of trying to contain and turn things round. Often the house can split into warring factions. Guests may hate each other or hate the RTs as a group, or hate individual RTs. The guest group may assume what Bion (1961) has described as the 'fight–flight basic assumption'. Sometimes the team leaders are the enemy to fight, sometimes an individual guest may be scapegoated, and so on.

In such circumstances the RT is in a difficult position and has to make a judgement as to whether to address a disturbing situation foremost as a group phenomenon or take an individual guest aside and focus upon their situation. There is no right or wrong approach. I do believe there is an understandable tendency to want to deal with a crisis by initiating an in-depth one-to-one meeting and recreate, often in the middle of the night, a mini team meeting. The RT working with a guest is in a unique and privileged position in relation to that guest – there with the guest in the formal therapy sessions and at the same time living with the guest in the house day and night. The RT forms a bridge between the formal meetings and the day-to-day life in the house. Like the guest, he or she is witness to both the importance and the inadequacy of the team, art and movement therapy meetings.

When things are breaking down in the middle of the night and a guest is acting out, I have found it helpful as an RT to try to find a way to respond which creates links to the thinking space of the team meetings without actually attempting to re-run the meeting of the day before. The RT can telephone the team leader on call at any time, 24 hours a day. In such a case the team leader can act as a container for the RT, but the guest does not have this direct link to their team leader. Consequently, the RT is often used by the guest as a surrogate figure, as a means of reconnecting to the team and team leader. I have found there is often a pressure (both from the guest and from within myself) to attempt to substitute for the absent team, to think about the guest's history and be interpretative. However, rather than recreate a pseudo-team meeting in the middle of the night, I have found that to acknowledge the absence and to work with the anticipations concerning future team meetings allows me as RT to stay 'in role'. It automatically puts a conditional tone to the exchange. It re-establishes the possibility of a link with the team in phantasy.

Where a guest is acting dangerously or destructively, the immediate task for the RT is to contain the acting out and, as it may be hoped, to introduce thinking that will allow the guest to transform actions into words. The change from dramatic act to words as an expression of feeling is to use the immediate future very differently from the immediate past. I like the word 'modulate' in this context because it captures an aspect of the sort of change that might be useful to aim at in working with the guest's dread of the future. To modulate in a musical sense means to change the keynote by the introduction of a new sharp or flat, or more simply, to move from one scale to another. But it can also mean to vary the tone of voice so as to give expression to some specific feeling or intention. Alternatively, it can mean to measure or to regulate. A module is a small quantity or small measure.

When confronted by psychotic or very disturbed acting out, the RT needs to make a small shift in the tone of what is happening. The drama may be big but that does not mean the response should be. To measure the situation and to change the tone of it may be all that is required. The shift I have in mind is for the RT to take the focus away from what has just happened and to articulate the phantasies about what might be about to happen in the house, in the group and in the team. This is obviously not simply spelling out the consequences of dangerous or disruptive behaviour, although this may be part of the process. Rather, what you are attempting is to articulate the guest's fears but shifting scale, moving to a different time frame, where fears exist but are modulated – they have not yet become actual.

The advantage of this approach is that it nurtures a specific type of transference to the RT. The RT becomes a thinking agent exploring the potential world. Good, bad or horrid, the exploration is not to avoid dread but to think about it together. This may be as simple as re-framing the options but it could also be an analysis of the guest's phantasies of the future – a kind of dream analysis, but one where the dream is really a daydream shared with the RT (even if it is in the middle of the night!).

Traditionally one thinks of the transference as meaning the therapist's representing a figure from the client's past. In the chapter 'Conjoint Therapy' (in Section Two of this book) Joseph Berke describes working within what he calls a 'differentiated team', in which the transference towards the team leader takes this form. But what of the transference to the RT in the house? Wanted or not, the RT will be a significant figure in the guest's remaining stay. What kind of figure will that be? How potent, how useless, how intimate, how loved, how hated, will the RT be?

In thinking about this, I found it helpful to identify what I call 'future transference'. The RT is very much responsible for the practicalities of future living conditions, and on one level the future transference may simply be based upon the RT as a role model. On a deeper level, however, the guest's future transference to the RT embraces the thoughts and feelings, imagination and anticipation, conscious and unconscious, which concern the whole future of their relationship with the RT, including leaving and follow-up. It is in effect the guest's view of the RT as a potential introject.

The future transference is a feeling in the here and now about how the relationship with the RT will be at some point in the future. It is thus a conceptual tool that the RT can use for thinking and hence for containment of both their own and the guest's anxieties. It is especially effective when the RT is working in a differentiated team, where the hope is that the transference, especially the negative transference, is generated with the team leader as the target. Anger and rage outside the team meeting can be thought of as a misplaced expression of this. Exploring the dread of the future team meetings becomes the RT's way of re-targeting the feelings and differentiating them from feelings about the house in the here and now. It is to be hoped the team leader will take it on the chin in the next session rather than the RT in the middle of the night!

This inevitably leads on to the idea of negative future transference, which I have written about elsewhere (Mak-Pearce 2001). Negative future transference may occur if a guest fears feelings of disintegration, for example. In this case the unconscious pressure could be to form a merging, idealizing relationship with the RT. This would be the guest's attempt to produce security in the future at the cost of present-day autonomy. Where this happens, the omnipotent control of the RT inherent in the merging tends to lead to a phantasy of the future relationship with the RT as a fated relationship. The RT can feel trapped and claustrophobically coveted. Thinking about the future with the guest would be very important in such a situation. How does the guest envisage maintaining the attachment while allowing a sense of separation?

The need to be able to live a life with a degree of ontological security (to borrow Laing's term) embraces having a reasonably comfortable sense that existential needs will be met. These needs may be as basic as the need to be safe, to eat, sleep, to relate to others, to exist in the present, to remember a past and to anticipate a future. The loss of a sense of time either through the suppression of memory or a loss of the ability to anticipate, judge or be an agent in the future is such a catastrophic experience that it is understandable that it has the hallmark of a psychotic breakdown.

As an RT, one is the target of such intense projective forces that it is predictable that sooner or later one will suffer (hopefully temporarily!) a loss of sense of safety, and loss of control over food, sleep and all the other elements necessary for a basically contented life. What I had not banked on as an RT was the experience of losing my own sense of time. This strikes at the heart of one's sanity, for it brings into question the 'hopefully temporary' proviso above, which makes anticipating such losses bearable.

In his chapter 'Psychotic Interventions' (in Section Three of this book) Joseph Berke describes how therapists sometimes may enter into the madness prevalent in the house and may then intervene in unhelpful ways and generally make things worse. I am sure anyone who has worked residentially for any length of time has witnessed this. In my experience when I have 'lost it' in this way, and been unable to contain a situation, the warning precursor was often a sense of a distortion of time. The pressure of making decisions if someone has cut themselves badly, the frustration of waiting for colleagues to return calls with advice, the sense of threat or intimidation in the air, the fear when suddenly the group seems menacing: all go to generate anxiety of unbearable intensity. In these sorts of situations I found I could lose my usual sense of time. Time no longer was experienced as constantly heralding in change, different resources and choices.

The best way I can think of describing this distortion of time is to offer the image of being in a car about to have a crash. I am certain I am not alone in having had the experience of racing towards another car at speed and yet experiencing the final moments before collision as unfolding in slow motion. I remember that one strange feature of this bizarre experience of time slowing down was that it allowed me the luxury of all sorts of useless and irrelevant thoughts while leaving me aware that I was unable to alter the inevitable!

Perhaps a more everyday experience of temporal distortions for a psychotherapist is sitting in a fifty-minute session that experientially has duration of about half a day! Equally, such a session can be followed by another that seems to pass in a flash. I have sat in many group supervision sessions hearing other therapists talk about such feelings, so I take heart in the knowledge that such distortions do not affect me alone. Obviously, time dragging on or passing quickly is not in itself a precursor of psychosis. A session may drag but one still manages to end it on time, one's sense of agency remaining intact. The analogy with the car crash is probably closer to a psychotic breakdown. It is intense traumatic moments when time really plays wild. One gets an impression of what it must be like to have had a childhood with numerous traumas. It seems fair to assume that the more traumatized a person felt in childhood the more likely they are to be left with a disposition to regress to a distorted sense of time as an adult.

In thinking about containing psychotic and borderline behaviour by focusing upon anxieties in the immediate future I was interested to learn that research by Whitrow (1988) presents the case that, developmentally, the concept of 'future' precedes that of 'past'. How do we learn the concepts of past, present and future? Whitrow, like Winnicott and others, puts an emphasis on developing a capacity to wait. The mother, through a series of gradually introduced and carefully monitored frustrations, teaches the infant that it is separate from mother in space and time. Infantile omnipotence is gradually deflated through a process of waiting. The infant has to wait for food and attention.

> The first intuition of duration appears as an interval which stands between the child and the fulfillment of desires… Up to the age of 18 months or more children appear to live only in the present… Between then and 30 months, they tend to acquire a few words relating to the future, such as 'soon', but almost none that concerns the past…the use of 'tomorrow' precedes that of 'yesterday'… (Whitrow 1988, p.95)

Working with future phantasies can potentially address some very primitive elements of the mind. It is understandable that we have evolved to be concerned about what is just about to happen. Our survival depends upon it. For most people most of the time what is just about to happen bears some relation to the recent past. Our behaviour has consequences. Many therapists have noted how in deeply regressed borderline psychotic states of mind this causal link gets broken. In relation to such a state of mind interpreting an individual's mad or bad past behaviour can easily be experienced as persecution. By contrast, by attempting to establish some link with phantasies about the immediate future the RT can help a paranoid or regressed guest to re-establish their own sense of causality.

That the modus operandi of psychotherapy is to work with historical material is hardly surprising; the compulsion to repeat and the awful consequences of early deprivation and abuse are constantly witnessed in the consulting room. However, for the RT working in the milieu of the Arbours Crisis Centre I feel it is essential to keep a sharp eye on the future – the guest's future, the group's future and, last but not least, their own personal future. Future phantasy is a way of talking about what has not happened yet. It is therefore plastic and with a degree of luck and skill can be shared without humiliation or accusation. It can even be treated with humour, opening the door to a richer and lighter form of relating – particularly important when one is working residentially.

References

Bion, W.R. (1961) *Experiences in Groups and Other Papers.* London: Tavistock.

Mak-Pearce, M.G. (2001) 'Engaging Troubled Adolescents in Six Session Psychodynamic Therapy.' In G. Baruch (ed) *Community Based Psychotherapy with Young People.* London: Brunner Routledge.

Whitrow G.J. (1988) *Time in History: The Evolution of Our General Awareness of Time and Temporal Perspective.* Oxford: Oxford University Press.

CHAPTER 2

Beyond Medication

Richard Lucas

During the last decade there has been a major change in the setting for the management of psychosis with the closure of the large mental hospitals and the move to care in the community. Before the closure of the asylums there was in general ample space provided in mental hospitals to contain patients during episodes of acutely disturbed behaviour as well as the more chronically disabled. The primary debate centred between the caring aspects provided by the asylum and the negative aspects of institutionalization.

In the days before the introduction of effective anti-psychotic medication, and in reaction to an excessively physical approach to psychosis, which included insulin coma treatment and leucotomies, those working within psychiatry were challenged to develop an alternative approach. R.D. Laing's and the 'anti-psychiatry' movement's response was to approach the patient as an individual human being. They saw aberrant behaviour as a problem of acceptance for a narrowly conservative society. In Laing's terms, the patient had to put on a false self for society. The problem with this approach was that it appeared to ignore the fact that there were entities called psychotic illnesses that presented management problems in their own right (*see* Lucas 1998).

After an initial period of euphoria following this new approach of liberating patients from hospital, the demanding nature of the work of containing patients with psychosis in the community became apparent, and Laing's enthusiasm waned. A few pioneers persisted and set up more permanent community homes, adding to them a caring psychotherapeutic dimension. Arbours remains an example of such an organization. The

Centre provides both crisis and more long-term community home-place-ments and uses a PsychoSocial approach (*see* Berke 1987). Its aim is to enable people to get a better understanding of themselves through the ex-perience of relationships in the community household, with provision of both group and individual therapy.

The approach offered by such dynamically run group homes and hostels and the general psychiatric approach, with its medical emphasis on physical treatments, have led separate existences. However, recent closure of the asylums has now brought the two approaches into closer contact.

When it was decided that the asylum in which I was working was to close, the management's initial reaction was to repeat the path followed by Laing. The philosophy adopted was that the patients' illness was the result of their having been treated in an institutionalized manner, and that, with time in the community, they would become self-sufficient and able to live independently in their own residential homes. Indeed the initial euphoria was so great that I was even told that a replacement ward would not be needed, as all patients would be contained in the community.

The following vignette serves as a vivid illustration of the prevailing attitude at the time. A man had been in hospital for over thirty years. On the old, yellowing hospital notes, the original admitting interview, it was recorded that he sat in the doctor's chair and said, 'I am the Messiah!' Peri-odically over the years he would exhibit outbursts of rage requiring more close supervision, but at all other times he resided on an open, long-stay ward. He was one of the long-stay patients chosen to be moved into a newly designed community home. In this house, it was decided, there would be no separate room for staff, as that would be like re-creating a ward rather than a home.

The aim was that patients would gradually take responsibility for themselves. Yet, this patient became increasingly disturbed. The staff found that they had no privacy and had to talk in whispers on the landing. Eventually, the patient assaulted a nurse and had to be readmitted to hospital.

Following tragic isolated acts of violence towards strangers in the community, the pendulum swung the other way. Anxieties escalated as to our ability to contain potentially unpredictable states of mind in the community. Government's response was to increase the number of medium-secure units to contain severely disturbed psychotic offenders, but it neglected to ensure that there would be sufficient district-hospital beds for when the asylums finally closed. Instead, for the less extreme cases, anxiety about containment has resulted in an increase in bureaucracy, and an attempt to replace asylum walls with walls of paper.

The care programme approach (CPA) was introduced to ensure proper reviews and follow-up of patients, with a designated key worker. Detailed risk-assessment forms were introduced, in spite of the knowledge that risk assessments remain essentially clinically-based, related to each individual case.

An outcome of all this is, and remains, the danger of having created a culture of blame, whereby, if unpredictable tragedies occur, such as an in-patient suicide, internal management inquiries may make staff feel that they are being held to account. This may foster a climate of defensive psychiatry at a time when a creative and flexible approach is most needed, with respect and encouragement for the skills and abilities of all staff working together as a multidisciplinary team.

A flexible attitude requires to be maintained when the psychiatric team and the residential and rehabilitation staff jointly consider the future needs of a patient with a history of psychosis. The approach has to incorporate contributions on diagnostic assessment and the need for appropriate physical treatment, coming from the medical side, along with the wider issues of containment and setting realistic therapeutic goals, emanating from the residential and rehabilitation side. Each side needs to understand the other's concern in working together within a new and pressurized environment.

This becomes a constant learning process for staff, patients and their relatives. The psychiatrist's biological approach and the residential carer's PsychoSocial approach may be addressing different facets of a mutually shared agenda. I have found that it is possible to bring together the biological and PsychoSocial attitudes within a psychoanalytically based framework of understanding.

I will first describe the thinking behind the medical model and then the development of analytic understandings on psychosis, before illustrating how they can be incorporated within an integrated approach.

All medical models relate to a background system of classification. In psychiatry there are two main classifications: the International Classification of Diseases (ICD 10) and the American Classification (DSM IV). As well as national and international classifications used for research purposes, psychiatrists carry with them a more simple classification for everyday purposes. For some this may include headings of neuroses, psychoses, personality disorders, learning difficulties and adjustment disorders.

Practically speaking, psychoses can be divided into the so-called 'functional psychoses', schizophrenia and affective disorders, and the organic psychoses. The organic psychoses may be divided into the acute toxic confusional states resulting from infections, drug abuse or metabolic disorders, and the chronic disorders, the dementias.

The main critics of classification have been psychotherapists who complain that attempts at classification ignore the individual and their unique characteristics. A rejoinder has been that psychotherapists have been more concerned with individuals with neuroses or personality disorders than with the more severe psychotic disorders and the management problems that they pose.

Of all the psychiatric conditions, schizophrenia remains the most difficult to define. When it comes to diagnosis in medical terms, there are levels of precision. We may have specific biochemical tests, or isolate the causative bacteria, for, say, tuberculosis. With schizophrenia, we still have to rely on the method advocated by Hippocrates for diagnosis – namely a cluster of symptoms to form a syndrome.

To address the diagnostic difficulties, psychiatrists have made use of Jaspers' concept of phenomenology (Jaspers 1963). Its aim is to be objective about subjective experiences through defining and classifying psychic phenomena such as hallucinations and delusions. In this exercise theoretical views of causation have no place, indeed they would be felt to interfere with the aim of achieving objectivity to the description of the subjective experiences.

Nevertheless, a problem remains in how optimally to use the phenomenological approach in defining schizophrenia. K. Schneider (1959) tried to make the diagnosis more reliable by describing certain symptoms as carrying more weight – the so-called Schneiderian 'first rank symptoms'. These include hearing your thoughts spoken out loud, voices talking about you, being made to feel things, experiences of thoughts inserted, withdrawn and broadcast, as well as delusional perception. However, the system is not fool-proof, as some 25 per cent of patients with manic depression show first rank symptoms, while some 25 per cent of patients with established schizophrenia do not.

Junior psychiatrists in training spend much time on the mental state examination, developing skills in eliciting first rank symptoms using the phenomenological approach. However, the mental state examination is only a snapshot taken at a moment in time, and as such it lacks a dynamic element. For example, a patient in a stressed state may one day present with a picture suggestive of depression and a few days later in a more paranoid state. There is also the danger of overemphasis of the importance to the formal mental state examination in training, as it may encourage development of a somewhat one-sided, rigid, organic attitude to psychosis that leaves out room for dynamic thinking.

In the pre-war period there was no effective medication for treating schizophrenia. The first effective anti-psychotic medication, chlorpromazine, was introduced in 1952. The tricyclic antidepressants were introduced soon after, with Imipramine in 1957. Over recent years, newer anti-psychotic and antidepressant medication, with fewer side effects, have been developed.

The priority in the psychiatric treatment of schizophrenia remains the controlling of the psychotic symptoms through medication. In some cases, where compliance is important, depot medication (injection) supervised by the community nurse may be the preferred option. Rehabilitation issues are addressed only after the psychotic symptoms have been brought under control.

The aetiology of schizophrenia continues to be sought through neurological studies of the brain, and through the psychopharmacological action of drugs. We now recognize that as well as defaulting from medication, living in an emotionally over-pressurizing environment can lead to relapses. We recognize too that educating the family to lower their expectations of the patient may reduce the relapse rate (Leff 1994). However, though emotional stresses are acknowledged as potential precipitants for relapses, the general psychiatric approach to schizophrenia is firmly rooted at the phenomenological and psychopharmacological level. Within this context, there would be felt to be no need for an analytic contribution; indeed, the patient would be felt to be too unwell for any psychotherapeutic approach other than supportive work or a cognitive behavioural approach that reinforced reality. One might reasonably ask, then, how an analytic approach could make any meaningful contribution to the management of schizophrenia.

Although Sigmund Freud was pessimistic as to the effectiveness of the analytic technique in influencing psychotic states, his insights lie at the root of all analytic thinking on the subject. In his paper 'On Narcissism: An Introduction' (Freud 1914) he described two basic ways of relating. The healthy way of developing is through taking in styles of relationships from a parent or teacher. In contrast, the narcissistic way is a self-centred state, where there is no taking in and no development occurs.

At this juncture Freud referred to the psychoses as the narcissistic neuroses, and held that psychoses were not amenable to classical analytic technique. He believed that transference phenomena were generally lacking due to the dominance of a narcissistic self-centred state. Over forty years later Herbert Rosenfeld was to refute this. He described the transference as being present in psychosis but having a concrete nature, with the 'as if' quality missing (Rosenfeld 1966). An example would be of a patient who takes a nurse, literally, to be the persecutory mother figure and makes an unprovoked assault on her.

The withdrawal into a narcissistic self-centred world is a prominent feature in many cases of long-standing hospitalized patients. It is not surprising that Freud questioned the possibility of influencing such states. However, his theory raises an interesting issue of considering two separate parts to the personality, the anaclitic and narcissistic, foreshadowing Wilfred Bion's later theory of psychotic disorder, in which each was considered to need to be addressed in its own right. An example to illustrate this would be a young patient diagnosed as suffering from schizophrenia and seen for consideration for analysis. On this occasion his healthy part said, 'Dr Lucas, I am really in need of analysis!' However, his narcissistic part then followed with, 'But man to man, as adults, there is nothing wrong with me.'

In 'Beyond the Pleasure Principle' Freud introduced the concept of the death instinct, an innate self-destructive and aggressive force (Freud 1920). This features most powerfully in psychotic states. In a similar vein, Melanie Klein saw envy, a projective spoiling process, as the external manifestation of the death instinct. Bion later referred to the never-decided conflict between the life and death instincts as the central clinical feature of the schizophrenic condition (Bion 1957). In other words, as soon as some progress is made in rehabilitation, negative forces threaten to destroy this. Caring for people with such disorders thus becomes a life-long commitment and means having to live with their ups and downs.

Following the introduction of the structural model, the ego, id and superego, Freud amended his theoretical formulations (Freud 1923). Psychoses (schizophrenia) were now seen to be related to a conflict between the ego, siding with the primitive feelings coming from the id, against the demands of external reality (Freud 1924).

The structural model lay behind the development of the Ego Psychology School of thought in the United States. The view came to be that in psychotic states one used more primitive defensive reactions against stress, and only through intensive psychotherapy could more mature ways of coping develop. The problem with this approach, practised at a renowned centre, Chestnut Lodge in Washington, was that it assumed a lack of differentiation between neurosis and psychosis, and that all patients could be understood using the clinician's or therapist's ordinary sensitivities.

Meanwhile, in the UK, Klein was developing her own theoretical formulations about psychosis. She was struck by similarities between the phantasies expressed by small children and the delusional world encountered in schizophrenia. She held that the psychopathology in schizophrenia arose during an early stage of development, termed the paranoid schizoid position, a stage where the main defences were of splitting and projection, creating a persecutory surrounding world. Klein viewed the origin of psychotic states as an excessive use of normal emotional defences of splitting and projection in early infancy.

Klein introduced many concepts fundamental to our thinking about psychotic states. While her theoretical contributions have helped enormously to form a better understanding of psychotic processes, they do not primarily address the difference between psychotic processes and major psychotic disorders. There is a great difference between regressing into a temporary persecutory psychotic state of mind under stress and having a life-long condition that requires specific consideration in its own right.

Bion introduced a quite new way of looking at schizophrenia. His theory arose from detailed psychoanalytic studies of individual schizophrenic patients (Bion 1957). He distinguished between two separate entities: the psychotic and non-psychotic parts of the personality. They function quite differently, the fundamental issue being how they cope with psychic pain.

Early on in life the psychotic part acts as if it can split the perceptual apparatus that registers emotional experiences into minute fragments and project them into objects. From the onset of life, the mental apparatus needed for judgement and for differentiating internal and external reality is attacked. The splitting is quite different from an excessive use of normal splitting and projection related to unbearable pain as described by Klein.

There is according to Bion always an underlying non-psychotic part capable of taking in and thinking, and through tolerating frustrations – experiences not quite matching our preconceptions – learning from experience. This means that even in the case of the most disturbed of patients one is invited still to seek an unaffected part of the patient with whom to communicate.

A vivid example of this seeking out of the part of the patient with whom one can communicate was provided by the case of a man with a history of severe chronic schizophrenia, hospitalized for over thirty years. When the asylum closed, the man was placed in a group home, but he became too demanding and returned to what was now the district-hospital unit. He would repeatedly say that he was not Mr Smith but another person, Mr Jones, born six years earlier, who had owned the asylum, and who possessed 80 million pounds. Moreover, he averred that I, Dr Lucas, had stolen his Ford Granada car. But the man would not associate as to why he was Mr Jones. He just insisted that it was a fact, and it seemed to give him a licence to behave in whatever infantile way he liked. In the end I said to him that I was not talking to Mr Jones but Mr Smith. I said to Mr Smith that we have got a problem with Mr Jones, who acted as a big baby, having outbursts and always wanting everything his own way. This approach stopped the patient in his tracks during one of his usual tirades about his being owed millions of pounds. It temporarily took the wind out of his sails and he quietened down and smiled.

The psychotic part cannot learn from experience. Intolerant of psychic pain and frustration, the psychotic part uses the mind as a muscular organ to evacuate feelings and the part of the mind that registers them. Bion held that from early life a gap appears between the psychotic and non-psychotic parts, widening until it becomes unbridgeable.

If the evacuated feelings were verbal in origin, then the projection forms an auditory hallucination. If the feelings were evacuated through the eyes, then visual hallucinations result. If feelings, developed through the work of the non-psychotic part, are concretely projected into an external object, they form a delusion. Bion referred to a process where past memories, termed ideographs, are stored for the purpose of the evacuation of disturbing feelings in the form of delusions. He thus invites us to consider the relationship between hallucinations and delusions and the purpose behind the communications.

A young man who came into hospital saying that he was Edward, son of Henry the Eighth, illustrates the presentation of an ideograph requiring understanding. The question was why he needed to bring up this piece of history. What feelings were being projected? He had no associations to the delusion. It later transpired, from feedback from the social services, that he had been beating his wife, who was now in a refuge. The psychotic part had to evacuate the awareness of its behaving in a manic, omnipotent state. This awareness was arrived at through the work of the non-psychotic part. The psychotic part, on the other hand, disowned and distanced the awareness into the stored ideograph of being Henry the Eighth's son; that is, the psychotic part had been behaving like Henry. Thereby the man was able to create his own rules and religion and treat his wife in any way he felt like.

Most general psychiatrists do not ask, dynamically speaking, how hallucinations are formed. They describe how the patient hears voices but never how this occurred. Bion excitingly and convincingly demonstrated the genesis of hallucinations through the idea of the mind being used as a muscular organ to evacuate feelings. Common examples of witnessing visual hallucinations in the process of creation occur during everyday ward interviews with new admissions. A patient with a diagnosis of schizophrenia may answer factual questions on his life history in a straightforward manner. However, when one turns to asking emotional questions, he may stare around the room, evacuating his feelings through his eyes. He may then turn to a person sitting next to him with a look as if saying, 'Who was that funny doctor who asked the emotional question in the first place?'

The commonest symptoms of psychosis are not, however, hallucinations or delusions, but denial and rationalization. The latter are present in well over 90 per cent of cases. The patient's communication from the psychotic part attacks one's sanity and invites one to accept that there is nothing wrong with them. Bion's theory invites one to consider, in all communications from a patient, whether the communication is coming from the non-psychotic part or is a rationalization from a psychotic part, covering up what is in fact a murderous state of mind.

This has important practical implications in all assessments related to formal hospital admissions. A good illustrative example could be taken from a patient who, having stopped his medication, became disturbed. His mother alerted the authorities that he was becoming aggressive in his attitude towards her, indicating that he was relapsing because he had stopped his medication. When seen by the Approved Social Worker (ASW), the patient presented a defensive picture, implying that he had just not got around to going to see his GP for his medication and was intending to rectify this. He said that his mother had a poor understanding of him, presenting a convincing case for acceptance of his version. The next day he was apprehended by the police, following a serious unprovoked attack on a stranger.

A lesson from such a case is that the nearest relative makes the diagnosis of a psychotic relapse and it then becomes an issue whether the professionals accept the relative's version or succumb to the patient's rationaliszation. At least having a coherent operational framework in mind when approaching psychotic disorders, as is provided by Bion's insights, allows one to be forewarned of potential pitfalls. As Bion put it, he had an advantage listening to Hitler on the radio before the war. The advantage was that he understood no German. As a result he only heard a dangerous madman ranting and raving, and was not open to being seduced by the words.

David Rosenfeld observed that if dreams are the royal road to the un-conscious in understanding the mind of the neurotic, then the counter-transference is the 'via regia' to understanding in the case of the psychotic (Rosenfeld 1992). Let me now demonstrate how it is possible to use a counter-transference experience in order to understand a delusion. A patient, on admission to hospital, complained of having a rat in his stomach. He said this in a very cold, angry and detached way. He made me feel that his state of mind was entirely organic in origin and I could feel no associations in my mind to the rat. However, after he had a stay in hospital and medication helped him to calm down, my counter-transference feelings changed. It emerged that he suffered from chronic schizophrenia and had been moved out of a group home into a non-supported place on his own. He did not have the emotional resources to cope. The psychotic part dealt with his disturbed feelings by projecting them into becoming the rat in his stomach.

As he became more relaxed, I felt the 'rattiness' that he couldn't stomach on being left. Initially it seemed that he had nowhere else to project these rat-like feelings other than into his own body. Subsequently he found he could thrust them into me. He had wanted people to respond to his needs for help. When I put this to him, he thanked me. Thus one's feelings about a psychotic patient's communications can change with time, and dynamic processes can be seen to be occurring even in what are apparently the most inaccessible of cases.

One should also note from this vignette how medication was needed to help settle the patient's state of mind. Anti-psychotic medication viewed at a psychological level helps to provide a calming-down effect, so that emotions can be contained rather than continue to be violently projected. Medication does not have to be seen as just producing a mental straight-jacket or as an alternative to dialogue, but can be recognized as facilitative within the rehabilitative process. In other words, medication should be considered for its helpful effects, rather than as a short cut to avoid meaningful emotional involvement with the patient.

Patients with psychotic disorders tend to fragment and project their problems, and different members of staff and relatives are recipients of the projections. They need to come together, bringing with them the missing pieces of the jigsaw puzzle, for the overall picture to emerge at a multidisciplinary meeting. Such a meeting typically occurs during a hospital admission, where there has been a relapse of the illness and where reasons for the relapse need to be explored.

An approach that carries within it an integrating, analytic core can help in providing a meaningful framework of reference when staff are coping with the pressure of demanding situations and heavy work loads. As Y.O. Alanen describes, when treatment staff are able to work in a way that makes use of dynamic thinking about psychosis, they gain an added interest in their vocation. A further bonus is that they are less likely to be afflicted by two of the major pitfalls of working with psychotic patients: 'burn out' and severe pessimism (Alanen 1997). This method creates a space for thinking in a pressurized world, summarized to me by a nurse on the ward: 'The "revolving door syndrome" has been replaced by a "cat flap".'

The following vignette demonstrates how it is possible to deploy an integrated treatment programme in practice. A 37-year-old woman started to be troubled, for the first time in her life, by noises from a neighbour's bedroom. She was eventually admitted to hospital. Doctors had considered differential diagnoses ranging from borderline personality disorder, depression with obsessive features, to the possibility of the start of a paranoid schizophrenic illness. Yet her condition had failed to respond to a combination of anti-depressants, anti-psychotics and individual counselling. In his counter-transference reaction, the junior doctor felt that it was his responsibility to get her out of hospital and that he would never be able to do this.

On assembling information from the involved multidisciplinary team, it emerged that she had lived all her life with her parents. When her father died, her mother felt that her daughter should now be helped to become more independent and so intended to sell the family home and buy two smaller places. Her daughter could then still live nearby but no longer with her. The daughter's fears of an enforced developmental movement were projected into the neighbour's bedroom as the persecutory noise, and her reaction was then to come into hospital, as if returning to the womb. The strength of her wish to remain looked after was projected so concretely into the junior doctor that it led to his powerful counter-transference experience that she was his personal responsibility and that he would never get her out of hospital.

Identifying the central dynamic of the separation anxiety, together with understanding the junior doctor's counter-transference experience, freed the team from feeling in a stuck position, allowing them to start to address the anxieties with the patient and her mother.

However, the problem remains that we are working in a changing environment in relation to psychosis. With the closure of the asylums, and the reduction in hospital beds, concern has shifted to containing patients with histories of psychotic episodes in the community. The challenge is to bring closer together the medical and PsychoSocial understandings of psychosis; and for this to occur there needs to be a mutual understanding of the position of each. Being familiar with the general psychiatrist's approach, as described earlier in this chapter, will help those with a predominantly PsychoSocial attitude to see the psychiatrist's stance. Helping the psychiatrist to appreciate defence mechanisms in operation, and joint discussion of shared counter-transference experiences, also helps in developing a closer rapport between the two groups of carers.

For both sides, it is important to carry a diagnostic framework in one's mind. For example, a patient with a so-called borderline personality disorder may have quite different emotional requirements during a period in a psychotherapeutically orientated community environment from a patient suffering from chronic schizophrenia. In the latter case, the real need may be for instigating provision of a life-long supportive environment that will be responsive to the ups and downs of their moods, rather than intense individual therapy.

Any placement in a community setting requires open and honest joint discussion between those responsible for psychiatric referrals and the potential community-home workers as to suitability and anticipated outcome. Work needs to be done by both sides to create a good rapport. To improve on and refine this joint process, for the benefit of the patients, remains a challenge for the future.

References

Alanen, Y.O. (1997) *Schizophrenia: Its Origins and Need-Adapted Treatment*. London: Karnac Books.

Berke, J.H. (1987) 'Settling-in, Settling-down, Leaving and Following-up: Stages of Stay at the Arbours Centre.' *British Journal of Medical Psychology 60*, 181–188.

Bion, W.R. (1957) 'Differentiation of the Psychotic from the Non-Psychotic Personalities.' In *Second Thoughts, Selected Papers on Psycho-Analysis*, 1967. New York: Jason Aronson.

Freud, S. (1914) 'On Narcissism: An Introduction.' *Vol. 14: The Standard Edition of the Complete Psychological Works of Sigmund Freud*. London: Hogarth Press.

Freud, S. (1920) 'Beyond the Pleasure Principle.' *Vol. 18: The Standard Edition of the Complete Psychological Works of Sigmund Freud*. London: Hogarth Press.

Freud, S. (1923) 'The Ego and the Id.' *Vol. 19: The Standard Edition of the Complete Psychological Works of Sigmund Freud*. London: Hogarth Press.

Freud, S. (1924) 'Neurosis and Psychosis.' *Vol. 19: The Standard Edition of the Complete Psychological Works of Sigmund Freud*. London: Hogarth Press.

Jaspers, K. (1963) *General Psychopathology*. (*Allgemeine Psychopathologie*, 7th edn, 1959, trans. J. Hoenig and M.W. Hamilton.) Manchester: Manchester University Press.

Leff, J. (1994) 'Working with families of schizophrenic patients.' *British Journal of Psychiatry 164*, 71–76.

Lucas, R. (1998) 'R.D. Laing – His Life and Legacy.' *International Journal of Psychoanalysis 79*, 1229–1239.

Rosenfeld, D. (1992) *The Psychotic Aspects of the Personality*. London: Karnac Books.

Rosenfeld, H. (1966) *Psychotic States: A Psycho-Analytical Approach*. New York: International University Press.

Schneider, K. (1959) *Clinical Psychopathology*. New York: Grune and Stratton.

CHAPTER 3

A Spin in the Toyota

Mats Mogren

In 1986 I spent a summer in Argentina as a guest of Dr Angel Fiasché.[1] Together with a colleague he had purchased a run-down hotel in Los Cocos, Argentina, and was working to renovate it for use as a treatment centre. Behind this project lay quite a special and simple idea. The patients came primarily from Buenos Aires, and the idea was that the move from an urban environment to a small rural community would involve a re-adjustment that would challenge stereotypical patterns, 'shake up' the person, and thereby open the way to new opportunities for learning.

The first goal of the project was the restoration of the hotel itself. The carpenters and the 'patients' did the work together. Every day we gathered by the swimming pool to drink Argentinian maté generally accompanied by lively discussion over day-to-day situations. However, it was not only manual labour that stood on the day's agenda. With help from professional artists, musicians, and journalists working in the project, creative activities such as music, painting and writing gave the patients an opportunity to express their inner dramas, and develop and cultivate their gifts. One important principle was that the local community assimilate the institution for the purpose of mutual ecosystemic enrichment. The surrounding society's resources were relied upon, and in exchange the locals were provided with concerts and other forms of help. A café was opened, along with a movie theatre, which had previously been non-existent in the town. These meeting places gave the townspeople a chance to revise their prejudices concerning psychosis, and the 'patients' an opportunity to contribute to the life and culture of the society from a position other than that of dependency; they were no longer passive consumers of health care, inferiors, but participants in the social contract – equals. Dr Fiasché's interest in institutions and institutional forms of working with the psychoses connects him with the Italian psychiatrist F. Basaglia, as well as with R.D. Laing, with whom he worked during the 1960s.

The work at Varpen and Gyllenkroken, in Gothenburg, Sweden, facilities that provide services for people in psychotic states, builds partly on experiences from Los Cocos. On the basis of our social contact with our guests, and with an in-depth knowledge of their often disorganized lives, we try together to establish organized habits. The co-operative restaurant, the heart of Gyllenkroken's facilities and its meeting place, is run by the staff and guests together, and offers inexpensive, nutritious dishes. This generous, basic provision for the body, together with the hospitality it implies, is a way for us to show our often suspicious visitors that the world isn't always so heartless. In addition, the restaurant has become popular among the residents and workers in the neighbourhood.

My intention in this chapter is to introduce the reader to the organizing ideas behind the work being done at Varpen and Gyllenkroken and to place them within the wider context of PsychoSocial thinking, and other views on psychosis. From their inception I have participated as a supervisor, contributing my theoretical and experiential knowledge during their formation and development as well as to their day-to-day clinical work. Both centres were established with the aim of providing an alternative to the traditional, authoritarian, drug-based psychiatric treatment, with its tendency to understand human nature by reference to a purely biological paradigm. In this context, these facilities share the ethos and aims of the Arbours Crisis Centre, the British mental health facility set up in London in 1973.

'What do you do if a patient becomes psychotic?' asks a representative of traditional Swedish psychiatry of a staff member at Varpen in a question-and-answer session that has begun to resemble a steely cross-examination.

'Oh, we take them for a spin in the Toyota,' replies the staff member.

'Don't you give them any medication?'

'No, we sit outside their rooms or read to them if they are suffering from anxiety attacks. We don't believe in medication; we believe in relationships.'

Varpen Psychosis Treatment Centre lies an hour's drive from Gothenburg in a beautiful, rural setting. The Centre is situated in a newly-built, aesthetically-pleasing house. The emotional atmosphere within is broad and generous. The staff is currently 12 strong, and the patients are there voluntarily.

The goal of treatment at Varpen is to be with the patient in his attempt to find himself and his place in life, and to help him reconstruct and work through his experiences. Thus, we do not consider the patient 'sick'; rather, we see him as someone who suffers, but does not always understand why. Varpen's job is to try to break the emotional isolation that has led the person to insanity; to transform the neurotic/psychotic suffering to everyday suffering that allows for an existential choice with the only curative tool we can trust – the human relationship.

Of the first six patients, all in their twenties with different varieties of psychotic conditions, five no longer live at the Centre. The sixth, who had been severely mistreated under traditional psychiatric care, killed herself very dramatically after a stay of about six months. For the others, it took five to six years of treatment at Varpen to begin to establish a wavering, though medicine-free life. Today these individuals consume no psychiatric services other than the follow-up therapeutic contact that is regularly included as a part of Varpen's leaving process. Instead, they spend their time at vocational training, university studies, or work, with a focus on developing their social lives.

We are kindred spirits with the Arbours Crisis Centre, in London. This link has helped us maintain and develop further a tradition of PsychoSocial interventions with psychotic patients. Dr Joseph Berke has given several seminars at Varpen since the first contact was made with him at a public seminar at Gothenburg Psychotherapy Institute in 1992. Since then, almost all the members of staff at Varpen have visited Arbours on separate occasions. Similarly, people from Arbours have visited Varpen. A member of staff from Varpen is currently in psychoanalytic psychotherapy training at Arbours and works at their Crisis Centre as Resident Therapist.

Gyllenkroken is not a treatment centre; rather, it is a meeting place, a space for activities, and a residence organized and run by the staff, the tenants, and the visitors together. It was founded in the 1980s by a former psychiatric nurse and the parents of two adult, seriously iatrogenically[2] damaged children. Gyllenkroken's guiding principle is that insanity is the result of both inner and outer solitude. We are social beings, and become human only in relation to others.

The facility has grown quickly and today employs some 20 full-time staff members, who organize between 50 and 60 visitors a day. Around 25 people live in its residential accommodation. Gyllenkroken offers a number of activities, from woodworking to the tango. Music occupies a particularly important place and has come to provide a sense of identity for both the centre and its musicians. Recently a CD of original music was released.

From its inception Gyllenkroken has received financial support through public funds; but it was not until the project demonstrated its viability that it began to receive regular support from the local authorities. Today Gyllenkroken is recognized nationwide, enjoys the support of the Swedish Board of National Health, and receives over 2000 study visitors each year.

The activities at Varpen and Gyllenkroken proceed from a specific set of underlying principles: an ideological infrastructure of tradition and theory enables us to 'see' the person within the insanity, and to organize our institutional and clinical work accordingly. These principles can be summarized in a few key concepts: historical consciousness – an awareness that our current understanding of what constitutes 'health' and 'sickness', 'normal' and 'abnormal', is a historically and culturally determined construct; humanism – the belief that human beings can learn from experience, differentiate between good and evil, give respect to each other and work for mutual improvement; psychoanalysis – especially the socially conscious PsychoSocial philosophy developed in Argentina by Enrique Pichon-Rivière and his followers; and, finally, an absolute existential–phenomenological respect for the experiences, integrity, and life choices of another.

Images of insanity have been part of human history and its cultural expression from the earliest known mystic and religious tracts to today's current cultural gestalt as expressed in literature, theatre, art, religion, film, law and science. Concurrently with Shakespeare's dramatic meditations on the nature of human passion and the rise of the capitalist system, the modern conceptualization of insanity began to take form. The unemployed, the vagabonds and the mad were confined together in settlements and hospitals that had at one time housed lepers; perceived as the carriers of pestilence and moral decay, the members of these groups were isolated and demonized. Confinement reduced social problems to the level of the individual, where they could be observable and classifiable, the very prerequisite for the establishment of a medical–psychological conceptualization of madness.

Humanist protests against confinement began to make themselves heard during the time of the French Revolution. Reformist movements in France and England strove to transform the asylum from a prison to a medical institution. The aim of these new institutions was the cure of the mentally ill by persuading them to admit their 'guilt'; thereafter they were gradually re-integrated as useful members of society. This was the institutionalization of the hand of power.

Towards the end of the 19th century, Darwin's theory of evolution was combined with Morel's theories on degeneration and heredity into a new paradigm of abnormality. A promiscuous immoral lifestyle was believed to lead to the degeneration of the nervous system, from depression to spinal disintegration and collapse. At the same time, Freud put forward a revolutionary alternative thesis that such symptoms resulted from a conflict between instinctual drives and the disciplinary demands of culture, an expression of an eternal battle between Desire and Necessity.

The 'subject that speaks' emerged as a central figure from within psychoanalytic discourse, and with it arose a new understanding of psychological suffering. In general, mainstream psychiatry was not influenced, but there were a few isolated exceptions, such as the Burghölzli hospital in Switzerland, where, around 1910, Eugen Bleuler, Jean Piaget, Ludwig Binswanger, Karl Abraham and C.G. Jung constructed the concept of 'schizophrenia' and other models for understanding psychosis. In the traditional asylums, individuals were consistently dehumanized and correctional methods developed and employed: cold water baths, strap-down chairs, ECT and, during the 1940s, lobotomies and forced sterilizations. The height of this medical–psychiatric tradition was finally reached, we may hope, with the Nazi doctors' extermination of 'degenerate elements' in the mental hospitals. It is probably this historically determined and deeply-rooted picture of psychosis as a disease that presents the largest obstacle to our attempts to listen to and respect the life and existential choices of the other.

The treatment of psychosis in Scandinavia has a mixed history. Swedish psychiatric practices were until the 1960s completely dominated by the biological paradigm. The psychiatrist Herman Lundborg, founder of the world's first state-run institute for 'racial hygiene' in 1921, had great influence on the psychiatric community. Like many other countries, and beginning in 1935, Sweden passed laws for the forced sterilization of the 'mentally ill', that is people not living according to the prevailing narrow definition of normality – a practice that continued until the mid-1970s.[3] During the 1940s and 1950s the academic world in Sweden was entirely dominated by Uppsalian analytic philosophy (logical positivism), which meant that such areas of knowledge as existentialism, phenomenology, psychoanalysis and Marxism were looked upon as metaphysical.

Throughout the 20th century mainstream psychiatry had its detractors, however – those who believed that it pathologized and then locked up essentially healthy (albeit outspoken) people, and those, doctors from other fields, who felt that it was unscientific and authoritarian. Inspired primarily by the Anglo-Saxon 'anti-psychiatry' movement, this criticism reached a peak in the 1960s, when psychologists, counsellors, social workers, psychiatric nurses, and many others, began to challenge the psychiatrist's exclusive right to understand and treat the mentally ill. This in turn led to bitter conflicts during the 1960s and 1970s, which found psychiatrists pitted against even the smallest reforms, in their attempts to maintain their professional dominance. Even to this day, many Swedish psychiatrists do not accept therapy as a form of treatment in its own right but see it rather as complementary to antipsychotic medication.

One of the earliest experiments in the alternative treatment of the psychoses in Scandinavia began in the 1950s, with the implementation at Ullevals Hospital in Norway of 'milieu therapy', a tradition developed further by the influential Norwegian psychiatrist Svein Haugsgjerd. In Finland Professor of Psychiatry Dr Y. Alanen has also been influential in non-biological-oriented psychiatric circles, especially during the 1990s. The central idea behind the 'Aabo model' put forward by Professor Alanen is that the way the person in crisis is met the very first time he seeks help determines the outcome. With a combination of individual and family therapeutic interventions, and if necessary a small dose of benzodiazepines, around 60 per cent of clients turn around at the door and never require further psychiatric treatment. Of Finland's five current professors in psychiatry, three are psychoanalytically trained and have taught philosophy in the humanistic tradition of Georg Henrik von Wright.[4]

Meanwhile in Sweden ground-breaking work in the treatment of psychotic states was done by Barbro Sandin in her psychotherapeutic work with schizophrenics at Saeter's Hospital during the 1970s. There have also been attempts to copy the 'Aabo model'. Despite this enthusiasm and the involvement it generated, numbers of therapists drowned in the drug-oriented psychiatric system.

In the 1980s the 'psychiatric reform', an overhaul of this entire system, began, and the huge, monolithic mental hospitals were dismantled. Today the number of treatment centres in Sweden is quite large (albeit far too few in relation to the need), and yet most of these centres are still dominated by the traditional psychiatric view. Even today, the claim that human relationships are of themselves the curative element is very controversial.

It is interesting to consider the view of psychosis as a survival strategy. In his analysis of Schreber's autobiography, Freud revolutionized our understanding of the psychoses by demonstrating that it was an attempt to solve an impossible relationship to reality. On the other hand, Freud expressed little interest in psychotic persons, claiming that the narcissistic basis of their pathology hindered them from developing transference, the basis for psychoanalytic treatment. However, during the 1940s, many of Freud's conceptualizations were placed in new contexts and redefined, especially in relation to the psychoses. The Argentinian psychoanalyst Heinrich Racker created new possibilities for the analysis of psychotic conditions through his extensive work on the concept of transference.

In the 1960s the work of R.D. Laing gave new perspectives on 'psychotic states'. According to the existential–phenomenological perspective, a person's existence in the world is formed out of the essence of his experiences. The psychosis is a subjective 'rational' survival strategy in an impossible reality, *not* an illness in the medical sense of the term. For example, at Varpen most of our patients have been sexually abused.

The overwhelming violence inherent in the psychiatric interpretation of these underlying motivations as expressions of an illness can be emotionally devastating, and the instant when meaninglessness is transformed into meaning irrevocably lost. The result: hopelessness and chronicity. In our work the most important task is to create and sustain hope in the search for meaning. The essence of the existential–phenomenological perspective, in the meeting between people, can be summarized in a few lines from Laing's *The Divided Self*: 1) I recognize that the other is who he believes himself to be; 2) He recognizes that I am who I believe myself to be. It is this mutually reinforcing confirmation of the other's existential being that establishes the basis for a transformative learning relationship, if necessary sometimes via deep regression, which Laing's co-worker Joseph Berke has demonstrated in his work since the 1960s. Arbours is the bearer of the traditions from Kingsley Hall, and the bridge to us at Varpen and Gyllenkroken.

Among the influences on our clinical practice are the ideas of Argentinan psychiatrist and psychoanalyst Dr Enrique Pichon-Rivière (1907–1977). The following vignette expresses the essence of his attitude:

> Enrique Pichon-Rivière spent his entire life investigating the mystery of human depression and helping to open the cages of non-communication. He found an effective ally in the game of soccer. During the 1940s Pichon-Rivière organized a soccer team together with his mental patients. The Crazies proved impossible to defeat on the soccer fields of eastern Argentina and at the same time applied with their game the best social therapy imaginable. 'The soccer team's strategy is my most important task,' the psychiatrist would explain, who was also the team's trainer and one of its best forwards. (Galeanos 1998)

Marxist Pichon-Rivière felt driven to make psychoanalytic treatment available for broader social groups. His goal was to transcend the traditional boundaries for psychoanalysis and develop new forms of therapy for the psychoses: group and 'milieu' therapy, 'the therapeutic society', and other such projects. Some of his theoretical contributions can be summarized as follows:

- The Human Bond:[5] He expanded the concept of object-relations and referred to it as a bond. He emphaized the mutually dialectic relationship to the other, and his theory encompasses both behaviour and affect. The human bond describes the context in which the human being emerges.

- The PsychoSocial Group: The inner psychosocial group is formed from early experiences. It constitutes the prototype for understanding and acting within the various sociodynamic groups in the external world. This conceptual distinction can be used to help the clinician/patient differentiate between the world as it is and the world as we interpret and experience it. At Varpen, we combine collective co-existence with individual therapy. Imaginary persons from the patient's historically established inner drama find or create roles that impose themselves within the social life of the group.

- The Drive for Knowledge: Klein's concept of epistemophilia – the drive to knowledge – reveals itself in the communications between patient and staff. One of the aims of the treatment is that the patient should discover the distinction between inner world and external reality. Problematic areas, cliffs and distortions, reveal themselves, and stereotyped, frozen tranquillity is set in motion.

- The Operative Group: Pichon-Rivière worked as a psychiatrist at a large hospital. At one point, due to his participation in a political protest, he had his entire staff taken away from him. To resolve the resulting crisis Pichon-Rivière created 'the operative group'. He trained those patients who were in the best condition to take care of their fellow patients. This solution, of course, expressed a rather inopportune and radical belief in the capacities of mental patients – after all, they were supposed to be incurable! The operative group's ability to think within the terms of a goal-oriented learning process is of central importance, as well as its ability to contain the fear which accompanies change when the Uncanny is mobilized.

Beyond the neurotic attitude in which most of us live drifts an incomprehensible, chaotic, magical, concrete, and occasionally terrifying psychotic world. In Pichon-Rivière's theories, this dialectic is conceptualized in terms of the psychotic nucleus and the neurotic superstructure. In a crisis, when the superstructure fails to fully contain anxieties, the underlying, latent nucleus becomes manifest. The various expressions of psychotic symptoms reveal the seriousness and desperation in the patient's inner drama. With Pichon-Rivière's models it becomes possible to 'read' the expression of this inner drama psychically, bodily and socially.

'Every confused behaviour comes from an inability to learn; a blocking of the ability to learn from reality'. In the psychotic state you live in your own inner world and do not doubt your interpretations of it in relation to reality. The images generated in this internal world superimpose themselves on reality and dominate it. Panic, the fear of annihilation, threatens the ability to feel and think – the tools for solving of conflicts. Will the outcome be creativity or madness? Madness refers to the condition of non-learning. Only with emotional involvement in the other can you discover, through experience, that your picture of the other doesn't really correspond with the 'real' other. Here, transferential mistakes are welcomed.

As we understand the individual as an expression of society, of social and class membership, of family and surroundings, the 'psychotic' is the speaker who reveals that something in this context is wrong. Our scepticism in relation to psychopharmacological treatment results from the fact that the speaker is robbed of his voice as well as his emotional presence with his affect and thought – the very material necessary for transforming a dilemma to a conflict and an existential choice. Treatment of symptoms provides us with nothing to learn and no need for the restructuring of the inner world: 'Don't expect anything of me; I'm schizophrenic.' With medical treatment something alien is introduced, which strengthens the feeling of the Uncanny and the image that we fear of him. There is nothing to listen to with meaning. In the authoritarian relationship the person is turned into a diagnosis and forms himself accordingly. Hope is doused and panic intensified.

Our work proceeds from the hypothesis that the decisive force in becoming human is the human relationship of love, and that several generations influence the creation of an adult identity. The family is the most important institutional structure to introduce the human being to culture. Sometimes it fails to fulfil its task to guide the child from absolute dependence to the adult position of independence.

One patient at Varpen, who had been violently provocative, unpleasant, and antagonistic, was re-admitted to the psychiatric ward. The manic state protected her from her own destructive impulses. In her individual therapy she began to reflect on what was happening to her. It was discovered that she unconsciously followed her family historical tradition with precision. Both her grandmother and her mother had lost their husbands while their children were very young. Both had been sent into psychiatric care. As the patient became conscious of her dread of this 'inescapable' destiny, this terrifying enchantment of hers vanished. After this abrupt event her relationships took a different turn, expressing a new-found sincerity and openness. Her attitude changed; she sought out support from the staff and her previous arrogance disappeared. However, all was not completely resolved. On numerous occasions, in contact with her therapist, 'something' came closer to consciousness, despite her desperate, frightened attempts to hold it at bay. At last the explanation for her earlier, inexplicably violent outburst – which had something to do with the curtains at Varpen – was revealed. When the patient was five or six years old she had been used as a kind of 'mannequin' by a neighbour who sewed clothes. However, when the curtains were drawn, the patient was not only used as a model; she was also severely sexually abused. The discovery of these memories led to new qualities – depression and an urge to repair. She now has the ability to live alone and deal with the existential dilemmas in life and relationships that are the lot of everyone.

The PsychoSocial approach provides time and space. It takes time to learn the 'semiotic' of the other; to discover the hidden story. On one of Varpen's vacation ski trips a male patient develops severe stomach pains. The patient is terribly anxious. His therapist, who is also on the trip, suggests jokingly: 'Let's travel to another country.' They get into the car and drive off. On the way back from Norway into Sweden the therapist says, 'We ought to bring something home from our travels abroad', whereupon he stops the car in the middle of nowhere to jump out and cut off the branch of a tree with his knife. At this, the patient's panic becomes total; he behaves as if he has been physically attacked. Out of this apparently random and inexplicable event the contours of sexual abuse appear to the therapist and his patient. It turns out that the patient's father raped him in the shower during a ski-trip many years ago.

The term 'space' refers to a special place with specific rules and a contract that serves to organize the work. The task of the staff is to participate in the creation of different spaces: the intimate, for interpersonal trust; the social, for the interchange of everyday thoughts and experiences; and the practical, in which one learns 'know-how'. The patient chooses the person in whom he has faith, and with whom he is comfortable to be. In particular, we must be able to reside in those inner spaces where no-one else has wanted, or been able, to be. New praxis – emotional and intellectual – requires time and space to develop. When the patient leaves the external 'institution', he will be able to use the internalized 'institution' in situations that formerly led him to suffer psychotic panic. When reflection, symbolization, and feelings of depression replace inexplicable acts of irritation, the end of the work is in sight.

In this context the supervisory space is vitally important. Earlier we started with the idea of making a careful reconstruction, using Kleinian concepts, of the patient's inner drama from his biography. With the information available to us I suggested that the behaviour the staff experienced as bizarre represented the only alternatives the patient had in his battle against his terrifying phantasies. Today, the focus is not on how to handle the objective person, but on how to understand the way we experience him within ourselves. To this the work with transference and countertransference is central. Moments of transformation require that we follow the process without understanding it; our attitude towards the unknown and our ability to contain it are crucial. Sometimes as therapists we must bear the craziness to the extent even of becoming crazy, in order to successfully digest the introjected parts of the patient, create meaning, and return that to the patient. This in turn highlights the extent to which we see our patients through our own constructs – our values, prejudices, feelings and our own personal experiences. We learn who we are in relation to others. Time after time we discover the difficulties inherent in listening, and the ways in which we try to avoid unpleasant insights.

The concept of the social space also becomes important. The mundane social routines of day-to-day living, on the chair beside the bed, or in the car, are the main therapeutic tools in the battle against madness, together with the individual therapy. The social space conveys and maintains the elemental structures of social life as well as a given culture's social codes. The strength of the PsychoSocial approach lies in its capacity to provide for the patient a dual perspective: that of being seen both as a social being and as an individual. The interactions that occur as part of the social collective's activities and inside the individual therapist's room create possibilities for the person to learn to know himself and the other.

The staff must respect the patients as capable of making their own choices, and be willing to engage in confrontations. 'Technique' and 'treatment' are concepts we must reconsider because we believe that an unreflective relationship can lead to a non-affirmative, distancing emotional absence. This is probably a repetition of the person's childhood experience and the reason he has come to us in the first place. The ideal is that we do not treat people; rather, that we treat each other. It is preferable to be honest, spontaneous and wrong rather than cold and right. This attitude helps create the necessary mutual presence in 'the bond'. Our institutions need to be more tolerant than the surrounding society and minimize the consequences of a person's 'not knowing' the rules. Many of those acts that in normal social life lead to ostracization are a good starting point for reflection.

Psychoanalytic interpretations do not belong to the social space. This rule prevents the development of a subculture of 'interpretative terrorism' in daily life. Holding the function and rules of the social space separate from those of the individual's therapy is central in the work. Members of staff are forced to find innovative ways to communicate their basic values and to create a climate in which no participant has reason to fear another. Staff members had to intervene when they saw the destructive behaviour of one particular individual. His attacks were treacherous and concealed in such a manner that we could not fall back on our Swedish tradition of 'folkvett'.[6] Furthermore, we could see the way he would unerringly pick out certain guests and with cunning accuracy deduce the sphere in which their fears resided. He dealt with his own fears via projective identification. His victims would 'become psychotic' and let out terrifying screams. We learned to recognize the subtle pattern and finally we were forced to intervene. Horse-tied by the restrictions, the staff had to find a creative solution. We decided that the staff member who had the best relationship to him would remain on his guard until an occasion for action arrived. This opportunity arose in the form of a shriek and a defensive flurry of hand gestures emanating from a corner of the café. The scene was unmistakable. There the man stood with his victim. The staff member slipped himself momentarily into the scene and commented, 'Good job, man. You really scared him', in such a way that the attacker could not help but realize that he had been found out.

The PsychoSocial approach places the person in a social and moral context with new possibilities: an environment is presented that cultivates and promotes integration, not by virtue of the staff's reformative attitude but by virtue of their companionship.

To express unequivocally the essence of our work let me offer a shard from Freud (1971):

> We cannot avoid also taking for treatment patients who are so helpless and incapable of ordinary life that for them one has to combine analytic with educative influence; and even with the majority now and then occasions arise in which the physician is bound to take up the position of teacher and mentor. But it must always be done with great caution, and the patient should be educated to liberate and fulfil his own nature, and not to resemble ourselves. (p.399)

The key to understanding Varpen's outstanding result in the tradition of PsychoSocial treatment of psychosis in Sweden[7] is its outlook on humankind. We are capable of doing this work when we have exchange with and inspiration from other institutions, such as Arbours, which respect people as human beings. Facilities which protect and improve important traditions of treatment, while the spirit of neo-liberalism expresses itself in the desire for quick gains and short-term profit, even when caring for others. In Sweden today most of the research and teaching in psychiatry is carried out by or with the support of the medical–pharmaceutical industrial complex. Society and culture exist as a network of institutions. As a part of this framework our activities in the form of our interventions acquire a meaning beyond ourselves. They create a very particular climate of relations and way of understanding the human being in the society we all inhabit. In a deeper sense our work is political.

Acknowledgements

The author would like to thank Karl Mogren and Tim Spence for their invaluable help, and particularly with their help in translating it into English.

Notes

1   The Gothenburg Institute of Psychotherapy was founded in 1974 by the Pichon-Rivière disciple Dr Angel Fiasché and his wife, the Kleinian child analyst Dora Fiasché, together with a Swedish group.

2   Iatrogenic: caused or created through treatment; from the Greek 'yatros', meaning 'doctor'.

3   62,888 supposedly 'mentally ill' people were sterilised in Sweden between 1935 and 1975.

4   Prof. Y. Alanen, personal communication.

5   The term 'bond' ('vínculo') has a central and very specific meaning in the theories of Pichon-Rivière that unfortunately lacks a precise English equivalent. For Pichon-Rivière, the 'bond' describes a specific type of object relation – a kind of 'emotional linkage' possessing a distinct quality. The quality of the bond forms the basis of Pichon-Rivière's diagnostic system (see below).

6   Elementary rules for social life.

7   Prof. Bengt-Åke Armelius, Umeå University, personal communication.

References

Armelius, B-Å., Börjesson, J., Fogelstam, H., Granberg, Å., Hemphälä, M. and Jeanneau, M. (2000) *En 5-årsstudie av patienter och personal vid behandlingshemmet Varpen.* Umeå: Inst. för psykologi, Umeå universitet.

Berke, J. (1979) *I Haven't Had to Go Mad Here.* Penguin Books.

Berke, J. *et al.* (1995) *Sanctuary.* London: Process Press.

Bion, W.R. (1977) *Learning from Experience.* New York: Jason Aronson.

Foucault, M. (1973) *Vansinnets Historia.* Stockholm: Aldus.

Freud, S. (1971) 'Turnings in the ways of Psychoanalytic Therapy.' *Collected Papers volume II.* London: The Hogarth Press.

Galeanos, E. (1998) *Fotbollens himmel och helvete.* Stockholm/Stehag: Symposion.

Laing, R.D. (1968) *Det kluvna jaget.* Stockholm: Bonniers.

Pichon-Rivière, E. (1979) *Teoría del vínculo.* Buenos Aires: Ediciones Nueva Visión.

Pichon-Rivière, E. (1982) *Del Psicoanálisis a la Psicología Social Vol I–III* (Vol I: El proceso creador; Vol II: La psiquiatría. Una nueva problemática; Vol III: El proceso grupal). Buenos Aires: Ediciones Nueva Visión.

Pichon-Rivière, E. (1982) *Del psicoanálisis a la Psicología Social.* Buenos Aires: Ediciones Nueva Visión.

Qvarsell, R. (1993) *Utan vett och vilja.* Stockholm: Carlssons bokförlag.

Racker, H. (1968) *Transference and Countertransference.* London: The Hogarth Press.

Zito Lema, V. (1976) *Conversaciones con Enrique Pichon-Rivière. Sobre el arte y la locura.* Buenos Aires: Timerman Editores.

CHAPTER 4

The Power of the Play

Stella Pierides-Müller

Psychosis, as the denial of reality in the defence against psychic pain and anxiety, has always been present in the psychological history of man. The psychotic personality's attempt at repair – as opposed to true reparation – while arising out of the psychotic concern to heal and protect the ego (Bion 1958; Freud 1911) is, by definition, always misguided and lacks the proper means – such as reality sense, concern for the object – for doing so. Nevertheless, the mythical nature of the attempt to construct a life on a different plane of reality bears similarities to the creation of art and literature. The personal myth(s) thus created aim – quite literally – to take the mind away from the problems of internal and external reality, and bear an uncanny resemblance to social and cultural myths and fiction.

However, the relationship between myth and listener, audience and play, reader and book, viewer and painting, set in motion the potential for working through and change, as thinking and behaviour become possible. This relationship is either missing altogether or is attacked in the mind of the psychotic personality, with the result of a story that is incomplete, unsatisfying and circular. Repetition rather than development is the main characteristic.

Here I am concerned with the theme of myth and its development in tragedy, which elaborates and contains the more disturbing aspects of the myth. I link this process with the private myths and personal tragedies of individuals who require psychological treatment. I then illustrate how residential, PsychoSocial, psychodynamic treatment offers a valuable treatment alternative for severely borderline and psychotic patients. These patients need a consistent, continuous presence to help them metabolize new sensations, so that they can develop their personal mythologies and raw reactions into elaborate personal narratives that can be thought about and contained. The work of the Arbours Crisis Centre, providing as the Centre does multiple therapeutic layers – the team, housemeetings, art and movement therapies and the milieu – that interweave in complex ways, creates a 'fabric' which acts as a container. The Centre aims to contain the unbearable emotional loads the patients bring to it. Far from fearing splitting and taking precautions to avoid it, the therapists here expect it and actively look for and work with it. Drawing on the work of Wilfred Bion, especially on the themes of alpha function as the maternal tool for containment, I illustrate how raw emotional sensations, undigested over time, find in the context of the multi-system container of the Centre the opportunity to get transformed into sensible and digestible experiences. This sets in motion a process of reflection and a belief in the patient in the possibility of transforming insufferable mythical horror and chaos into emotional pain, acceptance of the limitations of the reality of one's predicament, and understanding. Often this provides the impetus for the long process of psychotherapy and healing.

The concept of myth involves the story of a hero dealing with major life themes such as alienation, ambition, family issues, love and its vicissitudes, fate or religion. Through the retelling of the heroic deeds, the listener is availed of the opportunity to work through issues in his or her inner life, by identification with the major figures of the myth. In addition, cultural and religious aspects are conveyed through its narration which result in the socialization of the individual. Sigmund Freud, Carl Jung, Joseph Campbell, and others, understood the significance of the myth in its symbolic representation of basic human issues and their resolution.

However, myths have been told in many forms; in their more concrete recounting, they connect with at least one form of literature, that of epic poetry, which tells of mythical acts and only slightly elaborates mythical reality as well as praising it. Now since both myths and epic poetry, in pre-historic times, were said to depict reality, in other words were taken to be historical descriptions, they had to be retold in as much detail and with as little alteration as possible – the 'reality' described being under the direct supervision and direction of the all-seeing gods.

An important difference developed between mythical 'reality' as sung in epic poetry and reality in the tragedy, plays, poetry and literature which followed. The latter, from Aeschylus onwards, was no longer linked to reality – whether mythical or historical – in a way that necessitated the re-production of 'facts'. Myth moved away from a historical role to one where reflection becomes important – where justice, compassion, forgiveness, fear and, above all, choice are recognized to be in the mind and the hands of the individual hero (Snell 1953). With the development of tragedy, external reality diminished in importance. With this, ideas of riches or quantities lost their appeal, and the soul, or the internal world, took on a new significance, explored, above all, by Euripides.

> In his plays the human being is made to stand apart from the variegated tapestry of divine and earthly forces, and instead becomes himself the point whence actions and achievements take their origin. His own passions and his own knowledge are the only determining factors; all else is deception and semblance. (Snell 1953; repr. 1982, p.111)

At a time when fifth-century Athens was differentiating itself from its mythical and theocratic chains, allowing its citizens freedom of speech in a democracy, Euripides, in particular, was exploring the struggle of individuals to change themselves from being a simple actor/actress or carrier of the gods' wishes to being creators of their own destiny. In Euripides' *Medea*, the first psychological portrait of its kind, the individual is heard struggling between reason and the irrational mind and giving way to the irrational instincts. Thus tragedy moved to the theatrical play, where imagination, form and artistic convention (the stage, too) were being used to contain and give further shape and appeal to the content. Thus the move from the mythical representation of the world to the fictional one, in which imagination is closely tied to narrative form and used to weave a multi-perspectival play, was one of psychological development.

In recent times a further distinction was made by Bion (1963, p.66), when he differentiated between universal myth, such as the Oedipal myth, and the private version of it, a personal arrangement of the elements of the universal myth. The private myth corresponding to the universal Oedipal myth enables the patient, in Bion's view, to make sense of his relationship to his parents.

> This private myth, in its investigatory role, if impaired or maldeveloped or subjected to too great a stress, disintegrates; its components are dispersed and the patient is left without an apparatus which would enable him to comprehend the parental relationship and so to adjust to it. The Oedipus debris will in these circumstances contain elements that are

components of the Oedipal myth that should have operated as a precon-
ception. (Bion 1963, p.66)

For treatment, the various separate fragments of the myth have to be identified, noted and interpreted; though their scattering over time is particularly challenging for interpretation.

We might add that a fragmented private myth is more often recognized
by the audience – that is, the family or the therapist – than by its creator.
Less severely distorted personal myths resemble bad fiction, in their pretti-
fied, horrified and horrifying or simply stuck aspects. But great art and literature treat mythical elements in such a way as to rise above the personal
to touch and connect with the universal needs of the human mind.
Sophocles, in his tragedic version of the Oedipal myth, performed such a
task by arranging the fragments of the myth in the particular form that
appeals to mental development. Goethe, in his version of Faust, lifted the
Faustian myth from the numerous versions that circulated at the time (and
which still circulate in the minds of patients in psychiatric hospital wards
today, who feel themselves to be in constant communion with the devil),
and elevated it to a great piece of literature. It might further be said that the
distinction between universal myth and great art and literature on the one
hand, and personal myth and poor quality artistic and literary productions
on the other, relates to the state of mind which predominated at the time of
their creation.

Bion (1963) saw the Oedipal myth 'as an essential part of the
apparatus of learning in primitive stages of development'(p.47). The
psychotic mind suffers from the inability (dis-ability) to transform unbearable sensations into bearable experiences to be stored for future use; there
is proliferation and storage of undigested facts and fictions, which leads to
defences against the anxiety they provoke. At the same time, through projection, they invoke in others feelings which are not easily translatable into
thinking. Words are therefore used by the psychotic personality primarily
to rid the psyche of unbearable contents; instead of communication there
takes place evacuation.

Even the senses may be taken over to expel rather than receive information (Bion 1958):

> …if a patient says he sees an object it may mean that an external object
> has been perceived by him or it may mean that he is ejecting an object
> with his eyes; if he says he hears something it may mean he is ejecting a

sound – this is not the same as making a noise; if he says he feels something it may mean tactile sensation is being extruded, thrown off by his
skin. An awareness of the double meaning that verbs of sense have for
the psychotic sometimes makes it possible to detect an hallucinatory
process before it betrays itself by more familiar signs. (Bion 1958, p.67)

In such a situation, perception is entangled with hallucination, and improvement results from a careful and painstaking elucidation and differentiation of the two. These reversals of activities may be in the service of a
belief in repairing the ego, or may be camouflaged as such.

Bion postulated the existence of functions of the non-psychotic mind
which produce conscious awareness. The alpha-function in particular is
said to metabolize incoming sense impressions related to an emotional experience and transform them into alpha elements, which in their ways of
relating to each other form what he calls 'the contact barrier'. This is a
moment-to-moment formation of alpha elements standing both as a point
of separation and contact as well as an establishment of difference between
conscious and unconscious elements of experience. In Bion's view of
psychotic illness, it is an inability to metabolize incoming emotional impressions that produces this distinct way of reading of reality we see in
psychosis.

It follows that any treatment of psychotic individuals needs to take into
account this particular disability and provide a suitable environment where
it can be directly addressed. PsychoSocial interventions address this issue
through providing 'whole environments', where a two-tiered approach is
available: first, an acceptance of the fact that the patient comes with their
psychotic mind and their symptoms which have to be borne, not
forbidden; and second, a day-to-day, hour-to-hour metabolizing of new
experience needs to take place through staff members' mindful presence
and facilitation. This is not to say that staff will be interpreting all day long.
They are present for the patients in a way that is similar to the parental
presence.

In the parallel with art and literature I am using, the above differentiation is important too, in that the individuals may be using myth or fiction
to work through or process their experience of painful reality; that is,
doing containing work. In non-psychotic thinking, transformation and
modification imply work on the experience of reality; in psychotic
thinking, modification and transformation imply misconception or falsifi-
cation of experience. One of the earliest applications of art to soothe and

calm maddening feelings is thought of by Euripides, who has Medea's nurse say:

> The men of old times had little sense;
> If you called them fools you wouldn't be far wrong.
> They invented songs, and all the sweetness of music,
> To perform at feasts, banquets and celebrations;
> But no one thought of using
> Songs and stringed instruments
> To banish the bitterness and pain of life.
> Sorrow is the real cause
> Of deaths and disasters and families destroyed.
>
> *(Medea, trans. P. Vellacott, pp.194–198.*
> *Reproduced by permission of Penguin Books Ltd.)*

Interestingly, it was Euripides who pushed the myth-telling and lyric poetry to the point of imaginative and pedagogic tragedy. In this, we might say that he was one of the pioneers in helping, through his plays, to contain the most painful and disturbing aspects of the human mind. Containment through affective understanding is what Bion (1962) calls the process of getting to know. Bion denotes this process by the letter of the alphabet K. It is, for Bion, the culmination of several processes and emotional experiences working together, not an independent facility. Therefore, when we say that someone x knows someone y (e.g. mother knows baby, therapist knows patient) we employ the results of several processes to convey that someone is involved in the emotional process of getting to know someone else, not that she, or he, already knows everything about that person.

So, while myths and epic poetry related what were thought of as indisputable historical facts, and personal or private myths are believed to relate 'historical', 'indisputable', black-and-white facts about one's life, tragedies, literature and art as well as insights into one's personal predicament relate a multi-perspectival view through which one is in the process of experiencing imaginatively and creatively one's past and present experience.

An illustration of the distinction I am using between myth and literature is the difference between the myth of Medea and Euripides' rendition of it in his play of the same title. The myth itself, like all myths, has various versions. Robert Graves (1960) recounts them with such variations as Medea being reported to have had not two but fourteen children, or to have killed them so that they become immortal.

Nevertheless, the shock and horror that the listener to the myth experiences when hearing of the mother who killed her children because her husband left her to marry a younger woman are moderated and changed in the reading of Euripides' play. Feelings of pity for Medea, sympathy, sadness, anguish, regret, disbelief, as well as horror at her crimes, arise during the tortuous emotional journey that the playwright takes us on.

This is due to Euripides' treating the myth and its psychological aspects to a full literary make-over. His Medea, wronged and then abandoned by Jason, who despite their marriage and their children marries a younger Corinthian princess, collapses in her rage:

> ... Scorned and shamed,
> She raves, invoking every vow and solemn pledge
> That Jason made her, and calls the gods as witnesses
> What thanks she has received for her fidelity.
> She will not eat; she lies collapsed in agony,
> Dissolving the long hours in tears. Since first she heard
> Of Jason's wickedness, she has not raised her eyes,
> Or moved her cheek from the hard ground; and when her
>   friends
> Reason with her, she might be a rock or wave of the sea,
> For all she hears – unless, maybe, she turns away
> Her lovely head, speaks to herself alone, and wails...
>
> *(Vellacott, trans.: 19–28)*

In this state of mind, 'No word from any friend can give her comfort' (ibid: 142), and planning her revenge, to kill the young bride and then kill her own two children to get at Jason, she decides consciously: 'Until the deed is done words are not necessary.' (Ibid: 818.)

Early on in the play, the chorus agrees with Medea that Jason needs to be punished, but not on what the punishment should be! At one point Creon, the new bride's father, appears to order Medea to go into exile with her sons because, he tells her, he fears her – he fears what she might do to his daughter. With hindsight he was right to fear her, though one wonders how much his decision to exile her contributed to her carrying out her actions. Creon stands for the reasonable, cautious Greek who wants to protect his family. He exiles what is not reasonable: the foreign Medea who uses the non-reason of magic: 'Go, you poor wretch, take all my troubles with you! Go!' (ibid: 336–337) he says to her.

By changing the myth where Medea's children are killed by the Corinthians to revenge her for killing the young princess-bride, and by having Medea herself kill her own children, Euripides created a story of unique power and of universal significance. His play shows us a situation in which the fruit of the union of human beings is being destroyed by a mind driven by the psychotic logic that the evacuation of feelings is nourishing in itself, and that a problematic situation can be repaired haphazardly and without concern, using omnipotent means. Metaphorically, the killing also refers to the wilful destruction and annihilation of meaning wherever there is a perception of betrayal.

The potential for thinking and working these issues through is enormous. Ancient playwrights knew the power of their plays, and Euripides in particular used them pedagogically as well as therapeutically to explore and bring to light the darkest aspects of humanity. It is said that fifth-century Athenians received a subsidy that enabled them to go to the theatre whatever their means. Plays, tragedies and comedies were used by writers, actors and audiences to teach and learn imaginatively. It is through this involvement that, culturally, the option of giving up personal myths and identifying with universal ones can be taken up, and the developmental step of being understood and contained achieved. Far from endorsing cultural and social excess, ancient playwrights helped their audiences reflect, consider, and think about the moral, ethical and personal dilemmas of their day: a PsychoCultural treatment of the psychotic as well as neurotic anxieties of their time.

Artists and writers have since used their creativity to present unpalatable reality in palatable forms. Indeed it may be said that one of the main reasons for art's appeal to its audience, as much as to its creators, is the offering of an inclusive arena, in the books, the play, or the work of art, where unbearable truths can be identified, thought about, and worked through. More importantly, art and literature offer an arena to the psychotic personality, which matches its own perspective and approach. The freedom and inclusion that the psychotic personality experiences through an opportunity for (acceptable) forms of evacuation is attested through the increasing acceptance of art classes and art psychotherapy in mental health treatment programmes. Sometimes it becomes possible to reflect on the contents of the outpouring; mostly the availability of framed space provides satisfaction enough. Equally, the appeal of art that seems pretty, uncontained, violent or disturbing may be said to reside within the mind that does not wish to know but which nevertheless wishes to be reflected, recognized and included. Although inclusion as such is not a link, it is a primitive, concretized experience of belonging, which affords satisfaction without questions asked – in both the painter and the viewer.

In acute psychosis, by contrast, the reality created becomes a different world with overwhelming power, that obscures both the painful emotional reality and the capacity to think. The idea of inclusion is itself excluded. The emotional problem is dealt with by killing awareness, and sometimes by killing the patient. Imagination is misused to create personal myths – such as that one is driven by the devil or an all-powerful machine – that drive the self to act in mad or bad ways with no opportunity for reflection. Consequently, these actions are seen as symptoms by professionals who treat them in the same terms, without concern for the personal meaning and origins of the experience. In effect, a reversal takes place whereby a person's individual myths are ignored – often by being labelled – so that he or she can be fitted into the currently accepted social framework. A sort of PsychoCultural endowment of psychosis, we might say.

In this context, the lack of elaboration towards a meaningful narrative involved in the classification of symptoms – however much this classifcation may be helpful to professionals – and the effect this has on inhibiting the development of personal myth into story makes the plot vulnerable to being usurped by the psychotic mind. Not only does Medea become the mythic woman who killed her children, or Faust the one who made a pact with the Devil, but also all authority figures are seen as abusers, and all mothers as witches: confirmation is easily found by this mind. This means no differentiation is possible, and excitement is produced at the cost of understanding.

Psychotherapy with these patients can undo this cultural reversal by its concentration on uncovering, demystifying and understanding the person's personal myths. However, a different quality of treatment is needed for these patients. Understanding their personal myths while resisting the desire to respond to them as a class of mythical monsters is not sufficient. These people have benefited from the rewards of enacting their internal dramas, and having been responded to in similar terms have great difficulties in relinquishing them. Often the treatment gets interrupted, the person is seen as not responding, and medication with life-long hospitalization is considered the only suitable treatment. The PsychoSocial treatment of psychosis provides the stage for individual dramas to unfold, to be experienced by the whole milieu, and to be talked about and considered from different perspectives. Likewise it allows for new and real relationships to form, and to be monitored, thought about, understood and accepted. This provides the option for the individual both to identify his or her personal myths and to differentiate them from the universal ones, which he or she can then enjoy and learn from.

The astonishment of patients who have so far thought of their problems as unique to themselves but who then hear others retell their own histories is often very striking. At the Arbours Crisis Centre one of the major benefits of the milieu as a treatment facility is this provision of a space where the patient (guest) can listen to, and sometimes see, others approaching their problems in a maladapted way. In the milieu, this can be understood as the provision of a concretely constructed triangular space, where one observes others who look like oneself thinking or interacting in a way detrimental to themselves. Often 'older' guests will comment on 'newer' guests' difficulties, because it is easier to 'see' oneself in others.

I once worked with a woman, 'Helen', who believed that killing herself would solve her and her children's problems. This conviction resembled a badly constructed mythical/heroic view of herself – the view that it would be for the best. It arose as a result of her realizing that she had been behaving destructively in front of her children, and was produced by a version of her who would rather have her killed than think about the meaning of her actions. Her actions had involved a slow and deliberately precise cutting and burning of her legs and abdomen in front of her children, as well as various elaborate and ingenious suicide attempts. Initially, on hearing these bits of information we reacted in a similar way to hearing the Medea myth being re-told. Though 'Medea' is an extreme case, and an extreme comparison, I think that often the initial information about many patients, which includes the elements of their personal myth, arouses such a reaction in the therapist. Helen's stay at the Arbours Crisis Centre was one that started with a suicide attempt on the day of arrival and continued with silences lasting for days. She did listen, however. Coming from a family who had not had an experience of psychotherapy, and having had herself a number of hospitalizations without any form of psychodynamic understanding, she opened her ears to the tragic life-stories of other guests who spoke more freely about them. Helen also opened her ears to the interactions of the other guests with the resident therapists and other therapists around the Centre. They cried and laughed together, they were horrified and openly angry together, they imagined and suffered pain together.

This had not been within Helen's range of experience so far. People had tip-toed around her, had spoken secretly or in hushed voices around her; they had taken decisions for her. Her partner, a well-meaning man but who was not able to cope with feelings either, had taken over the running of the family much as a military regime. As he was a part-time worker in an undemanding job he was able to devote plenty of time to his family, but without offering any space for their feelings. He himself, however, was at the end of his tether.

Helen's breakdown had occurred when her parents, who had moved to Australia when she was in her teens, returned to live in England. It seemed that her early childhood experiences, in particular her intense feelings towards her parents, had concretely returned to haunt her when they came back. Helen's childhood had been remembered by her as a difficult one, with her parents endlessly arguing, usually after what she thought were heavy drinking bouts. Eventually it emerged that her mother had been envious of Helen growing up and having a life of her own. Whenever Helen went out mother would complain about her own predicament of being stuck in the house. When Helen brought boyfriends or friends home, mother would complain about her loneliness, or her illnesses, or retire to bed. There was no place where Helen could go that would not bring out a mental allergic rush in her mother that would break out in some form of behaviour. The only way that Helen had found to deal with what she interpreted as her mother's jealousy was to leave home as early as she could. Her parents left home too, to go 'down under'. Upon their return, they found out that mother was seriously ill and that she would shortly be dying. The return for Helen of what she had successfully avoided for many years, by mythologizing it in a way that 'worked' for her, coincided with the forthcoming death of her mother. Her feelings went haywire, and unable to contain them she broke down.

The milieu offered to Helen a space where, initially, she could literally watch others' thoughts and feelings being contained in the here and now.

Like watching the actors of a tragedy battle with, and eventually resolve, issues, Helen went through what looked like a voyage of discovery. Elements of their stories appeared and shifted and re-appeared re-organized; their feelings ebbed and flowed, their comings and goings, especially to their team meetings, were watched with great interest. Eventually, Helen started bringing her own issues to her sessions and group meetings.

The Medeaic psychic assault on her own children, who suffered watching her attempted death by a thousand cuts, effectively repeated her own history of having had to listen to her own parents cut each other up verbally. This was experienced by the team, reflected on and interpreted. More importantly, other elements of Helen's story and her private myths were collected from behind the scenes of the team meeting, very tentatively by her, and more determinedly by her resident therapist, and were then brought to the team to be talked and de-mythologized. Helen's jealous feelings towards her children, fellow guests, and therapists, as well as her pattern of dealing with them by cutting them out in what felt like a surgical manner, were thought through.

The progression from the personal myth (the debris of elements organized in a personally haphazard way) to the universal one allowed Helen the space to be her own self. Interestingly, she also returned to the creative use of her imagination to sculpt — which, in her case, involved cutting into her medium. The need to know allowed free flow, and nourishment restored her imagination and creativity.

Another guest expressed her internal world in a somatic paralysis, to the point that she had, at times, to be carried around. She benefited from the PsychoSocial milieu of the Centre in an interesting way. Her first two stays at the Centre allowed her to unlock the prohibition on language; a third allowed her to put into words her own worries about someone in her who was planning to hurt her children. Helping her to think about these matters, and ensure her children's safety, released her muscles from the voluntary psychological restraining order under which they had been placed.

In both these cases, the Centre provided the space where the symptoms could appear — without being either forbidden or encouraged — and be understood. Until their impact, their force and their meaning specific to the person's character and history had been confronted, no meaning could be achieved — only standard textbook categorization of symptoms and behaviour. The outward performance of these individuals' psychotic minds could have led staff to consign their non-psychotic minds to the 'bin' as well, identifying the patient only in terms of their psychotic symptoms.

An interesting case of this is when the toxic effects of medication on the phantasy world of the patient are not thought about and worked through. Whenever the patient's uncontained feelings, what Bion called beta-elements, are responded to by a pill that takes them away, without any further discussion and thinking, there is the danger that the patient will be introjecting for the second time what is known as a terrible 'dread'. Furthermore, the introjected (concrete) pill may give rise to side-effects such as tremors and movements that can be seen as new somatized bizarre internal objects. That is, beta-elements, having gone towards and back from an impermeable container, wrapped into pieces of the personality and accompanied by a concrete capsule/pill, return to influence, on a concrete level, the person who may end acting involuntarily (jerking, involuntary movements) and with movements that neither have apparent sense nor make sense; a truly embodied and embedded performance.

When guests come to the Centre with their myths, which, however painfully real, involve concrete, repetitive, detailed versions of abuse, neglect and mistreatment, they are given the opportunity to investigate them and eventually to think about the ways in which they embody distortions of Oedipal and other universal myths. In this process of getting to know themselves, guests within the Crisis Centre explore the various aspects of their versions of their lives with a view to altering their mythical stories to create a more flexible and imaginative, multi-perspectival version of their lives and histories. The latter – in contrast to the detailed, black-and-white version centring on experiences of abuse and punishment they have either suffered or inflicted, which remains a part of the psychotic memory – allows for flexibility, imaginative play and the acceptance of what was previously felt to be mythically horrific. This elaboration may take place within the 'settling down' stage of their stay (Berke 1987) or later, after their stay at the Crisis Centre has ended, once they are settled in ongoing, long-term psychotherapy.

References

Berke, J.H. (1987) 'Arriving, Settling-in, Settling-down, Leaving and Following-up: Stages of Stay at the Arbours Centre.' *British Journal of Medical Psychology 60*, 181–188.

Bion, W.R. (1958) 'On Hallucination.' In W.R. Bion (1967) *Second Thoughts*. London: William Heinemann; repr. London: Karnac Books, 1984.

Bion, W.R. (1962) *Learning from Experience*. London: William Heinemann; repr. London: Karnac Books, 1984.

Bion, W.R. (1963) *Elements of Psycho-Analysis*. London: William Heinemann; repr. London: Karnac Books, 1984.

Euripides *Medea*. In *Medea/Hecabe/Electra/Heracles*, trans. P. Vellacott. Harmondsworth: Penguin Classics.

Freud, S. (1911) 'Psycho-Analytic Notes on an Autobiographical Account of a Case of Paranoia (Dementia Paranoides).' *Vol. 12: The Standard Edition of the Complete Psychological Works of Sigmund Freud*. London: Hogarth Press.

Graves, R. (1960) *The Greek Myths. Vol. 2*. Harmondsworth: Penguin Books.

Snell, B. (1953) *The Discovery of the Mind: The Greek Origins of European Thought*. New York: Dover Publications; repr. as *The Discovery of the Mind in Greek Philosophy and Literature*. New York: Dover Publications.

Section Two

Methodology

Introduction

Joseph H. Berke, Margaret Fagan, George Mak-Pearce
and Stella Pierides-Müller

In this section the authors look more closely at how a PsychoSocial approach can be conceptualized and how it can inform practice. The Crisis Centre is a comparatively small unit, but despite this it receives referrals from extremely diverse sources. Consequently, at any given time there is invariably a pronounced mix of backgrounds in terms of race, education, culture and religion. Moreover this diversity also pertains within the therapists' group. Thus, though the Centre is small, there is a PsychoSocial 'cocktail' – a mixture of rich but sometimes explosive elements. This part of the book looks at some of the clinical thinking in terms of which this richness can be harnessed in the service of therapeutic change.

Joseph Berke looks at the overall structure of the Centre and describes how it operates as an interlocking system of interventions. The work takes place at the level of the individual, the group, and the milieu. The intervention is thus 'multi-focused', and for every guest who comes to the Centre there are several therapists working with that person. When this work is done in the team Berke calls it 'conjoint therapy'. The team may be organized in a 'differentiated' or in a 'shared' manner, depending on whether or not overt manifestations of psychosis are present. The intense transference and countertransference feelings evoked within these different styles of working are illustrated through a number of examples.

In her chapter 'The Wednesday Meeting' Stella Pierides-Müller takes up the importance of the dynamics between the therapists themselves, and how difficulties in working together can be understood and resolved. Central to this process is the weekly large-group meeting of all the therapists working at the Centre. Pierides-Müller shows how quickly co-operation can breakdown under the force of intense projective mechanisms. There can also be break downs in communication between the Centre as a whole and those important to individual guests, such as their family or the referring agency. For this reason the Wednesday meeting plays a central role in facilitating communication and maintaining support among therapists and students.

Continuing these themes, Tamar Schonfield explores the role of supervision during work with borderline and psychotic guests. She reminds us of the difficulties of supervision when unconscious processes are enacted by a therapist or indeed by the team as a whole. The acceptance of very disturbing emotional experiences by the therapists and the development of the capacity to ask for help on the part of guests are the essential ingredients in transforming enactment into engagement.

Catherine Sunderland gives a resident therapist's perspective on moving into the Crisis Centre. Coming from a psychiatric nursing background, she highlights some of the differences in coping with anxiety in the two settings. Sunderland describes how she had to struggle with her own fears to work without the external controls provided by a hospital setting, particularly in the face of self-harming and dangerous behaviour. Tolerance and understanding among the resident therapists as a group becomes the container of anxiety, and one that can take the place of physical psychiatric methods.

Maggie Fagan focuses on working with those in the throes of psychotic and borderline states. She differentiates the psychotic from the non-psychotic state of mind, applying the thinking of Bion and others to the PsychoSocial work of the Centre. Adopting the use of a 'dual track analysis', she explores how the therapist can usefully try to understand the point of view of the psychotic thinker and how this point of view will have a 'narrative competence'. This approach is elaborated in the context of working with those who are dangerously self-harming.

The section concludes with a splash of colour from Julia Saltiel and Lois Elliott. They give a lively account of an experimental way of working, which combines art therapy and group therapy. Both the art therapist and the group therapist join in the activity and produce paintings themselves. The resulting collection of paintings, by therapists and guests alike, is discussed in the group and interpreted in terms of the group dynamics. This model of working has been further developed in order to provide ongoing support for those of our guests who have left the Centre. The use of this 'Support Programme' is illustrated, and some transference issues of co-working in this manner are discussed.

CHAPTER 5

Conjoint Therapy

Joseph H. Berke

Conjoint therapy is the use of several therapists in a single therapeutic intervention. Usually this takes place when working with troubled families, although therapeutic groups may also utilize a co-therapist. Moreover, conjoint therapy may be practised as part of a multi-focused intervention with individuals suffering an emotional breakdown, as in 'crisis intervention'.

I shall describe the deliberate use of two or more co-therapists in the direct psychodynamic treatment of severely disturbed men and women. This work has been undertaken at the Arbours Crisis Centre in London over the past thirty years.

At the Centre we begin every intervention by establishing a treatment team. This 'team' carries the primary responsibility of working with the individual, 'the guest', who has come to stay at the Centre. It includes a team leader, a resident therapist (RT) and often a third member as well. The team leader is an experienced psychotherapist who co-ordinates the intervention. The RT is the therapist who lives at the Centre and has the most immediate involvement with the guest. The third member is an Arbours trainee or other professional doing a placement at the Centre.

'The guest' is the person in distress. At the Centre we use the term 'guest' to denote hospitality and to avoid the medicalization and stigmatization that often accompanies mental, emotional or social chaos.

The guest is a member of the team that meets three or more times per week in formal fifty-minute sessions, and is an active participant in the unfolding relationships and ensuing dramas that take place. But besides these meetings, the guests usually have informal discussions with the RT or other team members several, sometimes many, times per week.

The team itself is part of a multi-systemic approach to working with people who can no longer cope with their lives for a variety of intrapsychic, interpersonal or situational reasons. They come to the Centre when they are depressed, withdrawn, panic-stricken, and/or self-mutilating.

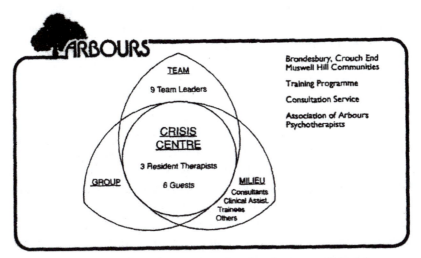

Figure 1 The Abours Crisis Centre's three systems: The mileu, the group and the teams

Sometimes they are in a state of psychosis during part or all of this stay. Figure 1 illustrates the Centre's three separate but inter-related and inter-relating systems. These are the milieu, the group and the team. The milieu is the Centre in its role as an overall therapeutic environment. The group encompasses the organized set of formal house meetings that take place four times a week. Consequently, the context of the team is the group and the context of the group is the milieu. One might even point out that the context for the milieu is the whole Arbours network. As I have also demonstrated in Figure 1, the Arbours network includes three long-stay therapeutic communities, the Training Programme, the Consultation Service and the Association of Arbours Psychotherapists. Thus, the Arbours, as a whole, involves nearly one hundred therapists, fifty trainees and twenty-five residents (those who live at the Crisis Centre or Communities).

Before focusing on the conjoint intervention of the team, it is necessary to consider the milieu and the group in greater detail. These two basic operating systems sustain, and are also sustained by, the work of the team.

The milieu is an active therapeutic environment. Perhaps 'active interpersonal environment' would be more correct, as the milieu can also be non-therapeutic or even anti-therapeutic, depending on who is at the Centre and what is going on. Its constituents include three RTs, six guests, nine team leaders, a clinical assistant, various consultants, an art therapist, a movement therapist, therapists in charge of our Follow-up Support Programme, and several trainees and professionals doing placements at the Centre. At any time one or more of these people can and do meet up with each other in order to help recognize, experience and tolerate the powerful, emotional currents that flow through the place. Specifically this milieu serves several purposes: it contains feelings; it sets boundaries for different and difficult behaviour; and it manages the expression or non-expression of feelings. Generally the milieu deals with the practicalities of day-to-day living together. In other words it mediates external reality.

The group consists of all the people who live in the house: the therapists and the guests. They are the ones who attend and conduct the house meetings. The only exception is that once a week the trainees are invited to attend. Essentially the house meetings provide the opportunity for mirroring, role playing and social feedback. They further often provide an occasion for one of the older guests, an individual who has been at the Centre for a number of weeks or months, and begun to reconstitute himself or herself emotionally and socially, to act as a guide, teacher and therapist for new guests. The house culture tends to be passed on during these meetings. For example, one resident, who came to the Centre because he could not tolerate his feelings and, indeed, looked like a Zombie, began to emerge from his shut-down state after six weeks. Subsequently, he took the lead in explaining to new guests at house meetings that the reason they had come was 'to learn to know what you feel'.

Moreover, when there are difficulties – someone being too disruptive or engaging in threatening behaviour – the first line of defence may be for the residents to call for an extra house meeting, to discuss and, as it may be hoped, defuse the situation.

The function of milieu and group (the house meetings) is to attend to external reality – what we do with each other – and to deal with some aspects of internal reality – feelings concerning the emotional tides and the undercurrents in the house. By contrast, the task of the team is specifically to explore, interpret and pull together the feelings and phantasies (the transferences) that arise with and within a particular guest, as well as the reciprocal feelings and phantasies (the countertransferences) that occur in and with the other members of the team.

In this sense we can say that the team mediates internal reality by focusing on the transference and countertransference relationships that emerge, towards the house, the group, the therapists and towards other guests as well. Of course there are many times when the work of the team overlaps with that of the milieu and group, but I think it functions best when the team is able to concentrate on the here and now of the team meetings – its own space and time.

In this sense one of the most important therapeutic goals of the milieu and group is to enable the guests to use the team and to explore their own internal reality. Often guests find this very difficult. When they first come, they may try to protect themselves against the impact of the other team members by silence, withdrawal, or by missing meetings. With these individuals you can follow the development of a therapeutic alliance by their participating in the life of the house, then in the work of the group, and finally by their actively attending the team meetings.

The team is a complicated therapeutic system in its own right. First, there are three or more meetings per week. Second, there are various informal meetings among the guests, RTs and trainees. These comprise a set of significant subsystems without which the formal work of the team would be relatively impoverished. Third, the therapists and trainees hold a regular supervision discussion each week and a variety of shorter informal exchanges. Finally, the team itself links up with all the therapists at an extended clinical discussion every week. (In between, many informal discussions take place.)

Moreover, the team itself can co-opt new members. This may occur when we work with the family of a guest and want to keep these family meetings separate from the regular team meetings. It also occurs when we are working with a very disturbed guest and the team needs an additional perspective. At such times another team leader or consultant will be asked to join the clinical discussions. From this outline of extended network relations one can glimpse the multi-levelled tiers of support that this system provides, both for the guest and therapists as well as for the Centre as a whole.

Significantly, the internal structure of the formal team meetings also varies. It functions in two different ways at different times – as 'a shared team' and as 'a differentiated team'. This organization and reorganization of the team is of particular relevance to our ability to work with severely disturbed individuals.

In the shared team the members can play any part and take any role. Thus a therapist may take on the role of a guest, or a guest may take on the role of a therapist. Some members may remain as silent witnesses, others may be active interveners. The RT and team leader tend to be equal partners, and each feels free to make interpretive comments.

In a differentiated team one member, usually the team leader, acts as the therapist, making interpretive comments and focusing the transference onto himself. The RT and trainee remain as silent witnesses, but active listeners. They take a much more direct and vital part after the formal meeting is over. Then they help the guest to digest what has occurred and what the team leader has said. Thus, in a differentiated team the RT and trainees act more specifically as surrogate egos for the guests.

Interestingly, my description of these two ways of working with guests parallels current developments in family therapy. These allow for two different forms of engagement according to the clients and issues involved. They are the 'partnership model' and the 'leadership model'. The partnership mode emphasizes an egalitarian relationship. Both therapists and client explore problems together and there is plenty of room for empathy and for self-disclosure by either side. By contrast, the leadership mode emphasizes a hierarchical relationship. Here the roles of therapist and patient are clearly defined, with one giving help and the other receiving it. In either case, the work is often carried out by a team which uses and integrates both partnership and leadership approach at different points in the therapy (Hoffman 1990/1).

When a guest is newly arrived at the Centre, the team will initially function as a shared team, that is as a partnership. Then the team may shift to a differentiated, leadership mode. When this actually happens depends on the degree of disturbance of the guest as well as the stage of the stay.

What do I mean by the expression 'stage of stay'? In a previous paper (Berke 1987) I have explained that all guests pass through five distinct periods or stages while they are at the Centre, regardless of their reasons for coming. These stages can be compared to five states of mind and greatly influence the feelings and actions of the guests while they are at the Centre. These stages are: *Arriving, Settling-in, Settling-down, Leaving*, and *Following-up*.

During the *Arriving* stage, the primary fears of the new arrivals have to do with leaving home, relating to a new place and new people, loss of control, regression and going mad. Whatever else, these fears have to be considered first, otherwise the new arrival will not be able to establish a therapeutic alliance with the Centre, the group or the team.

The second stage, *Settling-in*, is marked by a decrease in arrival fears and an increasing willingness to reflect on the underlying issues that have brought the guest to the Centre. It is during this stage that the patterns of basic work and organization of the team are decided.

The third stage, *Settling-down*, is the occasion for interpersonal association and intrapsychic consolidation. During this stage a lot of internal integration takes place.

The fourth stage, *Leaving*, may arouse a fresh crisis, because leaving necessarily arouses ambivalence, sadness and depressive feelings, which may seem too strong to bear. Therefore a wish to repeat the original breakdown may occur.

The fifth and final stage, *Following-up*, can extend for weeks or months after the guest has left and can be a period of further consolidation. The team holds two follow-up meetings at the Centre over the course of a fortnight. During this period we often arrange for a further course of individual therapy to take place, either with the person's previous therapist, or with a new therapist as needed. In addition we ask all guests to fill out a detailed questionnaire about their stay. This is a help to us and many people find this effort has a therapeutic impact. Recently the Centre has established an extensive follow-up Support Programme, which provides practical, therapeutic and social support during twice-weekly meetings. Former guests can participate in the programme for up to a year.

These stages have a separate, objective existence. This has been demonstrated by the fact that they occur in other, different facilities as well as in the Centre. Notably, this paradigm has been confirmed by colleagues at the Mount Sinai Hospital, in Toronto, Canada. In a paper on the intensive treatment of borderline patients they delineate stages which are practically identical to the ones I have described (Silver, Cardish and Glassman 1987). They describe these stages as follows: One − *Assessment or the Honeymoon;*

two – *Therapeutic Encirclement or Symptomatic*; three – *Therapeutic Engagement or Working Through*; and four – *Discharge–Liaison or Separation/Re-entry*. Although the Toronto group does not specify a Following-up stage, they do refer to the fact that in the period following discharge patients like to return to the ward.

Having considered the stages of stay, let us return to the basic issue: how, why and when does the team differentiate – or not? As I have indicated, at the beginning of the intervention the team is always a shared structure. This allows the team to explore the emotional range and relational capacity of the guest as well as to focus on diverse fears of arriving. Such fears are usually directed to the Centre as a whole but may be displaced onto a member of the team or resident of the house. At this point we pay particular attention to the kinds and extremes of feelings aroused in the team members. I previously mentioned the post-team discussions with the guests, which constitute an essential subsystem or subcomponent of our conjoint approach. Equally vital are the post-team discussions that the therapists have among themselves, where they can explore the tensions, associations and phantasies that develop in and among themselves. This subsystem focuses on the countertransference. Here each therapist can serve as a surrogate ego for the other and is an indispensable support in dealing with the confusing and destructive elements which the guests seek to evacuate into them.

Many guests are not in touch with their feelings. Therefore they cannot talk about them. In other words they are emotionally and verbally inarticulate. Instead they dramatize or act out what is happening or not happening in themselves within the team. This process also reflects what happens in the house meeting and the Centre as a whole: the tendency to externalize internal dramas. Thus, the shared team serves as a very sensitive barometer of events that occur outside conscious awareness.

I am reminded of one guest, a middle-aged Spanish man, who came to the Centre feeling suicidally depressed. Far from being withdrawn, he initially talked incessantly, barraging us with words, demands, questions, and more demands to the point where the RT felt severely under attack and wanted to scream at him – and at me – for inviting him to the Centre. This continued for several days. She felt very pressured by him. I also felt pressured by him, but more so by the RT, who also had to put up with his difficult behaviour in the house when I wasn't there. As for the trainee, she just withered on the vine, that is became more and more withdrawn. In our discussions we considered a lot of these experiences, but to no avail. We seemed to get increasingly acrimonious in our relationships with each other. It was painful to attend the team meetings. Then it occurred to me that this sense of intense pressure we felt, and were inflicting on each other, had to do with the very tensions which this man was suffering. He was not able to articulate them directly, but he chose to communicate and to get rid of the pressures by arousing them in us. As far as he was concerned, they were crazy-making and non-containable. He could not think and we were in danger of becoming like him. Yet, as soon as we appreciated this, the tensions in us became manageable. We didn't need to interpret this to him. At the time he would have felt that we were trying to shove the experience back into him. But our realizations to ourselves meant that we could approach things differently. In the sessions we became calmer and less hostile. Most important of all, perhaps, we could think again. The outcome was remarkable. Almost as soon as we accepted these pressures in ourselves, he proceeded to calm down.

In considering the interpersonal complexity of such a situation, it is not enough to say that the guest simply pushes non-containable experiences into the therapist. Rather, he acts to stir up an area of disturbance which is already pre-existent in the therapist. When this happens, the therapist feels as if he is under attack and will invariably attack back by withdrawing, by making premature interpretations or by actual verbal and physical abuse. The guest, in turn, correctly perceiving that he is now under attack, will tend to respond in kind. An escalation of aggressive tension ensues. Alternatively, when the therapist understands (and thereby accepts) the disturbance in himself, he is able to be less aggressive to the guest. This person is then able to calm down, because he no longer feels under external threat, and because he is less intimidated by his own impulses.

In another intervention, 'Ian', a young Scotsman, was referred to the Centre because his life had come to a standstill. He used to work and play cricket and socialize in pubs. Now he stayed at home, didn't see anyone and watched TV. He felt desperate and hopeless, but he was willing to give us a try. A month of meetings passed. He replied to almost everything we said with 'that's right', but remained impassive and blocked. In the house he kept talking about wanting sex, but kept aloof from the women. They, in turn, disliked and avoided him, especially when he seemed to stare at them from the corner of his eye. We found out that his mother had thrown him and his father out of their house in order to take in a variety of lovers. As a teenager, women had found him attractive, but when a girl told him she fancied him, he went out and smashed up cars. Then, after two very long months at the Centre, he began to talk about feeling depressed. He said that there was pressure in his head, that he wanted to turn off the valve, let it out, but that he couldn't. In doing so he engaged me, but studiously avoided Lois, my co-therapist. There was also a distinct tinge of hostility in his voice. About two-thirds of the way through the session Lois exclaimed angrily, 'You know, I really feel left out. I feel very jealous that you two are doing all the talking. I'm a nothing, just ignored and left out.' I hadn't appreciated this but immediately realized that I had been colluding with Ian to shut Lois out. So I turned to Lois and began to focus on her. Here was someone who felt 'bloody annoyed', and I tried to bring her jealousy, her upset, back into the group. At that moment Lois was the 'guest' and Ian the observer, watching the drama of himself played out before his eyes. Eventually I turned back to Ian. 'What do you think about Lois?' 'Oh, she's just a slag!' Then Ian was engaged and the jealous anger that he had tried to bury in Lois became amenable to discussion. As he retrieved his jealousies, a strange new current emerged in the team and in the house. The women began to like him.

These two vignettes exemplify some of the useful interventions that can be made by the shared team. With short-stay or less traumatized guests the team may continue on a shared basis until the end of the stay. But with psychotic or very chaotic individuals the sooner the team shifts to a differentiated organization the better. This allows the focal therapist, usually the team leader, to direct the strong libidinal and anti-libidinal or aggressive transferences to himself and thereby protect the RT, who is otherwise in continuing direct contact with these currents. It brings 'the craziness' into the team, and away from the house. It creates calm space, both within the house and within the psyche of the RT. From this we can see that in order to be effective, the team leader, along with the RT, has to be open to confusion, despair, fear, rage, worthlessness, fragmentation, panic and similar terrible experiences. Both therapists need to take in, and be willing to suffer, all the intolerable feelings that perfuse the guest, and from which he is desperately trying to escape by annihilating his states of mind.

In another paper (Berke 1981), I have described Peter, a North of England business-man who came to the Centre in the middle of a psychotic breakdown. This was an anniversary reaction connected to the death of a loved/hated brother. During the arriving stage Peter repeatedly tried to escape from the Centre or set fire to it. He feared being trapped inside what he perceived as a constricting, confining inferno. Slowly, as he settled down, the acting out diminished, but the RT and trainees were overwhelmed. They felt they were trapped inside a hell which he was orchestrating. In response, we decided to change the structure of the team. I would see Peter in a daily meeting for analytic therapy. The RT and student members of the team would serve as listeners and witnesses.

Peter missed the first session, but then began to come regularly. These meetings were wild and chaotic, but the acting out tailed off dramatically in the Centre. During the first week of the reorganization, he described a dream about a pyramid of bodies covered with blood. His associations led to seeing me as a bad, angry figure, like his father, like his conscience – someone who was out to decapitate and castrate him. Suddenly he froze and spat at my glasses. Then he cried, came over and flopped into my arms. After a couple of minutes, he got up, took my glasses and went into the kitchen of the Centre to get a rag to wipe them clean. He returned and put the glasses on a drawing done by another guest, which was a big sun with red marks on and about it. I interpreted that in attacking my glasses he was also attacking my breasts. They were covered in blood, the results of his angry, biting attacks on me. And this was another reason why he feared I would retaliate and cut off his head. Further associations and interpretations led to a great sense of relief.

Afterwards he went to his RT and carefully went over what we had discussed. He feared he would lose my words, my understanding, his understanding. Other guests in similar circumstances have gone to my co-therapist and complained about me: 'What's that crazy stuff Joe's been talking about?' In all these circumstances the function of the co-therapist, the witness, is to carefully explain what I meant, and help the guest digest my interpretations. So they functioned as Peter's surrogate ego, but also as my own.

I don't wish to suggest that the role of the co-therapist on a differentiated team is simply to agree with the interpretations made by the team leader and to repeat them to the guest in post-team discussions. Often the interpretations made during the course of the team meetings have been arrived at after a long period of thought and discussion involving all members of the team. Indeed, my colleagues helped me to understand that the attack on my glasses occurred on several different levels. Yes, it expressed a very primitive assault on a phantasized source of supply, my 'breasts'. But it was also Peter's way of telling me that he didn't want me, or himself, to see what was going on, because, as he later revealed, he was very ashamed of himself.

In the differentiated team the RT is an intermediary, a transitional figure between the team leader and the guest, between his craziness and the house culture, between inner reality and outer practicality. Then, by identifying with the RT, and his capacity to tolerate and assimilate my interpretations, the guest gains an intermediary space within himself. The expansion of this intermediary or transitional space within his own mind gradually enables him to regain what we might call sanity.

Peter stayed at the Centre for a couple of months. This period of time is what we call a medium stay. Long stays may last for up to a year. Both medium and long stays allow for the transference to be elaborated and for the team to shift to a differentiated structure. We do have guests who come for shorter periods of a few weeks. During these interventions we usually maintain a shared team structure. However, I now think that all teams can profitably shift from a shared to differentiated structure once the guest has overcome the arriving stage.

Leaving creates distinct problems of its own. It is frequently necessary for a shared team to revert to an analytic mode in order to cope with the massive outbursts of feeling that accompany this stage. At the same time the RT may also undergo a shift in his mental state that complements the guest's 'leaving crisis' and may find it intolerable to remain a witness. The feelings evoked here are not simply to do with countertransference. Having lived with another human being at a very high level of emotional intensity, the RT can and does feel tremendous loss, sadness and emptiness when his guest goes. As with the guest, we need during leaving to help the RT to assume his depression.

The conjoint therapy I have described allows for great flexibility in working with disturbed and disturbing individuals. It also allows us to provide crucial support for the therapists involved. Then they are able to assist each other in coping with the powerful projections that occur during an emotional crisis, to experience and contain them. At the very least this allows the guest to identify with, in the transference, a containing maternal/paternal figure who is able to modify otherwise impossible pain and despair. But the active role that the co-therapists play means that the guest, by the creation of a transitional, internal space, and by identifying with the therapist as analyst and the therapist as witness, is able to regain his capacity to perceive and evaluate reality.

In actual fact, our therapeutic goals are modest. We cannot turn around a person's life in a few weeks or a few months. What we can do is help people to tolerate their underlying despair, to identify their difficulties and conflicts, and to expand in some small ways their relational capacities – the possibility of intimacy, empathy and trust. In order to achieve this we do not remain passive onlookers. Rather we are active participants in the experiences they try to disgorge. Sometimes it seems that the main difference between the them and ourselves is that we are more able to ask for help in struggling with intolerable feelings and states of mind. In other words, as therapists we can turn to each other for support, for advice, for supervision, for understanding. And if we cannot get that from each other, we can, at least, turn to our colleagues, the multiplicity of healing systems which comprise the Centre and to other aspects of the Arbours network.

As one might expect, there remain many problems. I have not been simply describing conjoint therapy, but a co-therapy with colleagues who live in a residential milieu. They need to accept themselves the burden of the individual guests' turmoil both as members of a dynamic team and, on a continuing basis, from many different angles, as members of a dynamic household. RTs can easily feel used up and burnt out, all the more because we do not depend on drugs to force guests to stop feeling or acting distraught.

Interestingly, the existence of split transferences, which we expected would present great obstacles to a therapeutic engagement, does not seem to hinder the work. If anything the team is able to utilize the split transference – good and bad, self and other, maternal and paternal, as it emerges in and among the RTs and the team leaders – in order to reach the inner realities of the guest more clearly. In this respect, it is worth noting that the work of the team can never entirely remove the threat of the powerful transferences that are directed to the RTs. But by focusing these currents on the team leader, they become less oppressive in the group and milieu and give RTs more space to develop non-transferential relationships with the guests.

Whatever the difficulties, the conjoint therapy I have described has allowed us to effect significant change in severely disturbed individuals without relying on biochemical or other forms of physical restraint. We have also seen, time and time again, that a tangle of sorrows can lead to a tango of joy. Nothing is more uplifting both for the team leaders and RTs than to see someone who had been dismissed as a hopeless case regain hope and vitality. Before he left, Peter rediscovered a trove of lost affection for his wife. And Ian, who 'never felt nothing about no-one', exclaimed he felt better, although God knows why. Ian was happy/sad. He knew that he would miss Lois. He was also pleasantly surprised. When he came he expected his lot would be bread and water (prison food, deprivation, absence). Yet, upon leaving he realized he wanted and could enjoy the roast chicken, the chicken that Lois made for him at his leaving meal – the chicken which for him and for us came to symbolize our work together.

References

Berke, J.H. (1981) 'The Case of Peter and Susan: The Psychotherapeutic Treatment of an Acute Psychotic Episode at the Arbours Crisis Centre.' *Journal of Contemporary Psychotherapy 12*, 75–87.

Berke, J.H. (1987) 'Arriving, Settling-in, Settling-down, Leaving and Following-up: Stages of Stay at the Arbours Centre.' *British Journal of Medical Psychology 60*, 181–188.

Hoffman, L. (1990/1) 'How I Changed My Mind Again.' *Context: A News Magazine of Family Therapy 7*, 30.

Silver, D., Cardish, R. and Glassman, E. (1987) 'Intensive Treatment of Characterologically Difficult Patients.' *Psychiatric Clinic of North America 10*, 219–245.

CHAPTER 6

The Wednesday Meeting

Stella Pierides-Müller

'The Wednesday Meeting' is the weekly clinical meeting of the Arbours Crisis Centre. It takes its name from the day it takes place and it is the major meeting of the week. I shall describe some of its dynamics and ask what can be learned from the experiences of the people attending it. Though this meeting is specific to the Centre itself, it can be said that most mental health facilities have their own version of the Wednesday Meeting. Whatever the name, time or date of that meeting, it is the one which provides the venue for clinical issues to be discussed and thought about. The pressure that staff groups everywhere are under – in facilities where time is limited, patient turn-over is high, the group is short-staffed, and the expectations to perform are maximal – bears thinking about.

Professionals working primarily with borderline and psychotic persons face specific difficulties. Working psychodynamically with these people on a short-term basis is often a thankless task. Neither the patients, their families, nor other professionals discern the results easily, and the statistics are not always designed to capture the difference in improvements. There is no quick cure to be achieved and there are usually no major changes in a short period of time to brag about. The treatment pace is slow, insights ebb and flow, and visible changes in behaviour may be minimal. The member of staff or the whole group may be pleased with their, and his or her, work. And then, after a short or a long while, there is a stepping back, a relapse. If the patients are staying for at least a few months, some progress is consolidated and visible; if however they are due to leave, or be transferred, staff members may not be able to see any more of their further progress nor see them regain the fruits of their earlier work. Their relapse may even be due to the crisis unavoidably produced by the leaving process itself (Berke 1987). Then despair and hopelessness ensue, or even complete doubt about the treatment programme itself.

The reverse may also happen. Staff may actually see patients make progress and leave treatment before a relapse or regression occurs; patients may even postpone the relapse until after they have left the unit. This often results in unrealistic, saintly images of the therapists, the treatment and the person himself or herself. Recognition of this slowly-advancing forward yet quick-step dance of the process of healing in psychosis, and the differentiation from chance occurrences, or temporary relapses (the minute or small step forward followed by two or more steps back), requires patience, experience, expertise and, above all, time – not one or two of these factors, but all together.

It is now an accepted fact that professionals working together with borderline or psychotic individuals face major difficulties in their relationships with each other. Unfortunately, the collapse of professional co-operation under the influence of the specific projective mechanisms of the patient is rarely thought about in a constructive way by suffering professionals. Instead, professionals rationalize or act-out themselves the patient's problems, and the resulting unprocessed insanity often leads carers to their becoming less caring and helpful.

In this context it is important to take a long view of this 'dance', even when we are contributing a short-term part of the treatment, and to be ready to learn from each other's experience. In this chapter I give an illustration of how, during work with a psychotic person, the Arbours Crisis Centre's Wednesday Meeting – a microcosm of the wider mental health field – was tested to its limits: how different situations brought up different reactions as well as thoughts in the staff group. In the process, and on the basis of three decades of experiences of the Crisis Centre staff group's 'Working Together' (*see further* Pierides 2000), I consider issues to bear in mind that may be of relevance to other mental health professionals struggling within the field.

To begin with let me briefly describe the context of the Centre's Wednesday Meeting and I will then consider some important parameters of that group. The Arbours Crisis Centre is a small psychoanalytically informed facility, making use of its own unique blend of psychoanalytic thinking together with group and community therapy. Underpinned by the principle of co-therapy, or the working together of several professionals, the Centre is the space where this group of therapists meets formally to monitor, review, discuss and generally think about the ongoing work. In a sense it is the space which contains, supports, reflects and informs the direction of the work with individual 'guests'. The directors, the team leaders, art and movement therapists, resident therapists, trainees and others bring to the meeting their own experiences, interactions, feelings, perceptions and thinking to help form a picture of what is going on inside each individual guest, as well as in the group and in the milieu.

The model the Centre employs brings together various aspects of theory and technique. Individual patient-centred work takes place together with group work; psychoanalytically informed psychotherapeutic work together with movement therapy and art therapy; aspects of psychoanalytic technique rub shoulders with principles of therapeutic communities. All these ideas, techniques and professional interventions combine to develop and enrich each another so as to offer a suitable container for the needs of severely ill individuals.

The diversity of meetings, therapists and approaches forms a major part of the identity of the Centre. The Wednesday clinical group, much like an effective and functioning ego, relies on this diversity of perspectives and input. There is an awareness that under the pressure of immense projections from the work with the guests, a group will at times be divided along the lines of differing ways of combining these perspectives. For instance, there could be a division between those who emphasize therapeutic community aspects and those who emphasize working with individual psychoanalytic perspectives; those favouring group work and those who favour individual work; those who work with non-verbal therapies and those who work with verbal ones; those who live-in and those who only visit for meetings.

In addition, the therapists of the Centre share a history together and have learned to know and accept the various aspects of one another. This involves a collective working alliance of members, who have known one another over time, especially during calm times. Whenever regressed, although feeling confused, judgmental or cut-off from one another, according to their patients' dominant state of mind, they do not act out in too destructive a way, but are able to address countertransference feelings in themselves through the forum of the Meeting. The history of contained experiences of the group makes it possible both to work well in the present and to feel hopeful about the future.

At issue here is a commitment to working with each other, not in general terms, and not only in roles, but together, with the specific individuals that make up the Centre. In this sense, the Wednesday Meeting group has developed an emotional linking between its members, which provides a fertile space for reflection. Fear, intrusiveness and destructiveness attack this space and may temporarily fragment it, threatening its capacity to act as a mental container for its members. Joseph Berke has described this potential for psychotic intervention on the part of therapists (Berke 1995). However, over time, the clinical group, through its shared common experience, reconstitutes itself.

The Centre's therapists share common interests and aims. Through their involvement with the Centre they have made the commitment to work with borderline and psychotic persons in need of specialist residential care with minimal or, whenever possible, no medication. As a result, they have learned to accept, and work with, not only one another but also their patients' specific difficulties as these are stirred up and emerge in and through themselves. The therapists consider their own individual transferences as well as countertransferences to the guests. Underlying this is an acceptance of the fact that, working with such severely ill patients, one does not remain untouched. Joseph Berke (ibid.), in delineating the Centre's therapeutic goals, has noted: 'What we can do is help guests to tolerate their underlying despair, to identify their underlying difficulties and conflicts, and to expand in some small ways their relational capacities – the possibility of intimacy, empathy and trust. In order to achieve this we do not remain passive onlookers. Rather we are active participants in the experiences they are trying to disgorge. Sometimes it seems that the main difference between them and ourselves is that we are more able to ask for help in struggling with intolerable feelings and states of mind' (Berke 1995).

Partly due to the preceding points, therapists at the Centre work with a clear delineation of roles and responsibilities in mind, including the ambiguities built into their roles, respecting each other's space. The structure of each team is set up before the guest comes in and in most cases remains unchanged, with the exception of the occasional recruitment of an additional team leader for extended team supervision. Thus an identity develops which is specific to each team. With it, and within the wider context of the whole therapeutic environment of the Centre, the team members are ready to be tossed about in the storms of the guest's – and their own – transferences and counter-transferences. During this time, there will be uncertainties, splits, and projections. This will inevitably result in the therapists taking on their guest's disturbance to varying degrees (ibid.), but with the secure knowledge that they will be held by the wider Wednesday Meeting.

As the origins of the Centre draw in part from the therapeutic community background, the ethos in the group is directed to seeing the guest as involved in the treatment whatever their level of disturbance might be. There is an understanding that, however much the guest may be in the throes of psychosis, there is always a non-psychotic personality present to which verbal and other comments and interpretations may be directed (Bion 1957); even if that personality cannot respond at the time, the understanding is that it can hear and benefit from the interaction.

As a result of all these factors the Wednesday Meeting works as a peer supervisory space for those attending it. Trainees and long-standing senior psychotherapists equally report to and respect each other's thinking, each benefiting both from experience and fresh ways of looking into issues. Concomitantly, the Meeting can at times be experienced as 'the Mother of all Supervisions', with all the terrifying and final pronouncements one may associate with her, as well as the idealized overtones that can coat such an all-embracing figure. Nevertheless, the Wednesday Meeting moves forward the elaborate and agile structures of the Centre in a way that is well enough respected by its participants. Interestingly it is well respected by the guests of the Centre too, who, whatever state they may be in, almost never disrupt it or attack it in any way! There is usually an atmosphere of calmness and reflection around the house while the Meeting is taking place, with guests being more interested in rather than feeling paranoid about what is being said about them.

With this background description of the Wednesday Meeting in mind, I shall now describe a vignette where some of these factors and the emotional linking of the clinical group were under attack. 'Robert', a thirty-two-year-old man, who spent many years in hospital with the diagnosis of schizophrenia, came to the Centre for an initial six-month stay. Soon after his arrival he refused to attend team and house meetings, leave his room, or join in the life of the house in any way. The group in the Wednesday Meeting became divided. Some therapists saw the option of allowing him to continue like this as providing a hotel room for a paying guest, and as their acting as corrupt accomplices to his state of mind; their suggestion was for his stay to be discontinued. Others felt that we should make an effort as a group to accommodate his needs, different as they might be to those of the other guests. How, though, could Robert benefit from the Centre as a therapeutic community if he did not attend the house meetings? What message would we be giving to the other guests if we allowed Robert to miss meetings? Should we not acknowledge his individuality in terms of his history, severity of disturbance and needs by arranging a form of therapeutic intervention suitable, specifically, to him? Though divided, the group had the space for doubt and tolerance of the different positions, and allowed Robert to continue his stay utilizing the milieu and focusing on his resident therapist in the treatment programme.

This decision, based on a tolerant attitude on the part of the group, that has a long history, bore fruit and Robert started to come out of his room. Still Robert missed more meetings. In fact, his team meetings became one-to-one meetings between his resident therapist and his team leader. Finding ways of bearing the unbearable hopelessness, helplessness and contempt that were being passed on to them was the most important part of their work.

When the time came for Robert to leave the Centre, the holding situation deteriorated. Partly due to holidays, partly due to the confusional state our group entered for a while, it became nearly impossible to arrange a review meeting with his psychiatrist, social worker and ourselves in order to think about his future together. While the Crisis Centre clinical meeting had decided that Robert would benefit from a further six-month stay, this needed to be thought about with the other professionals involved. Robert's leaving date approached. He had his leaving meal – a ritual for those leaving the Centre, even for those who are offered a second stay. This leaving meal proved to be a moving experience for everyone and was followed by a week of saying goodbye. Without appropriate planning, however, it was not known when exactly Robert would leave the Centre, and whether he would be returning for another stay at the Centre or going to another facility. At the least, funding for another stay would have to be negotiated with the Health Authority. To make things worse, Robert's resident therapist, 'Marvin', who had carried the linking of the intervention, having reached the end of his contract with us, was in the process of leaving. This meant that even if Robert was to be allowed another stay by the review panel, he would still have to be allocated a new resident therapist. Robert had become quite attached to Marvin, as he had come to represent a major link between himself and his team leader, the containing object of the team space.

Not surprisingly, Robert deteriorated at this point. He was now seen sitting for hours in the house conservatory mumbling to himself, impervious to people's approaches, or suddenly becoming aggressive and threatening. The contact he had made with people seemed to have evaporated and he vacillated between rage, threat and total apathy. At the Wednesday Meeting individual members of staff described their experiences of him. Marvin's partner, 'Cathy', also a resident therapist, who was staying longer than Marvin, described how she had asked Robert to turn down the volume of the music he was playing and how he had stood in front of her, staring into her eyes in an alarming way. Cathy had felt very frightened, but has managed to acknowledge her fear to him. After a few minutes Robert had said to her, 'You have beautiful eyes', and had sat down again. Another member of staff had set a place-mat on the table for her coffee cup. Soon she had been confronted by a threatening Robert, who, grabbing it from her, said, 'This is *my* mat, *that* one is yours.' The group felt despondent and hopeless for him. His 'aggressively loud music' had entered our ears and filled our minds, blocking our attempts to think. The decision made previously that the Centre would recommend another stay for him was forgotten, and indeed for a while it became unthinkable.

Eventually, however, linking started. Cathy, as Marvin's partner, was indeed in Robert's way. Her 'beautiful eyes', that Robert connected to Marvin in his identification with him, made a man of him again, not a frightened child. Indeed, it was Cathy who had been frightened. Her fear however, at that moment of confrontation, had been contained by her. This fact, having been observed by Robert, had allowed him to appreciate the beauty in the containing 'I'. He could sit down and relax for a bit. And so could we sit together, and think about him. The clinical group felt for him and his predicament. It was truly 'maddening' not to know what was going to happen to him, to the work he had done at the Centre, to the good experiences he had had. The threat was a threat to his whole world, that was now coming undone. No wonder he had pitched his whole existence on the mat he could call his. At the same time, the mat and the other objects he tenaciously saw as his became parts of him that he protected with ferocious persistence from both the him and us who were aware of the strong possibility of impending separation and loss.

This Wednesday Meeting helped all those working with Robert to re-discover the good contact they had made with him before, to remember the decision to offer him a second stay, and recognize in themselves Robert's crisis. In this instance the Meeting worked as a supervisory space from which we drew insight and strength to continue the work. The seemingly 'impossible' – to arrange review meeting – was achieved. Interestingly, although Robert did not attend, he expressly communicated that his long-term aim was to 'get a flat and be able to drive a van'.

Meanwhile, Robert expressed literally, through his behaviour, how he felt about himself and the milieu he was in. Our clinical meeting gathered the information: 'Walter', the new resident therapist, who was now replacing Marvin, had been invited by Robert to watch television with him, and on another occasion to have a cup of tea. 'Maria', a trainee, having offered to make Robert a cup of cocoa, reported how she had been asked by him, 'How long will this take?' She had replied with a question: 'Why, are you in a hurry?', and they had both laughed amicably. Robert had then proceeded to pace up and down the kitchen, keeping busy with his thoughts. Indeed, Cathy remembered times he had been asked to bring from his room the plates, cups and saucers he had accumulated there, and when he had replied, 'Hmm, it's a matter of finding the time.' People's experiences of him were mulled over. We were all reminded of how Robert's time and space-frame was different from that of ours. Time and space – what normally separated objects in the external and internal worlds – had been attacked by the him that was unable to face separateness, or indeed frustration, to the point that they had become banned from his mind. He was so busy with a traffic of thoughts he felt crowded by, thoughts which he had very little sense of containing, that it was an effort for him to find the time for activities that would involve him in the life, time and space of the house. And yet, here he was, in essence welcoming the new resident therapist and trying to help him feel at home. Robert's behaviour towards Walter was the behaviour of someone who has a home and a place from which to invite and make welcome another. It was the behaviour of someone who has space for understanding what it is like to be a new group member. In the Wednesday Meeting of that time we did not know whether Robert would eventually find the resources to 'have a flat and drive a van'; and yet, we speculated, it was likely he would be able to find a space in his mind from which he would have the drive to acknowledge himself as existing within the same space–time context as others. The laughter he had shared with Maria, far from being denigrating, had been a moment of realization and of sharing the same moment in time with another human being.

This account illustrates a number of issues in the working-together clinical group. Robert's distress was such that it stretched and tested the fabric of the Centre. Where the strands of community therapy and psycho-analytic work met, a rift threatened to open. In addition, the resident thera-pists felt their work devalued when Robert refused to go to the house meetings they facilitated. Group work and individual work therapists were in danger of being at each other's throats. However, under the pressure of these enormous projective processes at work, although the Wednesday Meeting divided, it did not fragment. It went from questioning and doubting its identity to understanding its mental state in relation to that of Robert's, and so, eventually, managed to contain the projective fragments of his mind.

In this case it took the whole clinical group thinking together to un-derstand and contain a complex situation, aggravated by the threat of a relapse. Robert's situation involved the 'leaving crisis' of a very ill patient, experienced by our whole group as well as by outside professionals who, carrying Robert's confusion, found themselves unable to come together to arrange a meeting to think about him (Berke 1987). It was also a crisis pre-cipitated by the actual departure of a member of staff. In addition, our lim-itation in terms of what we offer as a time-limited therapeutic crisis centre – not a long-term staffed community – imposed a further burden on Robert, who needed a longer term placement, preferably open-ended, before he could effectively start thinking about leaving. For containment to take place, this guest's individual needs had to be acknowledged and taken into account. The therapists, too, had to be able to question, pull apart and reformulate not only their own sense of position and identity but also the Centre's. The container had to be moulded specifically around the patient in such a way that his contents could be contained. Expressed in another way, the therapists' group had to avoid the temptation of bringing up baby according to the specialist's manual with its strictly prescribed ways of handling and times of feeding. Rather, the group had to develop a baby-oriented approach, which responded to the particular baby in question. Had Robert been able to make decisions on what was appropri-ate treatment for him, attend therapy meetings, and be part of the social group, he would have been well on his way to recovery, perhaps not needing a residential facility but instead out-patient psychoanalytic psychotherapy. As he was, his needs were for an expanded therapeutic space that would allow for flexibility of thinking and flexibility in the treatment offered. For this to happen the Wednesday Meeting had to find a way of making the distinction between this and an 'anything goes' attitude. While the latter colludes with the psychotic personality of the patient, therapeutic flexibility allows for thinking to develop rather than stagnate under the pressure of mechanically standardized rules of behaviour (Pierides 1998).

It was bounded flexibility of the container that allowed for this particular person, on that particular occasion, to have a good experience. It was what allowed the clinical group to have a good experience too – of doing good work as an expanded team, and of succeeding in thinking with, and relating to, a very disturbed and disturbing person for an extended period of time. For a while, the container and the contained, through mutual contact, grew together (Bion 1984). Robert's needs had not been labelled and ignored; neither had they been rejected for not fitting a comfortable set of expectations of what the Centre offers and is about.

Unfortunately, but also predictably, the situation deteriorated once again around the next instances of leaving, both of staff and of guests. In the case of staff, this involved Cathy, Marvin's partner, who was now finishing her work with us. The resulting upheaval in the staff group led to a temporary deterioration in its containing capacities. Like a preoccupied mother, the staff group became less sensitive and receptive to its baby's needs. This happened at the time shortly after Robert's father left the country and when his mother was planning to leave to follow him. The parental couple, the literal basis of Robert's life, and the structure that underpinned his relationship to the therapeutic team, was abandoning him. Similarly, our staff group was losing Cathy, and, through her relationship with Marvin, Marvin himself, and the couple they made together, which for a long period had contributed a sense of stability to the Centre. At the same time, four of the six people of the guest group were in the process of leaving: a constant reminder to Robert of his own imminent leaving. Under this pressure, Robert 'took leave of his senses' in a way for which the only organizing principle was destructiveness. This time, it was not possible for the clinical group to contain him, and he had to go to hospital for a period of time. The container that the Centre provided had been less stable in the latter period, with less to offer. The Wednesday Meeting had to face once again the full impact of Robert's, and our, predicament – his and our limitations and relationship to reality, pain and loss; and the further injury to our clinical group's omnipotence as it saw its holding potential deteriorating at this time of change and loss.

Tired and wounded, the Wednesday Meeting nevertheless held itself together by means of its history, common aims and commitment. For all that, it took us longer than usual to recover our ability to communicate with each other thoughtfully and with insight about the events leading up to Robert's leaving. We have not heard from Robert since he left us. Our statistical entry for his stay will be a 'negative' one. However, one of our RTs saw Robert in the street. Robert was with his mother, crossing the road: first he looked left, then right, and then he crossed the road – something he could not ostensibly do while at the Centre. There he was, allowing himself to be aware of the traffic, of danger, of different spaces – but still with his mother. We felt pleased that some of the work we had done with him had been taken in and had taken root, and we could think that he was now able for a time to share the space and time of the world around him.

References

Berke, J.H. (1987) 'Arriving, Settling-in, Settling-down, Leaving and Following-up: Stages of Stay at the Arbours Centre.' *British Journal of Medical Psychology 60*, 181–188.

Berke, J.H. (1995) 'Psychotic Interventions.' In J.H. Berke, C. Masoliver and T. Ryan (eds) *Sanctuary: The Arbours Experience of Alternative Community Care.* London: Process Press.

Bion, W.R. (1957) 'Differentiation of the Psychotic from the Non-Psychotic Personalities.' In W.R. Bion, *Second Thoughts.* London: Karnac Books, 1984.

Bion, W.R. (1984) *Learning from Experience.* London: Karnac Books.

Pierides, S. (1998) 'Machine Phenomena.' In J.H. Berke, S. Pierides, A. Sabbadini and S. Schneider (eds) *Even Paranoids Have Enemies.* London: Routledge.

Pierides, S. (2000) 'Working together: Aspects of a Therapeutic Container at Work.' In S. Brooks and P. Hodson (eds) *The Invisible Matrix.* London: Rebus Press.

CHAPTER 7

Supervision in Team Work

Tamar Schonfield

The team, rather than a single therapist, carries out individual work at the Crisis Centre. This variant on conventional technique opens up interesting transference and countertransference possibilities, as well as raising issues of communication, and highlights the importance of supervision. I will discuss these issues here in the light of one guest's use of his team.

The team leader meets the guest only in the team meetings, while the resident therapist (RT) shares their life in the house and is also involved in the group work such as house meetings. The student on the team spends some informal time in the Crisis Centre, but does not live there or take part in most formal group-meetings. The team members, therefore, each have different relationships with the guest, and come together in the sessions and team-supervision meetings.

The need to have a team working with each guest arises from the high level of disturbance that drives borderline or psychotic patients to resort to splitting off and projecting as a way of both surviving and communicating their unbearable experiences. Like the guest, no one person on their own can bear the unbearable, and a team is necessary to 'in-patient' or 'out-patient' work with severely disturbed persons.

I regard team meetings as similar to one-to-one sessions in providing a safe enough space for the development of a relationship and for thinking about it. At times, as indeed with 'Mark', the guest I will present here, I, as team leader, hold a large share of the negative transference, thereby allowing the guest to be freer to use the rest of the Crisis Centre in more creative ways.

While I feel that a therapy session is complicated enough with only one person holding responsibility for it, I am aware of the confusion which could arise with two other active therapists in the session. With this in mind, I ask the resident therapist and the student on the team to contribute to team meetings, as they can make important links to the guest's other experiences in house meetings, art or movement or other interactions in the house. However, I ask them to refrain from adding new and different interpretations during team meetings, but to discuss them instead in supervision, where their observations can often contribute in very important ways to our shared understanding of what is going on.

An important feature of our work with the guests is the vulnerability of our thinking to conscious and unconscious attack from them. Aware of this, I tend to depend on the team to remember what I already know, and by sharing with them responsibility in this way am enabled as team leader to feel less anxious about remembering and thinking. This sharing of responsibility can sometimes work in a very productive way. In the team in which we worked with Mark we found that at times each of us remembered very different facts about the sessions and had contrasting impressions and feelings. Our remarkably different countertransference feelings towards Mark had the effect of creating splits in the team and promoting a competitive atmosphere, in which each of us claimed to hold the 'truth'. Thinking through the conflicts and holding these different parts of a 'divided truth' together gave us a strong sense of Mark's own intense defensive use of splitting, and his need to project elements that he could not bear to keep together. Team supervision in this sense is essential for restoring the team's thinking and containing capacities, repairing the links and bringing together and containing the guest's projected split-off elements.

In this way a team can enable a guest to have a differentiated relationship with its different members, to split rather than fragment, and to allow for a possible integration in team meetings. In other words, the team can function as an auxiliary-ego for the guest, with different members holding different parts of the person and bringing them together in a safe way. Overall the therapeutic value of the team depends to a great extent on communication and supervision, both in the weekly team-supervision sessions and in the Centre's larger weekly clinical meetings, where each guest and the team work are discussed. In her paper 'Working Together' (Pierides 2000) Stella Pierides has described the process by which the

Centre's weekly clinical meeting can temporarily lose and then regain its containing capacity; similar processes can be seen in team supervisions too.

These weekly clinical meetings and these team supervisions, which are peer structures, contrast with the individual and group supervision of the students and resident therapists, which are more hierarchical in character, involving an experienced supervisor working with people in training. In team supervision there is usually no supervisor, and more often than not the discussion is open rather than bound by detailed notes. The hierarchy of an 'all-knowing' supervisor and a beginner supervisee, who is closely involved with the patient, is absent because all participants take part in the therapy. What is discussed is alive for all, and the affective experience of the therapy tends to become a central focus for discussion. Emanuel Berman, an Israeli psychoanalyst, says that an 'open personal atmosphere' in supervision may 'evolve into a transitional space within which the dyad [or in the Centre, the team] generates new meanings not accessible by the intrapsychic work of each partner in isolation' (Berman 2000, p.285). Team supervision can become a safe space where the anxiety experienced in team meetings, the ambiguity born of splitting and projection and of conflicts between team members can be thought about. The ability to reflect openly, and to play with ideas in supervision, allows the team to be creative and in this way reverse the process of projective identification. That which has been split-off and projected, and which has been identified with, can be recognized, thought about and integrated as new understandings. These may be translated at a later stage into interpretations in team meetings with the guest.

No amount of conscious effort or supervision can prevent all the enactment of unconscious processes, however. This is particularly so when one is working with borderline or psychotic people, whether in individual therapy or in team work. Here direct conscious verbal communication presents only part of the picture, while important elements that are in conflict with the patient's accepted view remain split off and unknown to them but communicated by action or by projection. Michael Parsons, a British Independent psychoanalyst, in his paper 'The Logic of Play in Psychoanalysis' (Parsons 1999), views enactment as a rupture of the analytic playframe. Enactment breaks through the structure which provides the safe transitional space within which material can be played with and handled as both real and not real at the same time. Accordingly enactments necessitate an active process of repair of the analytic playframe. The basic assumptions about the safety of the space and its paradoxical nature have to be thought about and re-evaluated, and it is in this process of repair that the productive element of enactments lies.

From this point of view the team's structure can also be seen as a paradoxical space, where the material is both real and not real at the same time, and creative play can go on. However, when projected fragments are enacted in the form, for instance, of conflicts in the team, these conflicts feel very real, and as there is no unreality about them, there is no space for play or thought. The first creative task of the team supervision would be to repair and restore its framework, in order to enable the team to attend to the process of repairing the therapy space.

In team supervision, acknowledging the emotional impact of the therapy on team-members is crucial both as a medium for mutual support, by reducing anxiety, guilt, shame or embarrassment at having unacceptable feeling towards the guest, and as a key to unravelling the projected fragments. The process of reassembling these fragments and of repairing the thinking space, first of the team and then of the therapy, begins in the supervision space. The emotional challenge in supervision is to experience and to express at times very strong and difficult feelings, which more often than not can be felt as intense conflicts between team-members. The intellectual challenge is to reflect and think them through, play with the ideas and make sense of the ambiguities.

Let me now go into the details of our work with Mark, which will provide some very valuable illustrative material. Mark was a man in his late 30s, who always appeared to be a 'good boy', with a neat side-parting and a desire to please and be on best behaviour. As his presentation suggested, he was trying to repair and cover-up some of the real damage his uncontrolled rage had inflicted both on others and on himself, and which has resulted in a court case against him. He had been referred by Social Services to the Centre specifically to deal with these experiences of damage and loss, but he was hoping we might also support him in his impending court appearance resulting from this behaviour. We explained to him that our views would not be asked for, but the court-room dynamics were at times prevalent in the team.

Mark was sure we were judging him and tried to 'present his case' as he would in court. At times it was difficult not to comply with his desire to be judged. When he described in detail what he had done, we were simultaneously moved and drawn into judgemental positions. In our team supervision we were able to share our different experiences of his account and the judgemental positions we had reached. Alan, the student in the team, felt for Mark's victims, while I was more aware of him and his impossible predicament. Jude, the resident therapist, was preoccupied by the little-boy part of Mark. We each felt guilty, however, for holding one particular view to the exclusion of others and for judging. Evidently Mark himself feared unconsciously that were he to feel these different sets of feelings together a fatal explosion might follow. After we talked about it in his team meetings, the atmosphere changed and he was more able to use the meetings to talk about other aspects of his life. However, he was still on best behaviour hoping, despite everything, that our views would be asked for by the court.

Before my Easter break Mark was struggling with his therapy, pushing me away at team meetings but talking about me with anyone who would listen. He rejected any interpretations about my impending break with varying degrees of rage and contempt.

While I was away, the resident therapist, Jude, and the student, Alan, continued to hold two sessions a week. On our first session after my break, a Monday, I felt particularly unwell with flu, but decided to keep the session. Mark came in on time, but did not acknowledge my presence or my flu. He acted as though I had never been away and said, 'I've got a headache, I'm sick, ill. I want to go back to my mum and dad, I feel really bad.' I waited, bemused or shocked at his capacity to ignore my presence, and perhaps wondering also whether he had indeed noticed my state of health and had taken it on himself. Before I had time to gather my thoughts, and without further pause, Mark went on to talk about the difficulties he experienced in groups and his worries about confidentiality.

It seems that my failure to acknowledge straight away how bad Mark felt, and his wish to be a little boy and to return to his (idealized) mum and dad, led him into an attempt at falsely being an adult and using his therapy 'properly'. I took what he said at face value and proceeded to discuss trust with him. He then talked about how disappointingly distant Alan was towards him, effectively splitting Alan off from the team and blaming him rather than me for having been absent. I still did not pick up the resentful and defiant mood and Mark started talking about his parents and friends as the people he could trust. He recalled vividly the railway line at the end of the street near his parents' house. As a child he had been told he could be electrocuted, and as a result he was frightened of crossing the wooden bridge over the line in case he fell through the gaps between the planks. I said that I thought he was also describing his fear of falling through the gaps between team meetings, especially during my break. Mark replied adamantly that he was not, that he knew there were fifty minutes and that then he could leave. 'I don't want to think, I just want to talk,' he said, implying that for him talking was an action rather than part of a thinking process.

In the team supervision which followed the session the predominant feeling was of despair. Remarkably, nothing was mentioned about the beginning of the session or about Mark's wish to go home, which seemed to have been overshadowed by Mark's powerful refusal to think combined with his false co-operation in the therapeutic process. I expressed my lack of hope of ever making real contact with him. Jude was keen to share the unbearable murderous feelings towards Mark that she had been carrying over my break, while Alan, feeling less strongly, was somewhat critical of Jude's powerful reaction. The general feeling in the team was of separateness and pessimism: we felt isolated, stuck and unable to think. The play framework of the team, like the therapeutic one before, had been ruptured at this point and we needed time and help to repair it.

With hindsight it seems that we were projectively identified with Mark and not yet able to think about the situation creatively. We also had to deal with the team's reaction to my break. While I was away Jude and Alan had held the team meetings. Mark's negative feelings and destructiveness spilled over from the team meetings to their relationship in the house, making it clear that a team meeting without a team leader is a very different kind of team meeting. The absence of the person whose connection to the guest is an exclusive connection within this structure weakens the structure's boundary. Team meetings lost their holding capacity, and were no longer separate from the rest of the Crisis Centre experience. Mark must have felt increasingly unsafe, unable to leave his own unpleasant projections behind him in the team-meeting space, and was flooded when they came back at him in the persons of his resident therapist and student therapist. This must have caused him anxiety, against which he defended himself by being nasty to the resident therapists. When Jude opened the supervision with her pressing murderous feelings towards Mark it reflected both his terrifying, but denied, projected murderous feelings at being left in an unsafe situation, and her own rage at being left with him. Alan's reaction was more reflective of the therapeutic super-ego which forbids us, as 'good therapists', from having negative feelings of this sort, but it also echoed Mark's superficial attempts at falsely being a 'good patient'. As the one who had been away, I felt excluded from the team and hopeless about my ability to make contact with Mark, but quite probably also hopeless about my ability to repair the damage in any quick way. This perhaps reflected Mark's feelings at having been excluded from his family and his sense of being unable to repair the real damage he had caused.

However, at this point we were not able to think freely or to understand this. We needed time to restore our thinking space, and we thought we should ask another team leader, who would be free from these projections, to join us for supervision, an option which is always open to a team that feels it has lost direction.

And what happened to Mark's ideas about leaving?

Although little new understanding in this supervision meeting was reached, communicating among ourselves did open options for the work which followed. After team supervision Alan stayed on for his informal time in the house (four unstructured hours that each student spends weekly in the Centre). At this point, and in this setting, Mark told Alan that he was angry with me, frightened that he might get very nasty and worried that I had given up on him. He thought that this was what we had been talking about after his session that day, referring to our team supervision. The fact that he was in some way right indicates how perceptive Mark was. He seemed to hate his connection to the team, deny it, and split it off, but on some level always to be in touch with it. Alan talked to him about this horrible feeling of abandonment and wondered aloud whether it had prompted him to think about packing his bags in order to leave before he was asked to. Mark, sounding frustrated, responded that it would be a long time before our next team meeting when he would be able to find out whether I had indeed given up on him. But even then, he thought, I would not tell him.

Alan was able to help Mark process the day's events and to understand what no one had understood before – that Mark was thinking about leaving because he did not feel understood, and that he saw his departure as a prelude to his inevitable expulsion from the Centre. Why was Alan able to get further with Mark that day? One reason might be that since Mark had already let Alan know in the team meeting how frustrated he was with him, Mark was more open to communicating with him after the team meeting. Furthermore, Mark was clearly anxious about our supervision meeting, which at the level of phantasy he seemed to regard as another court sitting, the decision of which he would have to await anxiously and helplessly. On a deeper level still our team supervision may have felt like parents' secret conversation, in which the unbearability of the children can be discussed in private, enabling the parents either to cope or perhaps, as he feared, to decide to abandon the children altogether. After going through the anguish of the team meeting Mark felt at a loose end, hopeless about therapy, alone with his anxiety, frustration and rage, and frightened both of his own destructiveness and of mine. Not knowing what we had 'decided', he was desperate to talk to Alan. From Alan's point of view, the experience of the frustrating team meeting, and the emotional atmosphere of our team supervision, may have freed him to take risks, as he felt that Mark's therapeutic process could not have been at a lower point.

Over the following two days Mark was simultaneously preparing for his next session and for his departure – twin activities which seemed powerfully separated. He came to his Thursday session with two pages of notes, trying to be in control. He did not mention the idea of going home on this or the Friday sessions. His wish to leave was kept split off from team meetings and became a plan. I was not aware of the plan, however, and neither Alan nor Jude mentioned it. As we did not have another team supervision until the following Monday I had no way of finding out.

Mark's growing fears of 'failing therapy' and being rejected from the Centre were worked through out of the team meetings, and were not mentioned in the course of any. He could not accept his feeling of needing us and his anxiety of being rejected by us, and so, while keeping them split off from consciousness, acted them out. The feeling of failure was projected into the team and was to remain with us rather than with Mark, who was to take a break. We felt we were failing his therapy and it was we who were to be rejected.

Mark had split off his anxiety about the Easter break by turning the Centre, and myself in particular, into a bad, neglectful, non-holding mother, whom he had either to kill or flee from before he himself would be 'electrocuted'. By the time I returned from the Easter break words had very little chance of repairing this damage: the team meeting space was no longer a safe space for playing with ideas. Mark was compelled to act in order to achieve movement. This may throw useful light on how we as a team possibly colluded in an inevitable enactment.

So what happened to our team? Why did Jude and Alan not bring Mark's split-off leaving plans to the Thursday session? Why did they not make the connections? Was it because they trusted me too much and felt I must know what was going on without having to be told? Or was it because they felt the interaction between Mark and myself, which at times seemed tense and on the brink of a violent eruption, to be too dense to interrupt? Or perhaps the team, like Mark's mind, was split and unable to come together and think properly.

We used all of Mark's missed sessions for our own supervision and, as noted, invited another team leader to one of our meetings. Having a psychotherapist who was not involved in our intensive work and was free to think restored the transitional qualities of this space. We were finally able to discuss our feelings and to play constructively with our thoughts. I could air my own confusion at suddenly realizing that Mark was going; my anger for not having known or understood it earlier; my resentment at having been left out by the rest of the team; and my concerns about Mark, wondering whether I had lost him for good. These feelings seemed to reflect the vulnerability and anxiety that Mark could not own, and in particular his denial of any connection between the concerns he mentioned about being in a group and his experience in the team. Jude was able to expand on her murderous feelings towards him, dating back to the break discussed above, which she felt to have been too frightening to have been taken on board in the way they needed to be by the team. Alan talked of feeling marginalized, bound by the seductive quality of Mark's confiding his secret plan with him and of the gratitude he had expressed following their conversation together.

The opportunity in this expanded setting to discuss our feelings openly allowed us to come together at last, and we started to form a fuller picture of Mark. We had a sense of the intolerable vulnerability he felt when he was aware of his dependence and neediness, and of how frightening his destructiveness and murderousness must have felt to him. We could see how he could not bear feeling all this together in case he ended up destroying what he needed most, an experience he had very nearly had several times in his past. Working through this process, and reassembling the pieces, allowed us, first in team supervision and later with Mark, to contain the splits and move beyond the 'best-behaviour' phase to a more real kind of communication.

For Mark his break felt like an opportunity to regain control. It mirrored my break in that it was planned and announced in advance and ended at the time he said it would. He may have been aware that this would give us space to come together and think. It certainly gave him space to return to the Centre on his own terms – in a different state of mind, more able to think, and more able to use his team and the Crisis Centre in a more productive way.

The team's ability to recognize that we needed help in supervision, to ask for it, and to use it to restore our own safe transitional space, enabled us to be open about accepting Mark back on his own terms and helping him move on and take some risks in recognizing his needs.

Unravelling and understanding what had been going on in the team was at times difficult, not only because of difficulties in communication between team members, but because of the anxiety-provoking fragmented nature of what had been projected and enacted. The team's effort to make sense of and to follow the dynamics of the projections enabled each team member to work therapeutically with this guest in their varied relationships. Team supervision was the central space for sharing information and discussing technique, and also for sharing different emotional experiences and moving from fragmented conflictual ambiguity towards a very real sense of creative integration.

References

Berman, E. (2000) 'Psychoanalytic supervision: The Intersubjective Development.' *International Journal of Psychoanalysis 81*, 273–290.

Parsons, M. (1999) 'The Logic of Play in Psychoanalysis.' *International Journal of Psychoanalysis 80*, 871–884.

Pierides, S. (2000) 'Working Together: Aspects of a Therapeutic Container at Work.' In S. Brooks and P. Hodson (eds) *The Invisible Matrix*. London: Rebus Books.

CHAPTER 8

Containing Anxiety: A Resident Therapist's Experience

Catherine Sunderland

My background is in psychiatric nursing, and it is through my training as a psychiatric nurse that I came to do a placement at the Arbours Crisis Centre, before becoming a resident therapist. I did not realize at the time how influenced I was by the implicit and sometimes explicit assumptions embedded in the discourses of psychiatry and nursing, nor how some of these attitudes mirrored and fitted with my own attitudes and ways of coping. Some of the aims of psychiatric nursing are to make people feel better – eliminate symptoms, control feelings, get rid of or suppress difficult feelings – and at the same time maintain a 'professional' distance (which can mean not getting too involved with or emotionally impacted by the patients). I wanted to think that these were aims I never believed in, but they proved harder to shake off than I realized. At times they even felt more 'sensible' than living with disturbance in the way we do at the Crisis Centre. At times the Crisis Centre has felt like a mad place to live and work in and I have longed for the security of psychiatric terminology, hospital procedures, and the certainty (however illusory) offered by these ways of thinking about and responding to emotional distress.

The response by many mainstream psychiatric services is to treat the feelings of the guest and of those around them as abnormal and dangerous, something to be somehow got rid of. The anxiety felt by hospital staff is alleviated by adherence to a variety of procedures, which constitute the very fabric of the hospital structure. At the Crisis Centre we try to hold anxiety for our guests in a different way – to contain it in ways which give the guests the opportunity to begin to find ways of eventually containing it themselves.

Guests need to come to the Crisis Centre in general because they need to be 'inside' somewhere or something safe. Hospital can provide asylum/sanctuary in a certain way and to a certain extent. Patients are kept physically safer in hospital through the use of external controls: locked doors, seclusion rooms, medication and physical restraint. Giving sanctuary, a sense of being in a safely bounded space, is one function of containment (Britton 1998), and one which, in my experience, is in some way provided by hospitals, but provided in a different way by the Crisis Centre. The holding at the Crisis Centre is different in that it is, on the whole, not physical but something more mental. The 'nursing' provided at the Centre is a nursing with thinking rather than action. A second function of containment is giving meaning to experiences that feel unbearable and unthinkable (Britton 1998). It is in the provision of this second function that the Crisis Centre, being a psychotherapeutic facility, differs most from hospitals.

This work of giving meaning to unbearable experiences is internal – akin to the ways in which mothers contain babies. In Bion's words:

> The infant projects a part of its psyche, namely its bad feelings, into the good breast. Thence in due course they are removed and re-introjected. During this sojourn in the good breast they are felt to have been modified in such a way that the object that is re-introjected has become tolerable to the infant's psyche. (Bion 1962, p.90)

Put another way, if the resident therapist is receptive to the guest's state of mind and able to allow it to be evoked in herself, she can process it in such a way that in an identified form she can attend to the feelings in the guest and transform them into something more manageable, eventually enabling the guest to develop the capacity to do this themselves. Guests come to the Crisis Centre for many apparently different reasons, but a basic 'reason' is that they need help to contain their anxieties, which are usually enormous. Something is amiss and unmanageable and feelings are spilling over. Guests may express their anxieties vividly, perhaps through acting out or through psychosomatic or perceptual disturbance. Frequently it is those around the guest who feel this anxiety acutely. Guests who come to the Crisis Centre are invariably so full of anxiety that they need the containing space available in the resident therapist, the team leader, the milieu and the physical space of the house to hold it, bear it and, crucially, to process and understand it.

Monica came to the Crisis Centre after a placement in another residential facility broke down. After locking herself in her room there for several days she had been asked to leave and had spent some time in hospital. Monica arrived at the Centre bitter about how she felt she'd been treated in the previous place and anxious that the same thing might happen here. She presented herself as very anxious; people and objects in the external world seemed to be relentlessly experienced by her as obstacles. There seemed always in her mind to be someone or something obstructing her attempts to relieve herself of anxiety by making any significant or helpful contact with people. As her resident therapist I felt unable to give her anything or have any helpful contact with her. Monica expressed her anxieties by wanting immediate answers to concrete requests or questions. When an answer was given it was always either inadequate or not what she wanted to hear. She seemed to get very easily overwhelmed and said she could only deal with one thing at a time. She also told me she could only 'deal' with one person at a time, and would not come downstairs to meet the other members of the house. My phantasy was that her wish or need was to have me stay with her in her room – that this somehow was the only way she could feel in control.

Mary came to the Crisis Centre having had several hospital admissions in the past three years due to self-harming, through cutting herself and taking overdoses. She was a counsellor herself and found 'being on the other side of the fence' very humiliating and difficult. Prior to her initial consultation Mary wrote us a letter expressing how anxious and afraid she was of coming to the Centre and of what we were going to do to her. It was clear from her letter and from the initial consultation that relationships were very frightening to her. Having her pain and difficulties seen made her anxious, but not feeling understood left her feeling isolated. She expressed an intolerance to being on her own, and when at home she would ring up different professionals for help. She was afraid that she would destroy those around her with her neediness and seemed to despair of ever being able to be contained. Her previous therapist had been unable to continue working with her and Mary felt she was too much for everyone. Consequently she tended to hide her difficulties from us and attempted to deal with her difficult feelings in self-destructive and self-defeating ways such as overdosing on prescribed medication, cutting her arms, bingeing and vomiting, and isolating herself emotionally from her team.

I have felt many different types of anxiety in relation to these and other guests whilst living at the Crisis Centre. Monica seemed to induce in me lots of subtly different kinds of anxiety. With one comment or question from her I could feel immediate anxiety, as if she had just thrown me a 'football' of anxiety which I had 'caught'. At the end of one of her team meetings, as she was walking out, she looked at me and said in a very threatening voice, 'If you're interested, Cath, I feel like self-harming right now.' It felt to me that she was demanding immediate action from me, and since we were at the end of the session it was not possible to think with her about this as I was going straight to another meeting. I felt full of anxiety. But with the help of the team leaders and my fellow resident therapists I was able to continue to think, and able to hold onto and bear these 'footballs'.

In relation to Monica I often felt a sense of anxious dread – an anticipatory anxiety, which tended to escalate the longer she remained in her room away from the rest of the house or from her team meetings, for which she would frequently be late. On a couple of occasions she had hinted at how self-destructive she was feeling and at having razor blades or tablets in her room. She would then remain in her room in a mute state. The longer she was up there the more consumed and paralysed with anxiety I would feel. Short of remaining in the room with her I had no way of knowing if she would self-harm, or of how serious this would be, or what exactly she was feeling.

The anxiety we have to contain is often an anxiety of not knowing. What is happening in the house or to particular guests? What does it mean? What will happen next – in the next hour, over the weekend, or when a new guest arrives? This anxiety of not knowing is necessary, and finding a way to contain this anxiety is an important part of being a resident therapist. We help if we can allow something creative and new to occur, rather than getting locked into repetitive ways of reacting or responding to the distress (which could lead to an 'acting in' with the guests' acting out). That is, we have to let the guests use the Centre as a place to be unknown, so that they can be known in a different and more profound way, and not just as a label or set of symptoms.

Hospital interventions, which are usually employed to lessen or even diminish anxiety in the staff, do not allow the patients to know themselves in any new way. Guests have frequently been in-patients in psychiatric wards prior to coming to the Crisis Centre and are thus used to this kind of response. Indeed, we are often pressurized by guests to respond in this way.

When Monica let us know about feeling self-destructive but refused to let us help by allowing there to be communication between us, or by giving us the razor blades, I felt a pressure to respond in a hospital-like way. Had she been on a ward, the staff would have put her on close observation, and she would not have been allowed out of the sight of a staff member. She might also have been given some medication. This would prevent the self-destructive act from occurring temporarily, but do little to further anyone's understanding of what this act might or might not mean. The anxiety is not understood, the person is not understood or assisted in understanding themselves, and all those involved in the situation are caught up in a repetitive and unthinking process. To have succumbed to the pressure to act in relation to this example with Monica would not have been helpful. Learning how to respond in a different way, and in a way in which I could more likely be left feeling anxious, was not, and still at times is not, easy. I did go to bed that night with no reassurance that Monica would not cut herself, and our capacity to contain her at the Crisis Centre was very much in question.

Knowing when to allow anxiety to be borne, and when action to ensure the guest's safety must be taken, is not an easy task, nor one where we have any specific procedure (as in hospitals) to guide us. What we do have is our relationship with the guest – an intuitive sense of the strength of the therapeutic alliance between us; help from colleagues and at times other guests; and a trust in our own feelings borne out of past experience. It is exactly because we are *not* sure, that the work of bearing anxiety has to be done. When to bear not knowing and when not to is a difficult decision. Sometimes not knowing is part of a creative process, but it can mean being kept in the dark with regard to destructiveness.

Another common type of anxiety is what I describe as overload anxiety. This, in my experience, is what arises from an atmosphere or climate in the house where there is too much input/projection and seemingly limited possibilities for output/processing/feeding back. In the week of Monica's arrival we had a second new guest who we were concerned could become aggressive. My fellow resident therapist Jo was having a handover week with Patricia, her successor, and I was feeling the strain of coping with my feelings of loss and panic in relation to Jo's departure, welcoming the new resident therapist, and helping the existing guests during this period of transition.

On top of this came Monica, pressing me for one-to-one contact from the time of her arrival, and furthermore for contact which seemed consistently beset by obstacles. It was impossible to negotiate planned time with her; she would instead 'grab' me at unexpected moments. I was not sleeping well, and after one sleepless night she greeted me as I emerged bleary-eyed from the shower. I felt unable to think and was forced into a position where all I felt able to do was close the 'door' with a firm no. As for her use of the formal spaces, she either kept herself away, or, when she was present, remained impenetrably mute. I felt unable to process what was going on, as, presumably, did she. That week I seemed to move around the Centre feeling like an overfull balloon about to burst. It took me quite some time to unpick, understand and digest what was going on.

Guests frequently behave in ways that induce a great deal of anxiety in those around them. The fact that this is occurring can be a sign that the guest is allowing their feelings to be communicated and known. The anxiety I have felt in relation to Mary has at times felt like this. Mary tended to be secretive about her self-destructiveness, maintaining a veneer of being pleasant, coping and co-operative. I sometimes wondered about my lack of anxiety about her, so successful was she at hiding her difficulties. One evening, prior to the return of her team leader after the Easter break, Mary asked to speak to me before bed and let me know she had been storing her night-time medication and that evening had taken more than the prescribed dose. She said she felt desperate, and afraid she would take even more in the night. She was very reluctant to state clearly how many she had already taken, and was equally reluctant to hand in the rest. Patricia and I sat with her for some time talking to her about what was going on and trying to get her to hand in the tablets. It became increasingly apparent to me that for her, to hand in the tablets would mean preventing us from being anxious or concerned about her, as though our only interest in her was as nurses, wanting to prevent her self-harming behaviour in order to alleviate our own anxiety and appease our professional conscience. Hanna Segal has described the process by which the child, and by implication the patient, receives containment:

> When an infant has intolerable anxiety, he deals with it by projecting it into the mother. The mother's response is to acknowledge this anxiety and do whatever is necessary to relieve the infant's distress. The infant's

perception is that he has projected something intolerable into his
object, but the object was capable of containing it and dealing with it.
He can then reintroject not only the original anxiety, but an anxiety
modified by having been contained. He also reintrojects an object
capable of containing and dealing with anxiety. The containment of the
anxiety by an internal object capable of understanding is the beginning
of mental stability. (Segal 1975, p.135)

On this occasion Mary needed us to be anxious, to share some of the
anxiety she was finding too overwhelming to hold on her own. Voicing
these thoughts seemed to enable her to hand in the tablets and go to bed,
knowing that we also went to bed with feelings of concern for her.

A major part of my work at the Crisis Centre has involved being
receptive and sensitive to the atmosphere or climate of the house. This state
of receptivity is akin to what Bion describes as 'reverie' (Bion 1962), a state
of being that enables us to empathize with the internal experiences and
non-verbal communications of the guests. There have been times when the
atmosphere has felt difficult to put into words and very powerful.
Sometimes it has been as if the house was filled with a kind of noxious gas,
something that got into everything in a subtle but invasive way. I have
often experienced anxiety primarily in my body – a tension headache, loss
of appetite, fatigue or nausea. It can feel as if something is pervading my
whole being, paralysing my capacity to think. For the first few days of her
stay Monica remained in her bedroom, which was situated at the top of the
stairs. From here, with her door open, Monica would call out if I went by.

Interaction with her would centre on her demands for concrete
changes – all requests that could not immediately be met. My experience
of her at this time was that she was lying in wait like a spider in a web. I felt
that to walk by her room was to risk being ensnared with her in there. Experiences of this kind can be understood as important communications
from the guest: picking them up, bearing the power and intensity of them
and finding some way of verbalizing the experience is part of the containing work of the Centre. Something near-sensory and somatic – in Bion's
terminology, Beta elements – is transformed into something more mental –
Alpha elements, which can be used for thought (ibid.).

The work of the Centre is done in different ways by all who are
involved: team leaders, clinical assistant, resident therapists and students.
There are however aspects of life at the Centre that are unique to the
resident therapists. As we live at the Crisis Centre we have access to the rest

of the guests' lives: outside their therapy/the team meetings, we have the experience of sharing day-to-day life with them, which includes everyday contact such as at mealtimes, evenings and weekends, and sharing the physical structure of the house in terms of sharing its various living spaces. An important aspect of our role is to bring things that have happened in the house into the team meetings and house meetings, and use insights from the team meetings to give meaning and understanding to everyday contact in the house. Guests' knowledge that we do this provides them with a feeling of containment, though they frequently express resentment about it or show that they experience it as persecuting. Our continual presence and the function we fulfil of 'bridge' spanning the team and the milieu is a threat to the part of the guest that would rather things remained split off, separate and uncontained, and that has an investment in not thinking, not making links or not understanding. There is, however, another part of the guest that feels increasingly safe knowing that we do in fact hold on to and remember split off things and instances of acting out.

I became aware, from a conversation I had with Mary, that she had been storing tablets that she was feeling like taking to suppress her feelings of desperation. In the house meeting later that day another guest expressed his worry that Mary was feeling self-destructive. Mary initially remained silent but later, rather unconvincingly, said there was nothing to worry about. I then shared with the rest of the house my knowledge of the tablet storing and my view that there was in fact good cause for worry. I felt anxious saying this, as if I had somehow betrayed Mary and forced her to acknowledge things were not OK. This was one of a number of times when I felt at risk of being 'seduced' by the part of Mary that did not want to think or understand, and under its sway made to believe that things are better left unsaid.

Wishes and attempts to 'keep us in the dark' are a common occurrence. We have to strike a balance between accepting not knowing, and the anxiety of that, and being firm about the limit of our willingness to tolerate being kept in the dark which is often a manipulation on the part of the less healthy aspect of the guest. We often need to get help to stay with our desire to help the healthier part of the guest rather than collude with 'helping' the more destructive part. At times we must insist, for example, on cuts being shown to us, ambulances being called, tablets being handed in.

Earlier in her stay my relationship with Mary felt fragile. She herself admitted to feeling threatened and afraid of me; I at times felt I was persecuting her by encouraging discussion of her secret self-destructive actions. However, over time I've learnt that this is appreciated, at least by a part of the guest who feels relieved of the burden of carrying secrets, and helped by making sense of self-destructive urges.

Frequently, in fact, the resident therapist's role involves expressing or wondering about what is not being said or voiced. In a house meeting a day after a heated and angry explosion between Mary and another guest, Ann, both Mary and Ann claimed that everything was now sorted out between them as they'd apologized to each other. We, the resident therapists, had been anticipating a fiery house meeting and it was a surprise that things were apparently so smooth. I felt a pull to go along with this; Mary and Ann clearly felt that to explore what had happened between them and what was still going on between them risked another explosion. However, I said it was important for this to be voiced: I really had doubts about this resolution, and took the view that these feelings did need to be explored as they were otherwise likely to be expressed or acted out over the coming weekend in the house. Indeed, sometimes there is an atmosphere of eerie calm in the house: we have to be alert to respond to this by wondering where the uncalm is being expressed. I have learnt from experience that saying the difficult things that guests don't want to hear or think about is containing. And colluding in a view that nothing is wrong is not.

In a house meeting before Christmas Mary got very tearful and distressed and said she so much wanted a good Christmas both for herself and the resident therapists, who she knew had worked so hard on all the practical arrangements for it. She said she was afraid that she would spoil Christmas for everyone. In the past she had expressed worries about spoiling other important or celebratory occasions such as the leaving meals, to which I had always responded by saying, 'Oh I'm sure you won't spoil it, it'll be fine.'

This 'reassuring' response had never helped and Mary had managed to dominate these events by becoming distressed – crying loudly, sulking or otherwise diverting attention towards herself. This time I responded in a different way, encouraging her to explore what spoiling involved and also acknowledging her wish to spoil which seemed to be connected to her angry and envious feelings. It seemed that this was a much more containing response, acknowledging feelings that Mary felt were too negative and horrible to be admitted or articulated. In other words, I had to keep in mind the other part of Mary, who really was afraid of her spoiling and needed help with these anxieties not denial of them, which had always been her own way of attempting to deal with them in the past.

Because of their past experiences, guests frequently attempt, albeit unconsciously, to damage the container (the container being the individual resident therapist, the team or the Crisis Centre as a whole). These attacks come in different forms. They may be attacks on our capacity to think, such as the use of contradictory or 'enmaddening' communications. Monica would contradict herself so much or misrepresent something I'd said to her that I would be left feeling confused and unable to think clearly after talking with her. The attacks may of course be made on the physical structure of the house, or on the organizational structure of the Centre. From the day she arrived Monica seemed to be on a mission to enact changes: of the composition of her team, the layout of the kitchen, the meeting times and rooms. She also seemed to go to great lengths to avoid using the formal spaces while actively seeking one-to-one contact in the house.

A major part of my work as a resident therapist involves thinking about the different ways guests use me as a container and/or attack my capacity to be a container. Different 'parts' of guests want different things from the Centre. For one part the Centre can be a kind of theatre to act out in, and get others to act into, rather than a place where understanding and thinking can take place. For another part there can be a wish to somehow make the Centre into a hospital. One part prefers action to thought, another part wants understanding and help to make sense of their feelings and the predicament they find themselves in. Sometimes it feels to us as if we are being used mainly or only as dustbins for unwanted feelings or experiences.

Mary would frequently leave me feeling like this. She would often be silent in her team meetings, or drop hints about some self-abuse. At times it felt she was very drowsy, and we feared she'd taken an overdose. I often felt confused, anxious and overwhelmed, and hopeless – quite unable to make any helpful contact with her. I felt she would not allow me to think with her or contain her. As her stay proceeded and a relationship between us gradually developed, there were times when she allowed me to take in, digest and feed back in a more processed form the feelings she communicated to me.

She became more able to let me know what was going on inside her, and became less deceitful about issues such as her tablet storing, bingeing and vomiting, and cutting; she became more able to allow good contact with me and thinking to take place, without these having to be immediately attacked.

Guests use projective identification either to dramatize their situation and/or get rid of unwanted feelings or aspects of themselves. Projective identification can also, importantly, be used more benignly, as a means of communicating. Throughout a guest's stay these different uses will ebb and flow: sometimes I have felt used as a dustbin, at other times as a thinking, processing human, allowed to contain another's feelings in a helpful and insight-giving way. We therefore have to bear both the evacuation and the communication, and this requires flexibility and adaptability. This also needs from us the ability to enter into a state of reverie, which allows us to sense what state of mind the guest is in, and what they need from us.

Often interpretation alone is not helpful, as it can be experienced by the guest, when in a particular state of mind, as the therapist maintaining a protective distance from what the guest is needing to communicate, or as the therapist trying to force feelings back into the guest that the guest is unable to tolerate.

Sometimes the attack is on the psychological structures of the Centre. Guests make attempts to have one-to-ones in the house, usually wanting to tell only their resident therapist something. At times this can feel appropriate – as resident therapists we do have a special relationship with our guests as we are with them in their team meetings. There are other times when these one-to-ones seem to be orchestrated, unconsciously or consciously, in such a way that anxiety is 'lodged' only in one person, and that what goes on in these moments is split off (as, likewise, the resident therapist is split off) from the rest of the milieu. Both Mary and Monica tended to try to lodge anxiety with one person. On the evening of a leaving meal for my colleague Jo, Monica cornered me and told me she felt self-destructive. I suggested she come and join us downstairs – that being around people might help. She refused and went up to her room.

Throughout the preparations for the meal I felt paralysed with anxiety and preoccupied with Monica rather than with Jo. (It is possible to surmise that Monica sensed this.) I spoke to the team leader on call who said that all I could do was to check on Monica periodically and also try to get her to hand in her razor blades. Each time I went upstairs to Monica she was mute and unresponsive, occasionally appearing to be in some kind of dissociated state, which didn't feel to be genuine (but I couldn't be sure). I myself felt in danger of being held transfixed in her room. On this occasion the anxiety was shared out: it was decided that two resident therapists would go to Monica's room and Monica was firmly encouraged to come downstairs to talk with us.

There are times when only one member of the team or resident therapist group feels anxious. Carrying the burden of this anxiety alone leads to a sense of isolation and the doubting of one's own intuition. If, over time, things are routinely expressed to only one resident therapist and that resident therapist is left with a very particular bit of the guest's experience, he or she is more prone to end up overwhelmed, feeling an intolerable burden of holding and having to bear everything alone. I have realized that sharing this sort of burden with the other resident therapists can relieve not only some of my own anxiety but also some of the guest's. Others can help to look at the situation from another perspective and enable thinking to continue.

Guests benefit if they feel the milieu is containing them rather than just their team, or just an individual resident therapist. In order to contain in a way that is effective an expansion is needed, in terms of the number of people aware of and thinking about what is going on. In the weekly clinical meeting all the team leaders, resident therapists and students discuss and reflect on what is going on in the house and with particular guests. In this way our thinking space is expanded. At times I have mistaken the need to expand by increasing the thinking space for expanding in a more concrete way.

Earlier in my time as a resident therapist I felt I had to show the guests that I could bear and withstand anything, in part because of my wish to avoid their anger, in part as a way of attempting to avoid all kinds of anxiety. For example, I would sometimes feel I needed to stay up late with Mary, filled with an anxiety that she would hurt herself in some way if I left her, or feel full of unbearable feelings of anger at being abandoned.

It was important in these instances that I voiced my understanding of these feelings, and that I did go to bed. It is not containing experience for the guests if we continue to tolerate and appear to have no limits. The guests need to feel, and experience the fact, that there are boundaries – in other individuals and in the Centre as a whole – in order to feel safe. A permissive or over-tolerant attitude can in fact lead to guests upping the stakes or testing us – in some way or other asking to be given a limit.

If they are not it can be frightening to them. Mary often expressed fears that she would drain or destroy the container with her enormous needs and powerful feelings, a fear that could in fact have become reality without the limit setting by others and by myself.

I have struggled to find a balance between permissiveness and rigidity. These two ways of responding to disturbance are linked. If one is over-permissive one can end up so saturated and resentful – of being used as a dustbin – that one feels overwhelmed and intolerant. There then can follow a 'clamping down' – a closing down of empathy and an inability to 'take any more'.

At times I have responded to feeling used, or potentially used, as a dustbin by, as I term it, 'refusing entry'. This is an attempt to stop the difficult feelings coming my way or 'getting inside' me. Dodging guests, hiding in the office, being in a rush, using pat phrases, such as 'it's the weekend, talk about this in your team meeting', without any show of willingness to hear or understand, and feeling reluctant to talk or think about the guest in supervision or therapy, are all examples of refusing entry. In relation to Monica I found myself at times concretely 'refusing entry'. Such was my dread of succumbing to 'projective sickness' by being cornered by her and filled with overwhelming anxiety, I spent a great deal of time 'on the run': scuttling past her room, avoiding being in the communal areas when she was there, and hiding in the office. This felt like the only way to preserve my sanity and mental space. In a similar way to the exhaustion I would feel if I were physically running, this is what happened psychically. My sense of dread and fear was not understood and instead increased, and I sensed that Monica's awareness of my unavailability and lack of empathy led her to feel more desperate, angry and uncontained, provoking more attempts on her part to intrude herself forcibly: it felt like a vicious circle impossible to break.

It is containing for guests to hear what impact they have on us, if communicated to them sensitively and at a time when they are able to hear this. It is not helpful to them if they feel the resident therapist is unable to receive and feel their projections. Nor is it helpful if they experience us as entirely tolerant, taking everything without question or exploration. Both tendencies can reinforce a perception that we are superhuman robots, either unfeeling, or feeling without being impacted in any meaningful way. Guests need to see that we are human, to have a sense that they are in the presence of someone moved, but not shaken, by their anxiety. I've realized that it is better for me and for them if at times I admit my exhaustion and acknowledge my limits. They may feel disappointment or anger, but some aspect of them will also appreciate my humanness. It is important, too, that guests have an experience that these feelings of anger or disappointment can be successfully contained rather than avoided.

During their time at the Crisis Centre resident therapists go through, in parallel, the five stages of stay that are described by Joseph Berke for guests (Berke 1987). These stages are: (1) arriving, (2) settling-in, (3) settling-down, (4) leaving and (5) following-up. In my fourteen months at the Crisis Centre I can recognize moving through at least the first two of these, and possibly some elements of the third.

In my arrival stage I felt some of the anxieties described by Berke, such as a sense of inadequacy, a feeling of shame for not seeming to cope and at times a sense of helplessness in the face of the distress experienced by the guests. I often doubted my ability to contain, and, I think, also held the belief that I had to contain a guest, or indeed the whole house, single-handedly/single-mindedly, and consequently did not always find it easy to ask for help or recognize that I needed help.

Now, having settled in, though there are times when such anxieties re-emerge, I have a greater capacity for reflection and a growing ability to tolerate psychic pain in myself and that expressed by others. I think I am less prone to resort to 'nurse mode' as a defence – trying to 'make things better'. Experiences of getting through difficult times, through being contained myself by others, has given me greater faith in my ability to recover my capacity for thinking. I have learnt that surviving and functioning at the Crisis Centre is not about eliminating anxiety, but about managing it and containing it. Being helped to develop my own psychic space by sharing anxiety with others has expanded my capacity to contain my own anxiety and enabled me to be in a better position to contain that of the guests. Increasingly the Centre has become my home as well as my workplace, and I've realized the importance of limit setting in order to be able to sustain myself and continue living and working here.

I continue to learn that containing means being able to acknowledge and bear the fact that feelings cannot be taken away – something guests often want us to do. It is hard to stay with feelings such as despair, anxiety, anger and hopelessness. At times I have felt impotent and useless, which has undermined my sense of being a capable, helpful 'nurse'. Particularly in relation to Mary I have felt I am actively causing harm – by somehow allowing her (and at times by not 'doing' anything) to feel feelings she does not want to feel. It has been hard to hold onto a sense that 'help' is still being given when we are being criticized – told we are useless, or that we are simply making guests feel worse.

Joseph Berke writes: 'We make things bearable again by tolerating the pain and discomfort in ourselves, by suffering on behalf of another, and by trying to evaluate and understand what the distress is about' (Berke 1987, p.182). An important aspect of my learning has been how to be emotionally involved with guests in a way which enables this understanding while at the same time looking after and protecting myself, with the help of others. I have had to question and learn what is unhelpful, collusive involvement, which is ultimately not containing, and develop ways of being involved and emotionally engaged that will increase the potential for something new and creative to occur in the guests and myself.

References

Berke, J.H. (1987) 'Arriving, Settling-in, Settling-down, Leaving and Following-up: Stages of Stay at the Arbours Centre.' *British Journal of Medical Psychology 60*, 181–188.

Bion, W.R. (1962) *Learning from Experience.* London: Karnac.

Britton, R. (1998) *Belief and Imagination.* London: Routledge.

Segal, H. (1975) 'Psychoanalytical Approach to the Treatment of Schizophrenia.' In M.H. Lester (ed) *Studies in Schizophrenia.* Ashford, Kent: Headly Books.

CHAPTER 9

The Damaged Body: Working with Self-Harm

Margaret Fagan

The psychotic person encounters such overwhelming psychic pain and anxiety, that his or her mind turns away from reality in the hope of finding temporary relief in delusion. The psychotic mind comes to dominate the personality through the idealization of destructiveness and the development of the dangerous belief that within this delusional space there is freedom from pain. From a position of a fortress-like omnipotence, the psychotic mind starts to 'dish out' hatred and sadistic cruelty. These projections of a hatred of weakness can be forced into other people, and into other parts of the self, including the body. The net effect is to leave the non-psychotic part of the mind ever weaker and intimidated by powerful destructive forces. This prevents the subject, or damaged self, from obtaining psychic nourishment and help.

Many psychoanalysts (*see* Meltzer 1992; Rosenfeld 1987; Steiner 1993) have developed this account of how destructiveness becomes organized within the mind. Although each account is subtly different, they all accept Wilfred Bion's fundamental discovery that the psychotic personality co-exists with the non-psychotic personality: even in extreme states of psychosis, there is always some part of the personality, however small, which is non-psychotic (Bion 1984).

Some people in psychotic borderline states, who hover between sanity and insanity, cope with their fear of psychosis by making use of their body. Unable to deploy psychological elaborations, they bring their anxieties to a 'premature' closure: out of mind and into the body (*see* McDougall 1989).

However, although the person here is projecting their anxieties not into another part of their mind but into their body, he or she still has to struggle to find some relationship between the different split-off experiences and projections, that is an intra-psychic account of their state of mind. Although psychotic and non-psychotic ways of thinking are present in each of us, the 'volume', or the sway, of each perspective can change – and with this change comes an ever shifting relationship between the two parts of the personality, which constructs the intra-psychic picture. When the 'volume', or sway, of the psychotic perspective becomes louder, then the relationship between the mind and the body, and the therapy and the milieu, becomes especially important. It is these fluctuating intra-psychic relationships, and the use of the body, which I want to explore in this chapter. I will also discuss how each perspective in the mind presents its own account, or narrative, to make sense of its experience.

The Crisis Centre is a residential setting, where we aim to make our guests comfortable in pleasant surroundings, with good food and facilities. The very environment of the Centre addresses issues about how a guest looks after his or her body. Many of the guests who come to the Centre damage their bodies, often in response to the fact that something damaging has been done to their mind and body in the past. Their self-injury could be through an eating disorder, deliberate self-harm such as cutting, or extreme physical neglect. In this way they are expressing a hatred of the body and, in particular, a rejection of the sexual body. Such hatred is frequently part of a breakdown that has occurred in late adolescence, when the person tried to leave the parental home and face anew the issues of autonomy, responsibility and blame. Even though all our guests are adults, most bring with them the issue of how to relate to their parents, both externally and internally. Few have successfully left the parental home. Moses Laufer, a psychoanalyst who has worked extensively with young people, writes about developmental breakdown in adolescence (Laufer and Laufer 1989). He considers how the breakdown expresses the individual's need to hold onto a picture of himself or herself as someone 'who is victimized or persecuted or made helpless by inner forces over which he [or she] has no control' (p.12). The raging battle of who is to blame for the suffering (which Laufer re-frames as the question 'to whom does my sexual body belong?') is fought like a never-ending legal battle. In this battle all resources are consumed in the attempt to apportion blame and restore a belief in justice – that is, a belief in a good, helpful person, or, in the language of psychoanalysis, a good internal object. Many guests have the phantasy that team meetings are like a court room, with the team leader as judge and the guest on trial. The fact that a student and the resident therapist are also present can obviously easily fuel this phantasy, especially at the beginning of the stay.

The guests at the Crisis Centre are a self-selecting group, in that they have all had to be very motivated to secure a place at the Centre. This implies that each guest, in their very wish to come to the Centre, is challenging this sense of passivity which may previously have been part of their life for a very long time. Many of the guests at the Crisis Centre are so overwhelmed by the trauma of their experiences that they cannot enjoy a life separate to their preoccupation with what has happened to them – they think about their plight all the time. For most of our guests, ordinary daily life has come to a standstill. Laufer, again commenting on the adolescent, writes about this standstill as representing 'the adolescent's long-standing belief that he himself had little responsibility for his present crisis or that he was expressing, via his pathology, what he believed his parents had always wanted – a damaged, castrated, non-sexual child, rather than an potent sexual adult' (Laufer and Laufer 1989, p.23).

In this account the body contains the physical violence felt towards the mother and, in some cases, the violence felt towards perpetrators of sexual abuse. As the resident therapists and guests live together it is simply inevitable that issues to do with the body, such as sleep, food, and personal hygiene, are very much present. For example, the quantity of food eaten may sometimes be a comment on how much help the guest is going to allow (see Williams 1992). At the Centre we see a range of ways of relating to food such as 'stealing' from the fridge at night, only being able to eat specially bought foods, being unwilling to share in the evening meal, cooking vast quantities of food which can't then be eaten, not eating at all, over-eating and vomiting, going missing at meal times... The use or abuse of food is a powerful indicator or metaphor of differing states of mind.

In everyday language we talk about 'chewing something over', which means giving thought to an issue, whereas we might talk about a machine 'spitting out', to describe a very fast, unthinking process. When anxiety can't be contained, it has to be got rid of, spat out, or projected. One male guest said he couldn't come to his team meeting because he had 'an upset stomach' and needed to stay in his room, which was close to the toilet. When it was pointed out to him that he was looking after his upset stomach but wasn't able to think about his 'upset' mind, he came to his team meeting after all. Bion uses the image of digestion to illustrate the process of psychological understanding and containment. He talks about experience being 'metabolized' and 'digested'. The capacity to digest experience is developed as a result of the mother's ability to respond to her child's experiences.

Central to Bion's work is the poetic vignette of maternal reverie. In this reverie the child projects his or her unhappy and desperate feelings into the mother, and the mother cares for these feelings and offers them back to the child in a more manageable form. To do this, the mother must be able to tolerate the child's psychic pain – the pain that at that moment the child can't tolerate unaided (Bion 1962). According to this model, after repeated experiences of maternal 'containment', the child internalizes the process and so, eventually, can do it for himself or herself. At this point the child has introjected a model of containment. This is the basis of soothing.

At the Crisis Centre we work with people who despair that there is a maternal or paternal object who can contain their projections and so make things better for them – soothe them. Because they feel they don't have an object to project into – they have to do their own soothing. Like a short circuit, soothing that should take place in the mind happens instead in the body, often in ways which are difficult to understand. In very general terms, when a child can't rely on its mother to respond to distress, the child has to find alternatives. Indeed, one of the major 'tasks' of the infant–mother relationship may be to modulate levels of physiological arousal in the baby. For some people self-harm, paradoxically, is experienced as a form of soothing. Felicity De Zulueta, director of The Trauma Unit at the Maudsley Hospital, London, writes very helpfully on the subject:

> Victims of childhood abuse and neglect fail to modulate their arousal levels and may well need a much higher activation of the endogenous opiate system to feel soothed. These victimized people neutralize their hyperarousal by a variety of addictive behaviours, including compulsive re-exposure to situations reminiscent of the trauma... So while the self-mutilator slashes herself and the endorphins she releases calm her down, her sense of self may also find intense satisfaction in the act of controlling and attacking her body, now simply part-object in the enactment of her self-abuse... It appears that these people often feel ap-

prehensive, empty or sad: the trauma appears to act as the purveyor of the missing endogenous opioids: it has become an addiction. (De Zulueta 1999, p.193)

This account provides valuable understanding of the addictive nature of self-harm and the subjective nature of the experience. It shows us how self-harm is thought about within the mind. It also begins to explore how self-harm may be thought about intra-psychically; there may in fact be different views or accounts of self-harm within the same individual.

The capacity to describe one's life without undue repression or recourse to splitting appears to be linked to a healthier psychological life and to a stronger sense of self (Fonagy 1991). By contrast, when an individual is approaching a psychotic state of mind, the idea of a coherent narrative becomes more elusive. It is now even more apparent that the therapist has to listen out for two stories, each account having its own perspective. Michael Sinason, a contemporary British psychoanalyst with a specialist interest in psychosis, describes how it is possible to delineate an understanding of the meaning of a person's experiences in the case of both the psychotic and non-psychotic personality. According to Sinason (1993) the non-psychotic and the psychotic personalities 'cohabit' with one another. In fact he describes the phenomenon of their co-existence as 'internal cohabitation'. He considers each personality to be present from birth, each deserving of a full identity, or personhood, rather than simply manifestations or parts of the self. Understanding both perspectives helps the person to 'keep their bearings'. As a consequence the individual has a better chance of avoiding being overwhelmed or disorientated by a muddled or incomprehensible story that carries little personal meaning but just seems full of pointless suffering and loss. Sinason gives the name 'dual track analysis' to this process of following each distinct narrative and accurately assigning thoughts and behaviour to the relevant personality.

An innovative aspect of this theory lies in the therapist's commitment to try to learn to understand the point of view of the psychotic thinker. This commitment implies an acceptance that this point of view will have its own logic and 'narrative competence'. This acceptance (which does not imply agreement) often seems to provide significant relief. Previously, the psychotic self may have wanted to remain hidden because of his anticipation that the aim of therapy or treatment would be to get rid of him. I think that 'dual track analysis' greatly assists the guest to build up a stronger sense of self. The analysis of the 'logic' of the psychotic self's point of view relieves him of his fear that the sole aim of therapy is to get rid of him, anxiety is reduced, and he then has a greater opportunity to be looked after within the therapy without becoming increasingly hostile. As his hostility decreases, the psychotic self will still have his point of view but he may no longer dictate the action.

Overall, the model of 'internal cohabitation' allows for an exploration of destructiveness. Once a guest complained to me that she didn't get any credit for not having harmed anyone. 'It's not as if self-harm is criminal,' she said. When challenged about how she harmed herself, sadly, and predictably, she felt this didn't count. Her self-harm was an attempt to organize violent and destructive feelings intra-psychically – so that they remained within the orbit of the self. Eventually, a dual track analysis helped her to understand how each part of the personality related to the other through self-harm.

How do individuals express their awareness of the phenomena of 'internal cohabitation'? Two guests I have worked with each describe feeling not just that they are afraid of losing their mind, but that they are also afraid of being taken over by a stronger, more ruthless part of themselves – another version of themselves of whom they are aware and with whom they feel that they co-exist in a precarious status quo. Both guests are anxious about a fragile self 'falling apart'; but they also are aware of a well-organized other self waiting to take advantage of a vulnerable non-psychotic self. Both guests feel that their defences against psychotic anxieties are arranged in a hierarchy. One described a hierarchy of behaviour consisting in bulimia, self-cutting and 'topping'. The other described how he used drug abuse, then self-cutting and finally the threat of suicide.

Sinason's description of the 'cohabitee' elaborates the personality or way of thinking of the psychotic self, in particular a hatred of human contact and concern, and intolerance of feelings of vulnerability. In this eye-for-an-eye, tooth-for-a-tooth world, there is no such thing as help, or being able to depend on another person; to believe in help is naive. Part of the importance of this elaboration is that it allows the therapist to *predict* the concerns and preoccupations of the psychotic thinker in any situation. This is important in understanding self-cutting. Cutting appears to work like a funnel: complex ideas and identifications are funnelled out of the mind into the body through one 'simple' act. The task is to elaborate the complexity of these ideas to a person who is hell-bent on keeping them out of his or her mind.

In the borderline state, in which there is some capacity for the person to recognize that one part of them is doing something to another, the logic of cutting is always twofold. The person who cuts is at one and the same time pushing away and asking for help. The cutting then makes sense to both the psychotic and the non-psychotic parts of the mind. Precisely because this action makes 'sense' to both parts of the self it occurs as a reality rather than being contemplated as an idea, or phantasy, or rather than being kept secret as a plan by a more hidden and isolated psychotic part of the mind. In this borderline state a guest may self-cut because she is convinced she is plastic (a psychotic view), and so can do what she likes to her body; but she also cuts because she is worried that she isn't real and urgently needs to find out whether she is real, and whether she can remain real (that is, a non-psychotic viewpoint). Similarly a guest may cut because she has trusted in another to share her troubles (a non-psychotic view), but having risked depending on another, should now be taught a lesson for her foolishness in believing there to be meaning and value in talking to another (that is, from the psychotic viewpoint). In general the extreme view of the psychotic personality is more visible and more acted on when there is more inflammation of the psychotic way of thinking and a corresponding shrinkage of the non-psychotic.

A number of people I have worked with have talked about 'flickering' between these states of mind. I think the point is that to both states of mind cutting makes 'sense', and that therefore it moves unchecked from an idea into an action. In the sessions there has been more of a possibility of containment when we have been able to chart these shifting, flickering meanings. Carrying out 'a dual track analysis' has allowed us to uncover the fact that the same action can have different meanings for the different parts of the personality. In Sinason's conceptualization these different parts are actually perceived as two distinct persons with different names in one body.

One young woman, 'Joan', a resident at the Crisis Centre, described 'flickering' as a very fast, frightening movement, in and out of a psychotic state of mind. Joan recounted how it felt like 'changing channel' – it was like flicking from one TV channel to another but the switching got faster and faster so that she couldn't keep up. Joan very self-consciously used cutting to cope with her dread of psychosis. Recently the hospital offered

her an appointment to learn how to cover the scars with make-up. She
made this appointment to coincide with one of her therapy times. Then she
realized what was happening. Her psychotic mind was very excited by the
idea of make-up that could hide all scars: for her the visual impact of her
scars was the only drawback to cutting; with make-up she would be free to
continue to cut as often as she liked. With these insights Joan cancelled the
hospital appointment and came to her session which, up to this point, was
being juxtaposed as a poor alternative to 'cutting without cost'. She was
also now able to see the cutting as a punishment meted out by one part of
her personality to another. She was punished for being stupid enough to
trust another person...for being pathetic enough to believe that things
could be any different and change; she was being taught a lesson that it
wasn't safe to feel. Part of her sense of 'equilibrium' was restored by
entering a state of mind in which cutting proved that she no longer felt
anything, was indeed cut-off, as she substantially attacked her own body
without feeling any physical pain until some time afterwards, when as she
put it, she came to her senses. At this point then, the cutting was a triumph
over the non-psychotic self that dared to think and feel and experience
connections of love and affection between people. And yet, again paradoxically, she also cut to see blood and to reassure herself that she was real.
From another perspective this would be the logic of 'the ends justifies the
means', with the psychotic mind 'soothing' the non-psychotic one to sleep
so that she can have her way!

Joan also described going beyond this 'flickering' and entering a
psychotic world in which relationships are wholly replaced by cutting,
slashing, abuse and a sense that people can do absolutely what they like to
each other. In this world, life is lived on a see-saw: either you are up (at
someone else's expense) or you are down. At this point Joan reported the
further feeling that she was being told to cut by an abusive figure from her
childhood. To one part of her mind cutting still felt self-protective – a way
of stopping something worse from happening as it forestalled a move
towards psychosis. However, that part of the mind that was identified with
the abuser clearly held another, more deadly view. Whatever self-protection the cutting constituted could be compared to the protection offered
by the mafia. The protection money collected by the mafia, say from a
businessman, does afford him some protection. But the mafia is still the
mafia.

If cutting can be thought of, then, as a flawed form of self-protection, what happens if the individual moves into an environment in which there is a greater chance of the non-psychotic self being able to stand up to the psychotic self? Cutting, at the border between psychotic ways of thinking and non-psychotic ways of thinking, is a way of maintaining a vicious circle which does not allow the work of the depressive position ever to begin. For the borderline person, cutting is a way of maintaining 'life at death's door': cutting occurs in the place of the depression or mourning that would occur for someone supported by more stable and good internal objects – someone who is more optimistic that they can protect their good internal objects from their aggression and sadism. For the person who cuts, there is dreadful fear about whom they would harm if they weren't harming themselves.

The question then arises: if cutting occurs when it makes sense to both psychotic and non-psychotic personalities, does the person become more contained, and therefore cut less, if the pressures to cut are understood from both perspectives? It is my experience that the 'dual track' way of thinking helps patients to keep their bearings and so feel less over-whelmed. This diminishes the 'flickering' between different states of mind and moves the person towards containment, and away from cutting. At the Crisis Centre the 24-hour presence of thinking and caring adults means that the guest can tolerate more of their psychic reality without feeling that it is imperative to shy away from it, either by becoming more 'cut-off' in the self-punishing and self-effacing world of cutting, or by entering a world of psychosis in which there only is cutting and slashing and ruth-lessness, and the relief brought by identification with sadistic introjects. A stable 24-hour therapeutic presence, with the continuous support it offers to the non-psychotic mind, allows the guest to maintain a more solid, real-istic boundary between phantasy and deed.

As Anne Alvarez, a child psychotherapist who has worked extensively with borderline and abused children (Alvarez 1992), has noted, that it is vital to interpret 'the child's *fear* that he will stab', rather than his wish to stab. She goes on to explain how the child whose case she is presenting was 'searching desperately for an object that can contain and transform violent action into violent metaphor'(p.157). The use of dual track analysis, I think, also assists in this process.

For some guests at the Crisis Centre, both men and women, there is a connection between the issues of sexual abuse and cutting. Statistics from research at 'Hackney Off Centre' (Collins 1996) indicate that for those young people who self-harm, 75 per cent have been sexually abused in childhood. Individuals who have been sexually abused often describe overwhelming feelings of guilt and are convinced that they are responsible for what has happened to them. These feelings are also experienced by other victims of trauma. Likewise, their needs for control and revenge – the wish to preserve identity and a sense of continuity by doing unto others as it has been done unto them – can be achieved by a form of splitting that allows this repetition to be organized about different aspects of the self. Dawn Collins points out (Collins 1996) that the 'actions of the adult are so incomprehensible to the child that their only defence is to introject and dissociate'(p.467). But when internalization is an attempt at control, it serves only to transfer the problem to the child's inner world and the solution then is the splitting of the internalized object. In this conceptualization, self-harm is an attempt to control the splits in the self. In this complex quicksand, made up of a mixture of introjection and dissociation, there may be such a muddle in the person's mind that an attack on the self feels like a literal attack on the abuser.

A fragment from a recent session with 'David' illustrates this identification with an internalized aggressor, and the pain and confusion which result from this defensive move. David is cutting less. He says that it doesn't work for him in the way that it did, and he has mixed feelings about this. He now experiences times of severe depression during which he feels he is useless, deformed, ugly, and has little belief that things will improve. At such times he wishes he was an animal and could be put to sleep by a vet. He says, 'Look at me, you wouldn't want to live with this damage, these memories and feeling useless.' Before long his hatred of the differences between us is so extreme that it overwhelms his ambivalent feelings towards me and he starts to feel it is not safe to come to therapy because he wants to hit me. At this point David begins to abandon his feelings of depression as he no longer seems able to protect me, the good object, from his aggression, or he may feel that I'm not strong enough to survive it, so he resorts to splitting. I am split into an idealized, permanently available good object – but only available for my family; while he is left with the bad – the therapist who only does it for the money. In his flight from depression and the mourning of his own childhood, his experience of me is turned inside out as he projects into me his anger. I am experienced as dangerous, wishing him dead, slapping him about the face, plotting his murder. As he then identifies me as the owner of these violent feelings, and accuses me of saying things to him like 'I wish you were dead', I have the bizarre experience of thinking to myself 'I didn't say that, but it is what you are thinking.' At these points David has no ownership of his own hostility, he projects it all outwards, until eventually he sees everything he does in terms of self-defence. Before long depression is left far behind and it feels more like war on full alert – David is convinced he needs to wipe me out before I do the same to him. In the past, at this point, he would have been so terrified of his own aggression to me that he would forestall the situation and cut himself. But as he has grown a little more confident that we can weather the attacks, that the boundary between phantasy and deed has grown stronger, their ferocity has diminished. At this point David is projecting into me his feelings of being wrongly and unjustly treated, and showing me what it feels like to be accused of things which are untrue; while he is identified with a parent who feels justified in being cruel because the child is perceived as being so worthless.

It is to be hoped that over time, as he has an experience of me being there for him as his therapist, David's capacity to deal with his ambivalent feelings towards me will increase and so reduce his feelings of envy which lead to an intolerance of an experience of difference and separateness. Indeed, when he doesn't cut, and so doesn't cut off, there is eventually some poignant acknowledgement of how much he misses his parents and a variety of more precise related memories resurfaces.

The Crisis Centre is a household of intense relationships. For people who come to the Centre who use their body in some form of self-harm, the issue of living together can be central to their experience of the Centre. For these people the emphasis on a good physical environment as well as on the provision of psychotherapy has a considerable impact. The offer of psychological help in a very personalized setting may help them to keep more complex and challenging thoughts in mind without having to get them out of mind and into the body as a way of avoiding thinking or of remembering traumatic experiences. The use of dual track analysis, which allows the therapist to explore both the psychotic and the non-psychotic points of view, means that seemingly pointless and meaningless acts such as self-harm can be untangled to show the different meanings that the behaviour has to each part of the personality. This untangling, and the ability to assign motive and meaning to each part of the personality, means that in the dual track analysis two narratives emerge.

References

Alvarez, A. (1992) *Live Company – Psychoanalytic Psychotherapy with Autistic, Borderline, Deprived and Abused Children.* London: Routledge.

Bion, W. (1962) 'A Theory of Thinking.' In *Second Thoughts.* London: Karnac Books, 1984.

Bion, W. (1984) *Second Thoughts.* London: Karnac Books.

Collins, D. (1996) 'Attacks on the Body: How Can We Understand Self-Harm?' *Psychodynamic Counselling Journal 2*, 4, 463–475.

De Zulueta, F. (1999) *From Pain to Violence.* London: Whurr Publications.

Fonagy, P. (1991) 'Thinking about Thinking: Some Clinical and Theoretical Considerations for the Treatment of a Borderline Patient.' *International Journal of Psychoanalysis 72*, 639–656.

Laufer, M. and Laufer, M.E. (eds) (1989) *Developmental Breakdown and Psychoanalytic Treatment in Adolescence.* New Haven and London: Yale University Press.

McDougall, J. (1989) *Theatres of the Body: A Psychoanalytic Approach to Psychosomatic Illness.* London: Free Association Books.

Meltzer, D. (1992) *The Claustrum: An Investigation of Claustrophobic Phenomena.* Perthshire: The Clunie Press.

Rosenfeld, H. (1987) *Impasse and Interpretation.* London: Tavistock.

Sinason, M. (1993) 'Who is the Mad Voice Inside?' *Psychoanalytic Psychotherapy 7*, 3, 207–221.

Steiner, J. (1993) *Psychic Retreats: Pathological Organisations in Psychotic, Neurotic and Borderline Patients.* London: Routledge.

Williams, G. (1992) *Internal Landscapes and Foreign Bodies.* London: Duckworth.

CHAPTER 10

State of the Art

Julia Saltiel and Lois Elliott

'State of the Art' refers to how concretely artwork in the art therapy session of the Arbours Support Programme reflects the state of mind of the group and the individuals within it. The individuals with whom we work in the group often function on a level which uses concrete symbols, for example paintings, for communication. The title also refers to this new way of working: an art therapist and a psychoanalytic psychotherapist both painting in the group and thereby having access to concrete information about the transference and countertransference. This concept of combining art therapy and group psychotherapy in one group was developed from the work and experience of the Arbours Crisis Centre.

Art therapy was introduced to the Arbours Crisis Centre by Julia Saltiel in 1988. The model which she adopted was unusual for art therapy, as she painted in the group together with the other group members. This was found to be particularly helpful in working with psychotic and borderline guests, who seemed to be less persecuted when the art therapist was part of the process rather than what could be experienced by them as a punishing figure scrutinizing them. The art therapist's painting also offered them containment: they could identify with the images and themes in her work, and experience her as someone who could possibly know about and understand their internal world.

In the art therapy group at the Crisis Centre, as part of the conjoint model of working, everyone sits around the table and paints together; the resulting art is then discussed by the whole group. Group members are able to convey an image of their internal world through their artwork, which then becomes available for thought and understanding in the other therapeutic spaces of group, milieu and individual therapy. The work of the art therapist also reflects the images and themes of the group unconscious – material that is of vital importance in helping the team of therapists contain and manage the group dynamic in the house, and for wider psychotherapeutic understanding.

This model has been further developed in the Support Programme, in which equal emphasis is given to the artwork produced and to the analytic understanding of the verbal and non-verbal communication. This is possible through the art therapist and psychoanalytic psychotherapist both being present and having an active role in each therapeutic space.

The Arbours Support Programme, a facility of the Arbours Crisis Centre, began in 1990. It was initially set up to provide follow-on support to people leaving the Crisis Centre. It has since expanded its membership to include people who need support to help them remain in the community, as well as people waiting to go to the Centre. It provides two sessions per week: one psychotherapy group and one art therapy session. It is a small, intensive, open group with up to eight members, including the two facilitators, one of whom is an art therapist and the other a psychoanalytic psychotherapist.

To illustrate the work of the Support Programme we shall describe the work of one of the group members. Ben is a 23-year-old man, who suffered his first acute psychotic breakdown at the age of 21 following the completion of a college course. He initially went to the Crisis Centre as an alternative to psychiatric hospital, and after his stay attended the Support Programme for 12 months. Throughout this year in the group he only ever painted pictures of the Swiss cheese plant that was in the room where the art therapy took place. By the end of his time in the group he had painted a total of 39 pictures of the same object, but each painting was completely different, conveying his varied and fluctuating emotional state.

The therapeutic relationship is animated by the artwork. For Ben his relationship to us was described through his paintings of the cheese plant in the room. He would be completely engrossed in the mixing and the application of the varying tones of colour. Sometimes the leaves were all dark and sombre, at other times light and alive. Sometimes he would make eye contact with the art therapist, but rarely with other group members. We understood this as Ben's attempt to create an exclusive relationship with the mother/art therapist, and exclude the father/psychotherapist and siblings/group members. We understood that he was also planting himself in the art therapist to avoid the painful feelings that come with separateness. Painting the same plant throughout the time he was in the group was an indicator of Ben's narcissistic omnipotence. He strove to have mastery over the plant, which denied the reality of the wider setting and ultimately his relationship to the other therapist and group members.

In the group psychotherapy sessions, where the medium of communication is verbal, Ben was acquiescent and deferential to all group members. He claimed to have good, close relationships with all the group members, which was not the case in reality. His contact with others was superficial in nature, and he strongly resisted any attempts at linking the work of the art therapy session with the group psychotherapy session, attempting to preserve the fantasy of an exclusive relationship with the art therapy. Over time, by offering its particular space, and allowing him the constancy of the year of the Swiss cheese plant drawings, the Support Programme enabled Ben to move on to recognizing and at times actually valuing the presence of 'others'.

The group psychotherapy model that we use can perhaps best be described in the words of S.H. Foulkes and E.J. Anthony (1965) as 'the individual…being treated in the context of the group with the active participation of the group'(p.16). We take our knowledge of psychoanalytic concepts and apply this knowledge to the group as a whole, as if the group were one patient. An example of this was a session in which a new member came to join an established group consisting of three members. The new member arrived late, on crutches, causing a great deal of disturbance, which necessitated one of us having to leave the group in order to help her up the stairs. She came crashing through the doors and involved everyone in the rearrangement of the chairs amid much banging of crutches. However, this did not interrupt another group member, Jo, who was attempting to gain the group's sympathy by recounting an incident in which her ex-partner had not responded to her phone call. Jo's distress failed to evoke any compassion in either of us, particularly when she did not pause, even after a further fifteen minutes, to acknowledge the arrival of the new group member, Alice.

At length, Alice removed a handkerchief from her pocket and carefully blew her nose, after which she announced to the group that she had had social skills training and had been taught not to look into her hanky after blowing her nose. This succeeded in silencing Jo, and the rest of the group. The way we understood this was that Alice was letting us know that she had noticed our lack of social skills in not welcoming her into the group, but also acted out the group's feelings towards us for allowing Jo to monopolize the group. For Jo it had become another experience of not being responded to, like the phone call. We interpreted that something seemed to have got up the nose of the group and we thought that it was us, that we were viewed as the ones lacking the skills to look into what the group needed. This produced from the group a unanimous response of outrage that we had not responded to Jo's obvious despair, nor had we helped Alice to join the group – in short that we were incompetent and neglectful. We commented on how disappointed and let down they must feel, and how it felt that there was already not enough to go round without a new member arriving. Acknowledging this did seem to mobilize the group, and they were more able to interact with each other rather than feeling a need to compete for our attention. In fact, at the end of the session Alice left without her crutches, remembering them only when she reached the front door.

The different trainings of the art therapist and the psychoanalytic psychotherapist provide a deeper understanding of the work and a broader spectrum through which the work can be understood and fed back to group members. Our experience has been that our different perspectives not only complement each other but also expand our capacity for insight and understanding. We confine ourselves to interpreting the transference in the 'here and now', as illustrated above, using material from both the art therapy and the group psychotherapy sessions. In another art therapy session Jo painted a picture of a naked figure. The picture consisted of a small outline of the head and the rest of the paper taken up with huge exposed buttocks with blood dripping from the anus. She described it as her ex-partner 'being taken from behind' by the new lover. We understood this not only as a response to the new arrival in the group, but also as a wish to deny 'good intercourse' – the view being that only unproductive and abusive intercourse could take place. We felt that in the same way as Alice's nose blowing spoke for the group, so Jo's disturbing image communicated the feelings of the group. We interpreted to the group the view of our intercourse as being ineffective and unproductive at best, and at worst abusive and 'taken from behind', should the group members drop their guard.

In the co-working model we each take on the transference and by doing so we expand the possibilities for insight and understanding. The group's structure provides the opportunity for the family constellation to appear. Most commonly in our experience the art therapist becomes the mother and the psychotherapist the father, although there are continual fluctuations in this. Obviously each individual group member brings their own experience of their own family and internal dynamics. The art therapist/mother can be experienced as nurturing and nourishing by providing food and play through the painting materials as well as her understanding. Conversely she can be experienced as withholding and neglectful, especially when paper, masking tape and other materials run out, or when a group member arrives after the painting time and is not allowed to join the group. The psychotherapist/father can be experienced as strong and containing with her interpretative comments, but also stern and critical. The transferential relation may also be reflected in our different styles of painting, which would appear at first sight to be very different. The art therapist/mother paints figuratively providing a concrete representation of the group members/children, while the psychotherapist/father paints abstractedly giving an insight into the container in which the family is held.

Our own paintings incorporate our countertransference experience of being in the space of the group. We do not begin with set ideas or an image, but move the paint over the paper and allow the picture to appear in the same way associations are made in the mind of the therapist in individual sessions. At times we can be very surprised at the result of the process, finding it hard to recognize ourselves in the painting produced. On these occasions it is common in the discussion that follows for one or more group members to comment that the painting is expressing what they themselves are feeling. Rather than push this back into them we own the painting and describe the thoughts and feelings we had while painting, and give voice to our associations to the finished product in a deliberately contained and containing form. In this we follow parents' ways of communicating feelings and thoughts to their children – ways that keep the communication and what is communicated acceptable and safe. This information is then available to group members to make use of in whatever way they are able, but is also a very important source for our understanding of the group and individual members. This information is then kept in mind and sheds further light on the dynamics of the psychotherapy group.

In the transference the co-working relationship is of paramount importance. There are many attempts to split us into good and bad objects, at times conveyed through splitting the different spaces into good and bad. A group member may start attending only one of the weekly sessions, expressing a preference for either the art therapy or the group psychotherapy. This may be understood in terms of a transference issue with one or other of us. While Ben never missed an art therapy session, he did absent himself occasionally from the group psychotherapy sessions. We understood this as a transference issue, and interpreted it as such in the group.

The splitting of the different spaces may also be understood in terms of a resistance to the work. Non-attendance of the art therapy session results in no painting being produced, and therefore no material connection being made, with all the implications this may have for the connection with 'mother'. Non-attendance of the psychotherapy group denies the opportunity to verbalize the issues arising in the group and the painting, in order for them to be thought about and for connections to be made.

Splitting between us as good and bad object often occurs. What we have learnt is how important it is that we resist rescuing one another, but encourage the group to explore who we have come to represent for them. What we have found to be effective in working with the splitting is not only that we are both present and active in both therapeutic spaces but also that we talk to each other openly after the sessions and share our experience of the group. This transforms our ability to think and enables us to make links.

As mentioned before, our paintings would seem to be completely different; however, on further examination we have found that there are usually similarities in our paintings in terms of either theme or colour, texture or pattern. This has become more evident the longer we have worked together, which reflects our growing knowledge of each other, particularly each other's pathology, which is used to understand and strengthen our relationship.

We believe that the support we offer our group members is manifold. The artwork is used in many ways, group members having the option of projecting concretely onto the paper such feelings as anger, fragmentation and confusion. In the picture it is usually contained, but not always – sometimes it can spill over literally as well as metaphorically. The group member also has the option of going a step further and talking about what they have produced in order to mobilize and make use of the group's help in understanding it. The picture becomes a kind of mirror for the group, providing the opportunity for reflection and reflectiveness to take place. This reflectiveness is valued in itself by the members who draw support from it and is extended in the group session, where people get the opportunity to use insights from the art therapy group to think about current, everyday difficulties they are facing. Likewise, insights gained in the psychotherapy group are used by people in their paintings. For example, Ben's behaviour in the psychotherapy group could be seen as his planting himself among its members in such a way as to ensure he would not be uprooted or damaged by angry, sad, or loving feelings that could arise in him or others were he to be more alive and 'himself' in the group.

We consider the Support Programme to offer all that a group can offer in terms of belonging: the chance to be a respected and effective member of the group, to be accepted, and to be able to share and to participate with others. Further, the Programme offers insight and understanding through the use of the concrete as well as the abstract, giving more options for expression and communication to group members. It expands the information and experience available to them, and it provides us with concrete and abstract countertransference material that deepens and strengthens our analytic understanding and helps us to contain the group.

In the same way as each individual psychotherapy session forms part of the whole therapy, so the two Support Programme sessions offer the same cohesiveness. With the possibility of cross-referencing from one group to the other they form a whole, reducing the level of splitting and fragmentation and providing continuity. This is illustrated in Ben's final painting in the group. The picture is split into two – light coloured on the left and dark coloured on the right, portraying very different emotional states. One of the leaves traverses both parts, and the interface contains traces of vivid blue and red. The painting reflects Ben's growing ability to bring together two very different parts of himself – where not only can they both be present in the same picture but where the point at which they meet is alive with colour. This painting contrasts greatly with his first painting in the group, in which the colours are muted and the leaves are represented by uniform shapes, seemingly with no connection to one another. We feel that the contrast between Ben's first and last pictures reflects his growing ability to recognize and tolerate his own split-off parts, a capacity which enables him to become more whole. This growing ability also enables him to tolerate and value the presence of others and the diversity of perspectives that they offer, the increased number of leaves correlating with the increased number of group members from whom he is now able to take in and experience.

Acknowledgement

We would like to give thanks to Stella Pierides-Müller for aiding our analytic understanding of the group processes, and helping us to give concrete form to our emotional experiences.

Reference

Foulkes, S.H. and Anthony, E.J. (1965) *Group Psychotherapy, the Psychoanalytic Approach.* London: Karnac Books.

State of the Art

The photographs over the next few pages are of paintings produced by Julia Saltiel and Lois Elliott in various sessions of the Support Programme.

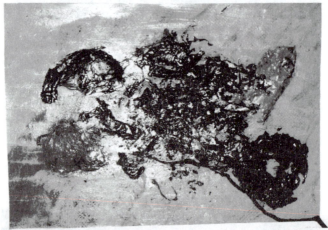

Section Three

Narratives

Introduction

Joseph H. Berke, Margaret Fagan, George Mak-Pearce and Stella Pierides-Müller

This section concentrates on the narrative or story of the guests at the Crisis Centre. As previously mentioned, in these accounts written by therapists about their guests certain details have been changed in order to protect confidentiality. Nevertheless, because the accounts focus on the interactions between guests and therapists, they capture the essence of the guests' experience at the Crisis Centre. These interactions are a 'window' into the internal world of the guests and to their general, but subjective, experience of the world. In this respect the narratives contrast with case histories, which often objectify patients.

Many of the guests find that they can begin to tell their story in ways they previously thought were impossible. Telling one's story is an important part of being human. For those whose life becomes so fragmented, because they protect themselves through splitting and projection, 'telling it like it is' is a very complicated issue. At the Crisis Centre the resident therapists become intense 'attachment figures' for their guests, and so provide a paradigm of a secure base. Frequently it is the Centre's capacity to offer continuous and consistent care – a secure base – that allows the guests to develop relationships with others, become less socially isolated and emerge more tolerant of themselves. Consequently, this provides the opportunity to begin to tell one's story with more coherence and less defensiveness, and, as it may be hoped, reducing the need for splitting and projection.

The living mixture of guests and resident therapist provides rich opportunities for a new experience of attunement – the attempt to get to know someone despite inevitable setbacks. For, surely, 'Psychotherapy is not about making clever and apt interpretations: by and large it is a long-term giving the patient back what the patient brings' (Winnicott 1971, p.137). The work described in the following chapters shows the importance of this 'giving back' and emphasizes how the Centre creates greater opportunities for this fine-tuned responsiveness. In the chapter 'A Fine Balance: Between Hope and Despair' Lois Elliott intricately describes the therapy of a young woman on the brink of a crushing despair. The account elegantly recounts how the team sought support and supervision so that they could remain in balance and continue to work with her. The beautiful quotations from several poets emphasize, too, that despair is the domain not only of the mentally ill, nor understanding the sole preserve of therapists.

Martin Jenkins' chapter is published posthumously by joint permission of his sister Ms Rhael Jenkins and his colleague Ms Stella Pierides-Müller. It was read at the Arbours Crisis Centre as part of the Team Leader Presentations series, and also at the Association of Psychoanalytic Psychotherapists Conference in 1993, entitled 'Psychodynamic Approaches to Psychosis: Survival or Revival?'. At that time Martin was starting to think about Dr Michael Sinason's concept of Internal Cohabitation through his supervision with Dr Manek Bharucha. Both Dr Bharucha and Ms Joscelyn Richards attended the Manic-Depressive Workshop facilitated by Dr Sinason at the Willesden Centre. Subsequently Martin worked with the concept of Internal Cohabitation and contributed to it through a major paper, published, also posthumously, in the *British Journal of Psychotherapy* (Jenkins 1999).

Martin brought a tireless and gifted enthusiasm to his work, and a remarkable memory for detail in the therapeutic encounter which was combined with considerable clinical acumen. His chapter portrays the intra-psychic world of 'Luke' as the latter faced a psychotic breakdown, and shows the importance of the differentiation of the psychotic from the non-psychotic personality so as to understand the 'psychotic one's' way of thinking.

In contrast, Joseph Berke describes the border between sanity and insanity, between what the Centre can and can't tolerate in the behaviour of the guests. This is the moment when many creative and insightful interventions occur. The chapter depicts several tense situations where unbearable feelings passed from guest to guest to resident therapist, to the point where it was difficult to tell whose feelings were whose. Berke emphasizes the necessity of being able to think on one's feet when seemingly overwhelming situations unfold.

Lizzi Payne introduces the children's game of hopscotch to explore the idea of how to avoid 'stepping on the cracks'. Subtly and creatively she explores a whole range of metaphors which include the notion of a 'crack' and, from different perspectives, discusses the sensitivity needed to help guests at the Centre loosen their defences in order to be able to tell the stories of their 'cracking up'. Miss Payne also includes some material from her work as a therapist on a hospital ward and illustrates the contribution a therapist can make to a multi-disciplinary team.

Similarly, Kate Hardwicke uses the magical Narnia story to ponder how guests are offered new opportunities – the opening of doors in their mind – when they stay at the Crisis Centre. In Narnia the characters have to overcome their fear of the dominating Snow Queen, who forbids the warmth of relationships, which would melt her kingdom. It is a powerful metaphor which describes the grip of destructive processes, which are sometimes inflamed by becoming a guest at the Centre. The chapter eloquently explores how guests react to the offer of help in a place where everyone has, literally and symbolically, the key to the front door.

Laura Forti presents not only the guests' narratives but also the story of the Crisis Centre itself. By taking a historical perspective in her 'Then and Now', she reminds us of just how much the Crisis Centre has grown and developed over its 30-year history. Forti describes several interventions which show how the containment provided by the Crisis Centre has become richer. She also points out that although the Crisis Centre is available to guests suffering a first episode of psychosis, many of the people who are referred nowadays have a long history of seemingly intractable mental illness. With its enthusiasm, history, and substantial experience in helping people suffering a psychotic breakdown, the Crisis Centre should be a first port of call. Sometimes, sadly, because of society's reluctance to pay for the psychological treatment of psychosis, it is only after several interventions have been tried and have failed, that the guest gains the funding for a place at the Centre.

References

Jenkins, M. (1999) 'Clinical Application of the Concept of Internal Cohabitation.' *British Journal of Psychotherapy 16*, 1, 7–42.

Winnicott, D.W. (1971) 'Mirror-Role of Mother and Family.' In *Playing and Reality*. London: Penguin Books.

CHAPTER 11

Survival or Revival?

Martin Jenkins

The Arbours Crisis Centre accepts people for a residential stay for relatively short periods of time, and generally not more than a year. In making a decision to accept a very disturbed individual, then, we need to think carefully about whether this person can be contained and work in the particular setting we offer and also what the eventual outcome of his stay might be, not least the further support and treatment he will inevitably need. A crucial aspect of the management of the case is the link up between ourselves and other professional agencies, family and friends – those who have provided support and who will continue to be the carers when the person leaves us.

Separating management issues from clinical ones is often vital in working with psychosis, and in these circumstances another team leader might be called upon to fulfil the function of maintaining links with outside authorities. This is particularly crucial owing to the intensity of the splitting mechanisms used by individuals with psychotic difficulties. A guest might be working well in the house and his team meetings while a split-off aspect of him is phoning up his psychiatrist or social worker and stirring massive anxieties in them about the nature of the work that is going on in the Centre. Where family and friends are concerned, if the degree of hostility towards and anxiety about the prospective guest is great, a different team may be set up to help the family or social network deal with such anxieties. Where relations have not completely broken down between the family and the guest, the guest's own team may also be able to work with the family.

We sometimes come under great pressure to accept a person into the Centre for a residential stay from other family members who are overwhelmed with anxiety and we find it vital to resist such pressure. In these situations we offer the individual or his family a number of out-patient consultations to help contain the crisis. I think this is very important because it conveys to the person and his network that we are taking his difficulties very seriously and are not resorting to omnipotence – that is, giving the message that the Centre could provide an automatic solution to his problems.

Very often in assessing someone suffering a psychotic breakdown one can detect the external precipitating life events of which the psychosis is the consequence. Frequently this centres on psychosocial or maturational transitions or separations, and where the intervention is of a fairly short duration it might be important that these events become the focus of the therapeutic intervention. However, our growing understanding of the nature of psychosis has helped us to differentiate the enormous difficulties the psychotic personality of the guest faces from these of his non-psychotic self. Bion's thinking on the differentiation of the psychotic from non-psychotic personalities is crucial here (Bion 1962). Without this clear distinction, the intervention would be superficial and lead to further breakdowns in the future.

I would therefore see our interventions with persons suffering a psychotic illness as important but limited: the aim being to provide an initial containing environment from which it would be possible to move into long-term individual psychotherapy when they leave the Centre. In addition, the Centre provides a setting for persons already in psychoanalytic treatment during the course of which psychotic difficulties have come to the fore. In these cases the Centre offers a holding environment which allows the treatment to continue. Unusually perhaps we work in teams: for each guest there is a team leader, a resident therapist and, where appropriate, a student in psychotherapy training. I think this way of working has many advantages.

Both the resident therapist and student have direct experience of the daily interactions with the guest and can witness at first hand how the guest relates to others in the household. This forms part of the material which can be brought into the team meetings and inform the work of the team. Equally, issues that arise in the team meetings can be worked through outside, in the house, in informal discussion between the guest, the resident therapist and the student. In this way both resident therapist and student become auxiliary egos to the guest whose capacity to hold onto understanding, and to tolerate the depressive feelings that the team meetings inevitably stir is so limited. And so a benign matrix of containment is set up: a to-and-fro between the daily life of the guest and the work in the team meetings. The psychotic self, dominated as he is by concrete thinking and an inability to symbolize, can only go by sensory impressions, tones and atmospheres, and quickly misinterprets intentions and motivations of those around him. A vital function of the resident therapist and student is to collect their own impressions of the guest's behaviour in the house into the team meetings, where understanding can be applied and split-off aspects of the guest can be thought about together. The resident therapists, who live at the Centre, and to a lesser degree the student, are on the front line with guests suffering from psychotic difficulties, and the need for support with this is recognized by the intensity of supervision that is provided, in addition to the weight given to their own personal psychoanalysis for help with their own internal difficulties.

A resident therapist can often feel quite overwhelmed in the face of the violence and hostility of projective identifications of which he is on the receiving end, and the team supervisions each week are a place where undigested experiences and overwhelming feelings can be brought to be made sense of and where the team leader can help the resident therapist or student to regain their thinking capacities. Sometimes the whole team can feel overwhelmed by the psychotic onslaughts of their guest, and the team as a whole needs help and containment from the weekly group meeting of all the resident therapists and team leaders.

I think it is important not to underestimate the enormity of the opposition that psychotic processes create to the therapeutic work of the Centre. We have found – and Dr Berke has written about this in his paper on the Stages of Stay at the Crisis Centre (Berke 1987) – that once a person has settled down at the Centre and there is an atmosphere of work in progress, this then triggers a massive flare-up of psychotic opposition in him. This seems to be due to two things: on the one hand the non-psychotic part of the guest is starting to be able to bear more depressive feelings and becoming more attached to the person of the resident therapist and team leader and other members of the household, becoming also more aware of the help received from the Centre as a precious commodity. This itself leads to a massive inflammation in the psychotic part of the guest's personality. On the other hand, the guest who has by now got some more reality-sense also becomes aware of the impending loss of his attachments, the fact that he will shortly have to leave the Centre and say goodbye. In such circumstances the guest often identifies with omnipotent destructive elements in himself. Such omnipotent destructiveness can be seen clearly operating at the Centre as the person becomes more aware of his dependence and so starts behaving in a powerful, menacing way in an attempt to destroy feelings of sadness and vulnerability, tyrannizing the household and particularly the resident therapists. When a guest is behaving in a very tyrannical way the risk is that the resident therapists themselves can revert to psychotic thinking: that their physical and mental survival depends on an instant removal of the guest from the Crisis Centre. In such an atmosphere, the team leader's understanding is not experienced as helpful but concretely as prevarication or manipulation, forcing the bad object (the guest) back into the minds and lives of the resident therapists. At such times we may need to ask the guest to leave for a few days, adding that he can come back for his team meetings. This conveys to the guest that we are not operating in a psychotic way, that is violently projecting the guest through the front door, but also gives the message that we are not willing for the therapeutic fabric of the Centre to be destroyed by psychotic hostility.

A complicating factor is that the resident therapist is both part of the team and lives his daily life with the guest. This contact, whilst it has many advantages, can be a problem for the guest with psychotic difficulties, exquisitely and concretely tuned-in as he is to how others behave towards him. Equally, this daily contact means that there is the risk that what the resident therapist or student says to the guest, in informal times in the house, may not be as well thought out or sensitive as what might be said by a psychoanalytic psychotherapist in his consulting room. Getting the words right for such a patient who feels so easily crushed and hurt is an extremely hard job at the best of times.

I now want to talk in more depth about a young man, Luke, with whom I worked for eleven-and-a-half months in all, although this was broken down into three separate stays. The first was for six weeks, the second for four months, and then he returned after a seven-month gap for a further stay of six months. The team was myself, the team leader; Ian, the resident therapist; Marion, the student for the first two stays, and Karin, the student for the final stay. During all three stays we met once monthly with himself and his parents for family meetings. The contact with the family actually proved crucial, in that between his stays Luke had to return to live with them. We felt it was important to support them in being able to hold onto the work that we were doing with Luke and that they come to see the seriousness of his condition and the fact that instant cures were not possible. In this way the family network became a strong source of support to our work and the family meetings helped avoid the risk of destructive splitting.

Luke had recently left a College of Performing Arts and had started to work in a garage in Kent. It was here, he claimed, that he first started to feel that people were talking about him behind his back, that there were people who were spreading disgusting rumours that he was a murderer, a prostitute and a homosexual. Voices were coming through the walls of his room, which he could not keep out. He held the delusional belief that a noxious and invisible drug had been injected into his room and that this had chemically castrated him. He complained that although he was attracted to women he now felt that he could not achieve an erection. Precipitating life events seemed to centre around separation: he had recently split up with his girlfriend, he had left the comforts of college life, and his parents were telling him that he now had to stand on his own feet. He had been admitted to psychiatric hospital and received the formal diagnosis of paranoid schizophrenic. He continued on the fairly low dosage of Largactil he had been prescribed in hospital until the third month with us, when our consultant psychiatrist thought it was appropriate for him to come off it.

When Luke first moved into the Centre he was very difficult to contain in spite of the medication he was on. He was very confused and would generally cause havoc in his insistent and indiscriminate demands on the resident therapists that they do something about his persecutors. The local press in Kent was writing scurrilous things about him in the newspaper, dragging his name in the dirt and blackening his reputation for ever. He felt that a gross injustice was being done to him. At first Luke managed to keep the persecutors far away and localized in Kent, and the Crisis Centre became idealized as a place where all his needs could be met: he ate voraciously and approached new female guests as if they were prospective brides. He expressed a view that he could stay at the Centre for ever, which soon became elaborated into a belief that he actually owned the Centre: that we were in fact his guests. His intrusiveness and the chaotic mess he created at the Centre first irritated and finally infuriated both guests and resident therapists alike, and it was touch and go whether or not we would be able to invite Luke back for a further stay after the first six weeks. However, in spite of all the pandemonium he stirred up he had been able to attend his team and house meetings, as well as go to the art and movement therapy sessions, even if this meant a member of the household team going to fetch him.

On balance, the team felt that Luke was workable with. In the team meetings, at first he would urge us to do something about the reports in Kent. How could he live with this muck-raking going on? All these damning articles were being written about him and there was nothing he could do about it! Using Bion's concept of the divergence between the psychotic and non-psychotic personalities, I suggested to him that he was letting us know about the activities of an ill one who was blackening his name and grossly distorting his image of himself. I felt it was important as quickly as possible to help him to differentiate between himself and another – a psychotic one who was assaulting him and sullying him from within. The matter of terminology is very important here. Because of the exquisite sensitivity of the psychotic self to words, the naming of this part of the personality is delicate work. On the one hand Luke seemed very reassured that such a distinction could be made, on the other the word 'ill' became a source of considerable anxiety. What kind of illness did he have, was it curable or terminal? Over time Luke renamed this aspect of himself as the less well one or the unwell one. Nevertheless I think that introducing this concept to him early on had a powerful effect and elicited some curiosity on his part about the activities and nature of this 'other'.

Nevertheless, he soon came to feel that his persecutors were much closer at hand than Kent and indeed had preceded him to the Centre. On one occasion he said that he had not been able to sleep because people were shouting disgusting things about him across the street through his bedroom window. I interpreted to him that I thought he was letting us know what minimal defences (presented by the thinness of the glass window) he felt he had against the ill one's allegations. As if to confirm this he whispered agitatedly that the walls in the consulting room might be too thin. The thinness of the walls seemed to represent the almost osmotic quality of the division between his psychotic and non-psychotic self. Not only could his psychotic self relentlessly pour horrible insinuations into his mind, but also it was there overhearing everything that was being said and distorting his communications. Early references to this came when he talked of photographs of himself having been stolen by the gutter press from his flat in Kent and that these reporters had left a pair of overalls in his wardrobe. I took this to mean that his psychotic self stole a sane image of him (the photograph was of him in his graduation gown) and replaced it with a denigrated image: he felt that the overalls had been left as a sign that instead of being a performer he would live his life as a garage hand.

In the team meetings the psychotic Luke had a very different experience of communication. This Luke held the view that communication served only to dig one's own grave deeper. Much later in his third stay he was able to tell of a delusional belief he had during this earlier stay that there were criminals in England whose punishment was to live underground. Communication was experienced as a confession of criminality: the more he said, the more heinous the crime and the more severe the punishment. Under the intense persuasiveness of this propaganda, and entangled as Luke was with his psychotic self, he would often succumb to the view that the best policy was to keep silent, take the Fifth Amendment – that anything he did say would be taken down and used in evidence against him. A question he would ask at the beginning of his team meetings was: 'Did I say too much last time?' On one occasion he asked Marion, the student: 'Do you know about me?'

Luke himself was aware of the importance of communication, but this awareness was constantly being interfered with by a propaganda that was relentless and like the invisible noxious drug of his delusions he could do nothing to stop. There were plenty of references to the relentlessness of this process. For example, he mentioned that the local free newspaper in Kent came through his front door unsolicited. These were bogus papers, claiming to be independent and factual, he said, but the news in them was grossly distorted. These papers could be dropped through the door day or night. We understood this to mean that the distorting propaganda could be dropped into his mind without his being able to predict when it would come.

On one occasion, he thought that the decorators who were doing some work at the Centre that day were reporters from the Evening Standard. What had previously been localized in Kent was now a national affair. I suggested to him that the ill one reported nationally a daily disgusting standard of himself. This seemed confirmed by scattered references, over all three stays, that when he woke in the morning he felt alright for a moment and then a horrible feeling would fill his stomach. His growing conviction that the reporters had preceded him to the Centre was a source of considerable despair to him. We understood this as a despair of ever being able to represent himself properly in words. If the gutter press had already got to the Centre, what hope did he have that his own communications could be properly received and registered in our minds? It was as if the psychotic one stood between us like a filter: spreading rumours into our minds about him before he had opened his mouth, and distorting his experience of myself and the team so that he would be too frightened to take things in. What hope did he have to communicate in a factual and independent way, or feel that we had independent minds able to register what he was saying, when the psychotic one was so close at hand? In anguish he said that he had been excommunicated, which confirmed the view that he had of himself as the victim of some very powerful figure which claimed to be infallible in its judgements on him. The word 'excommunicate' also relates to his despair about ever being able to use words to communicate meaning. His whispering, which was a feature on and off throughout his stays, although it became much less so as his stay progressed, seemed to be a concrete solution to the problem: like slipping a message past enemy lines.

Differentiating the psychotic thinking from non-psychotic thinking helped Luke considerably to disentangle himself from his own clutches. He would try vainly to maintain a split between the trustworthiness of the team and the persecutors outside. Obviously, when working as a team, aspects of the transference can be split between members of the team. On many occasions in his third stay, for example, he would seem to be talking to me but keeping a careful eye on Karin or Ian or the space between them as if trying to pick up invisible messages that were passing between them about him. This needed, of course, to be picked up; and throughout, I needed repeatedly to comment to him on his concern that what he was saying was producing a very distorted record of him in one or other of our minds – in other words, that one of us might be operating in precisely the same way as his psychotic self. Our capacity to put into words his psychotic experience of the team began to allow Luke to feel more contained and more able to be aware of the possibility of a good partnership between himself and his team.

One of his few dreams dreamt in his second stay was of a man saying: 'If you go to the party I'll skin you alive.' This dream seemed to represent the terrible threat the psychotic one posed to Luke making any good, straight contact with his team, represented by the party; but it also showed a terrifying image of myself in the transference as the one who sadistically opposed all progress and development or attempt on his part to reverse his excommunication. The psychotic transference would also attach itself to Ian or Karin. Recently he thought Ian was indicating by his body movements that he was going to arrange for a truck to come and take Luke away to the abattoir, where he would have to live with pig carcasses. What Luke himself felt to be sustenance and emotional food and understanding from the Centre would quickly be taken up by the psychotic one as greed; that he was a greedy pig and this view was projected into Ian. He had an image of looking down at everyone eating at the table as if they were chickens pecking at chicken feed. He said it was a terrible image. The psychotic one misinformed him that we felt he should only be allowed a subsistence existence. In other words the psychotic one took on chameleonic dimensions, at times creating a paranoid state of mind, at other times making him psychotically guilty about his needs. The psychotic twisting of needs could be seen in the Crisis Centre, too. After he had a good talk with another resident therapist in the house he then had the thought that she was thinking he was a prostitute. There was a constantly active reworking process that maligned his basic needs.

The psychotic transference had often to be got to through inference rather than by what he actually said. For example, early in his second stay Luke left the Centre for a period of hours and walked three miles to turn up at a mental health day centre. When he was returned, his feet were bloody and swollen. I think this was an example of the institutional transference and took this to mean that the psychotic Luke was demonstrating a direct link between the Crisis Centre treatment and abusiveness – that he had had to escape to a place of safety and show the wounds that he had received at our hands. The powerful embargo on verbal communication that his psychotic self placed on him meant that it was only over a long period of time that we could begin to build up a picture of the psychotic transference. For example, it was only several months after his first stay that he was able to talk about a delusion he had during that stay that I had placed a black lead across the coat rack by the front door which had some connection to excommunication. In other words, in the psychotic transference I was the one who wanted him banished and exiled so that he could not even come through the front door. For the psychotic Luke, dominated as he was by concrete thinking, experience of the therapy was like genetic engineering, an almost physical manipulation of himself by myself and the team. In early sessions he would rush out to the toilet during team meetings, not only to evacuate down the toilet what he felt to be the noxious substance of our comments but to physically check his penis – to make sure it was still intact, as if the therapy was felt by him as a physical castration.

The distorting and maligning process was not just a phantasy. The psychotic one could actually take him over completely at times, and make him behave in an obnoxious way at the Centre. His amorous advances towards female guests could be very intrusive. It was as if an intention (of making emotional or loving contact with others) coming from his non-psychotic self would be rejected by his psychotic self and perverted. This would actually create a view in other people's minds of him as a sexual abuser. At other times he would be sick in the kitchen sink or create a mess in the kitchen. Sometimes he would offer to help cook a meal with someone else but be so disruptive and chaotic that the person he was cooking with would become utterly exasperated with him: again, a good intention hijacked. In his art therapy sessions his noisy frenetic activity or his taking up the whole space on the table would disturb the whole art group. In team meetings he would be in anguish that the actions he had taken in his life were the wrong ones and that he had made the wrong decisions. He was very concerned that his team members would not be led to the belief that his actions were a true representation of himself. His earlier claims that a gross injustice had been done to him made sense in this light. The psychotic self took him over and made him behave in obnoxious ways, and then it was he who had to take the responsibility and blame for it. The way in which the psychotic self took over the non-psychotic self and made him behave in an alienating way was actually a source of considerable concern, and there was a risk that others in the Crisis Centre – the other guests or resident therapists outside the team – could take a snap shot of his behaviour and misidentify the non-psychotic Luke for the psychotic Luke, as if that was all of him, and not be able to see that a well-intentioned Luke had been taken over. This could also lead to collusions in the guest group's viewing of Luke as the source of disgust and fear and a target for mockery – the very characteristics attributed to him by his psychotic self. One of the great advantages of having the resident therapist and student 'out there' in the Centre was that they could pick up when this was happening, and their understanding of the dynamics in the other guests at any other time could help us to see how other guests might be using Luke's condition to serve their own purposes.

Another aspect of Luke's psychosis was his omnipotence. The psychotic Luke viewed the so-called treatment as an attempt to deprive him of all his potency. This was much more so in his first two stays than his last stay. At the same time as feeling he was being made out to be a criminal, he could also be convinced that he was a famous performer and that he was about to land a fabulous contract. At these times he could become convinced that the Centre was a film studio or that the team meetings were filming sessions. He would want to change the nature of the team meetings by making us watch him perform. We should just be full of admiration for him and his wonderful talents. On one occasion, after I had confronted him about his attempt to twist the team meeting into something else, he became silent for a while and then started to pick his nose and eat the pickings with a supercilious smile on his face. I suggested to him that he was now mocking what I had said and making a claim that his own nose pickings were superior to what was on offer from me. On other occasions he would say that we should all go to America on an ocean liner and there he would land this fabulous contract which would provide him with enormous material wealth and be the solution to all our problems. More commonly, he would feel that we were interfering with his plans and become highly agitated that we were standing in his way. He would feel that being at the Centre was the biggest mistake of his life and that he was missing so many opportunities to fulfil his career as a famous person.

In addition to this, however, by providing him with an opportunity to perform at the Centre (outside the team meetings), we were able to support a sane side and help give expression to his creative self and not unnecessarily provoke his psychotic self, who felt we were out to deprive him of all avenues of self-expression. Bion emphasizes that many of the symptoms of psychosis arise from attempts on the part of the patient to restore his damaged ego and reconstitute a world which has been destroyed. Luke had the conviction that he owned a mansion in America that was falling into disrepair and being invaded by squatters: if he could land the contract he would be able to reclaim it and pay for its reconstruction. His omnipotent solutions seemed to go hand in hand with the paranoid onslaughts. Each detail of his paranoia was reflected in his omnipotent solutions to it. For example, his fears that he could be overheard or that the newspapers were making him infamous had their counterpart in the phantasy that he was world famous, heard all over the world through his performances. In this way omnipotent solutions were used to triumph over his persecution. Some indication that such solutions did not work could be seen when he once said that whenever he performed there would be the adoring crowd, but there would always be one person in the audience who would be mocking and deriding him. Dr J. Steiner, summarizing Bion, writes: 'The psychotic part is preoccupied with the problem of repair of the ego and the non-psychotic part is concerned with neurotic problems centred on the resolution of a conflict of ideas and emotions.' Steiner goes on to say: 'This incompatibility of aims leads to a kind of enmity between the two parts of the personality and in the transference one or other parts is disowned and projected into the analyst. The enmity is then relived in the transference.' Luke would often project his non-psychotic self into the team, concerned as we were about his real relationships in the house, his conflicts about the future, and so on. By comparison with his omnipotent solutions our contributions felt derisory and weak or else were highly persecuting to him as if we were trying to control him and prevent him from fulfilling himself.

Disentangling the psychotic self from the non-psychotic self was, therefore, an important part of our work. So, for example, when he talked about filming contracts I suggested to him that there were two Lukes. That there was an ill one who felt the Centre to be a gross interference to his aim of becoming world famous through landing the fabulous contract, but that, side by side with *that* Luke, was himself, who had the sane wish to make a contract with us with the hope that out of such a partnership something creative could be produced. Luke at times seemed able to accept this. On the other hand I would at times find myself driven to an omnipotent state of mind myself, as if by excessive confrontation I could drive the psychosis from him or nail it down. Such states of mind in me never helped.

Luke became much more contained in his third stay, and his omnipotence and paranoia were much less disruptive. He became much more keen to get to his team meetings and use them as best he could, but there was a powerful and seductive pull in him which continued to twist communication. We did begin to have team meetings where a non-psychotic Luke was much more present, but this was always followed by a reassertion of his psychotic self, either in the house following the team meeting or else in the following meeting. Both Lukes were always present in the team meetings. Again it is here that Ian and Karin proved invaluable in being able to pick up in the session how Luke seemed to neutralize and dismiss my contribution or turn them into something exciting or a source of mirth. His psychotic self was less obstructive but not gone away. On very many occasions, something I said would be subtly twisted so that it lost all meaning or got reworked as a kind of fix to give him a bit of a lift. Something potentially emotionally painful would be repeatedly turned into something pleasant. Having independent witnesses in the room in the form of Ian and Karin helped on many occasions to rescue me from the insidious effects of a rose-tinted psychotic process that would effectively turn what I said to dust. He would hate this being pointed out and become easily persecuted again by this process being noticed. Confronting such psychotic processes is a very delicate issue, and as a team we became more skilled in being able to be firm with him without needlessly humiliating him. The psychotic part of Luke easily felt very hurt and humiliated and could experience us as standing for sanity in a triumphant and gloating way. It was extremely painful for Luke to give up some of the pleasures afforded him by his psychotic self.

A very strong theme in this last stay was humour. By this I mean psychotic humour. He would often try to stop himself bursting into laughter during a team meeting. When we enquired what was funny it would usually be the way one of us was looking. He was highly reluctant to let us know what was making him laugh because of the intense humiliation he felt when we didn't find it funny too. He would then defiantly state that there were some people who found the same things funny as he did. What was terribly painful to him apart from the humiliation was that by talking about the source of his humour he has to give it up. He complained on more than one occasion that he did not like talking about it because it took the humour away and he was then left with a sad feeling. This is another variation on the theme that the psychotic Luke viewed therapy as theft, taking away his potency, self-expression and pleasures.

Over time, the gaps between team meetings were felt by him more acutely, especially over the weekend break. He talked about this concretely in terms of travelling: the difficulties of getting from A to B. He found travelling very difficult because on the train or bus he always got pounced on by hostile, bullying fellow passengers. This was quite a shift, as if he was letting us know how problematic gaps between team meetings were and how it was in these gaps that the psychotic self, represented by the fellow passengers, barged back in. This state of affairs showed a marked difference from the Luke of earlier days, who was so taken over by the view that the Centre was the source of abuse. He became more aware of the further help needed when he left the Centre, something vehemently denied during his earlier stays, and seemed keen to continue in individual therapy. More importantly, I think, there was a little more awareness of how his non-psychotic self was so tangled up with his psychotic self. This was movingly demonstrated in a later team meeting in which he was talking of his concerns about leaving the Centre and finding himself in the vicinity of others at work, who might get at him and bully him. These bullies, he said, would be people who were quite off their heads and would not know it. At this point, as if to demonstrate these bullying activities, he jerked his fist towards his head. These would be people who would really need therapy but not know they needed it. If he was left in their company he might start to degenerate, he said. I said that I thought he was letting us know about the serious predicament he was in when he felt left in the vicinity of the ill one. He then went on to talk about an awful sensation he was having outside the sessions of fainting, as if the blood were rushing from his head and creating disturbing feelings in his stomach. I said that I thought that he was telling us about the effects of the ill one's stranglehold on him – that it took away his resources to think at the moment when thinking became a possibility. He replied that he now knew that therapy was very important to him. At this point he fell silent and then tried to stop himself bursting out laughing. This vignette highlights an important point: that as soon as the non-psychotic Luke had managed to communicate something of the degenerative effects of the psychotic self (represented by the fellow passengers) on himself and the effects the psychotic one had on his mind (represented by the blood rushing from his head) – that is, to make a differentiation between himself and it – the psychotic one burst forth in mad laughter and took him over again. It was as if with each step the non-psychotic Luke took, the psychotic one felt squeezed out and barged back in.

In another later session Luke talked about the difficulty he was having with his glasses. They kept slipping off his nose. Could Ian fix them for him? The trouble was, he said, that he was not technically minded. I thought this was very significant. His comment that he was not very technically minded seemed to be an awareness of the state of disrepair he felt his mind to be in and his incapacity to register an accurate record of his experience and progress at the Centre. This was again a very moving experience, where he seemed in contact with the damage that the psychotic part of his personality had done to him. But he also said that he had been given a video camera for his birthday. This, I think, was a communication that he was present from his birth: that he had been given the equipment but it was in a state of disrepair and, as with his glasses, he needed help from outside himself to repair the damage. This is in marked contrast to the psychotic one's claim that he had been there before him – to his omnipotence, where all solutions to the disrepair of his ego could come from himself alone.

In conclusion, I think that some important groundwork was done with Luke. By the end of his stay he was much saner and very keen to find a therapeutic community to live in and to continue individual psychotherapy. But, as I say, we are only just at the beginning. Finally, I think the Arbours Crisis Centre offers an important, if limited, resource. I would view the Centre as providing a first port of call for some psychotic individuals. Through the team work and the therapeutic milieu of the Centre such people can have the opportunity to be sufficiently contained to begin the groundwork for longer-term individual psychotherapy. We are working with extremely disturbed individuals who risk a career as mental patients, and many of those who stay with us do not end up with such careers.

References

Berke, J. H. (1987) 'Arriving, Settling-in, Settling-down, Leaving and Following-up: Stages of Stay at the Arbours Centre.' *British Journal of Medical Psychology* 60, 181–188.

Bion, W.R. (1962) *Learning from Experience*. London: William Heinemann; repr. London: Karnac Books, 1984.

CHAPTER 12

A Fine Balance: Between Hope and Despair

Lois Elliott

The title of this chapter is taken from the novel by Rohinton Mistry *A Fine Balance,* in which one of the characters describes life as a fine balance between hope and despair:

> The proof reader nodded, 'You see, you cannot draw lines and compartments, and refuse to budge beyond them. Sometimes you have to use your failures as stepping-stones to success. You have to maintain a fine balance between hope and despair.' He paused, considering what he had just said. 'Yes,' he repeated. 'In the end, it's all a question of balance.' (Mistry 1995, p.282)

Without wishing to spoil the story for those of you who have not yet read the book, I found it excruciatingly painful to read. It takes one on a roller coaster of a ride through different levels and stages of hope and despair. It confronts one with life's unfairness and injustice and divests one of any illusions one may have in believing in the triumph of good over evil. In the book the author beautifully portrays the despair and hope in the lives of the main characters, and describes how hope comes not in the triumph of good over evil nor the reversal of fortune but *through change.*

The emotional journey that this book took me on is very reminiscent of the emotional journey I made together with my fellow team members, colleagues at the Crisis Centre, and the guest whom I shall call 'Brenda', with whom we worked during her stay. When Brenda came to the Arbours Crisis Centre her life had become one of total despair. She was 18 years old and had spent most of the previous two years of her life in a psychiatric hospital under close observation owing to several suicide attempts and episodes of serious self-harming. Those around her – her family and the staff of the hospital – were also in a state of despair as to what to do with her. The environment of the ward was recognized as not being a healthy one for a young woman, but they were at a loss as to what else to do. The Crisis Centre was approached as a source of hope.

'He has no hope who never had a fear.' (Alexander Selkirk)

I think at this initial point we were able to achieve a fine balance between hope and despair. We had two assessment consultations with Brenda, during the first one of which she was mainly silent, and during the second one of which she told us about her situation, her desperation and her hope that we could help her. We did not know if we could offer sufficient containment for Brenda to allow her to begin to engage with us without inflaming her self-destructive impulses to the extent that they would take over. This was her first experience of psychoanalytic psychotherapeutic treatment and it was, therefore, unknown whether she would be able to make use of this form of treatment. On the other hand, Brenda herself had expressed the wish to come to the Centre and the hope that we could help her. Also, the assessment team had been able to establish a connection with her and together forge some links that provided insight into her situation. With this balance in mind she was offered a stay. It was to be some time before such a balance was found again.

Brenda's stay began slowly, ourselves ever mindful of the powerful destructive forces that we knew to be inside the passive, compliant young woman who sat with us taking small tentative steps to let us know something about herself. In the second month of the stay Brenda seemed to have 'settled in' (Berke 1987). Joseph Berke describes this stage as 'marked by a significant decrease in arrival fears and an increased ability to reflect on the underlying issues which brought the guest to the Centre. During this time the therapeutic alliance between guest and therapists should become more fully established, and the framework of meetings firmly fixed.' (1987, p.184)

This indeed appeared to be the case with Brenda. She was developing relationships with other people in the house, and had a good relationship with her resident therapist. In the group therapy meetings she was alert, although mainly silent and responding only to questions directed to her.

She was able to participate in the art therapy although unable to attend the movement therapy sessions. She was struggling in the team meetings to allow us to introduce her to the alien concept of her internal world, but always arrived on time and never missed a session. It therefore came as an enormous shock when shortly before dinner one evening she presented herself to one of the team members with a laceration to her wrist that was almost the full circumference of her wrist, and deep enough to expose the bone. She stood there mute and apparently unaffected while an ambulance was called, and she was taken to hospital.

'So farewell hope, and with hope farewell fear.' (John Milton)

The shock that we felt at this incident reflected not only the horror of the act itself, but also that we had allowed ourselves to hope – the hope that things could be different for Brenda. Our feelings of hope were not conscious. In the team meetings we were very much aware of Brenda's struggle to put into words what were felt by her to be unthinkable thoughts. Her internal world continued to be largely unknown to both ourselves and to Brenda, but in spite of this our shock at this incident reflected that somewhere we had forgotten that she was capable of such self-destruction; somewhere we had lost sight of her despair.

Herbert Rosenfeld has written that the 'fact that projective identifica-tion can be used to vacuate and to deny psychic reality has to be recog-nized alongside the fact that when a patient is trying to push unbearable mental content into the analyst he is also compelling him to share the un-pleasant experiences' (Rosenfeld 1987, p.165). In a very concrete way Brenda was handing to us evidence of her psychic reality which she found unbearable, and was compelling us to share the unpleasant experience. This was a time of great despair, when it was hard to find any sign of hope.

The Oxford Dictionary definition of hope is 'expectation and desire combined, e.g. for a certain thing to occur'. The definition of despair is 'the complete loss or absence of hope'. Despair is defined in relation to hope, the complete loss of it, but hope is not defined in relation to despair. Through the process of engagement and the resulting empathic feelings that had grown in us towards Brenda we had developed an expectation and desire for things to be different for her. In our hope we had lost sight of its relation to despair: unwittingly we had abandoned Brenda to her despair, the complete loss or absence of hope.

As the Crisis Centre is a small, intimate residential facility, the shock and horror of what had happened reverberated around the house. Interestingly there was little anger felt towards Brenda, although on one level her actions could be viewed as an attack on the house and the work taking place. Rather the atmosphere was one of despair and horror at what had taken place. R.D. Hinshelwood (1987) has written that despair

> results from phantasies about destructive objects and feelings, and they are connected with phantasies of the loss, death or fragmentation of the 'good object'. Anger, hatred and envy also occur, but in my view they are attributed to the patients by members of staff too often, and by patients to each other or to the staff. Despair may not be recognized often enough. (Hinshelwood 1987, pp.57–58)

The feeling for the team and the house was one of despair, our consolation at that time being that Brenda was safe, and where she needed to be, within the secure setting of a hospital. We did at least understand that Brenda was communicating to us her feeling of hopelessness and helplessness in the face of the violence and destructiveness of her internal world.

'He that lives on hope will die fasting.' (Benjamin Franklin)

In the following weekly clinical meeting the incident and events leading up to it were discussed. The other team members and myself found them extremely difficult to think about and gain insight and understanding into what had happened. We had gone over in detail, time and again, the incident itself and the events leading up to it, trying to find some clue or explanation, some sign or symptom that we had missed, that might provide some respite from our painful feelings of despair. We hoped that the clinical group might furnish the missing clue.

On reflection I am struck by how the team's situation in relation to the clinical group mirrored that of Brenda's to the team. In these early days of her stay Brenda found it almost impossible to speak spontaneously, preferring to be asked direct questions to which she would respond in the affirmative or the negative. She visibly squirmed in the team meetings when I said I wondered what her thoughts were. Without the tools that would enable thinking and the processing of thoughts, she too had tried to glean clues and explanations that she hoped would provide her with some respite from her psychic reality.

Instead of furnishing the missing clue, the clinical group began by helping to counterbalance our despair. It was pointed out that Brenda had not lacerated the full circumference of her wrist, which would have involved the cutting of a major artery. Also that she had been able to seek out help before completing this deadly task. We took comfort from this, and the realization that not all of our work together had been severed: a small connection had survived. This small glimmer of hope came not in a reversal or reparation of events – indeed at that point there was no question for the team of Brenda returning to the Crisis Centre – but in finding some balance to our overwhelming despair. By balancing one thought with another, a mental space was created in which other thoughts could develop, and the clinical group provided the container in which the thinking about these thoughts could take place.

Differing views were expressed in the clinical group regarding the incident itself. Some viewed it as an attack on the help being proffered by the team and the house. Others drew attention to it being Brenda's right hand, her masturbation hand, and it being an attack on her developing sexual feelings. It was also pointed out that in some countries the punishment for theft is cutting off a hand. Did Brenda feel that she had stolen something from us, or had we stolen something from her – the cutting off of the stay being our punishment? Rosenfeld points out that a negative therapeutic reaction can follow on from progress in the analytic treatment, or can indicate a failure on the part of the analyst/therapist to understand (Rosenfeld 1987). There had been some small signs of progress with Brenda, such as her engagement in the house and her attempts at communication in the team meetings. Yet the horrific, negative therapeutic reaction conveyed in the attempt to cut her hand off did feel like a response to our failure to understand her despair.

As we struggled to gain some insight and understanding into what had happened, Brenda remained withdrawn and disconnected. Lying in the blood stained sheets of her hospital bed, she was unable to acknowledge or communicate with the hospital staff or the team members who visited her. Maybe at that point, we could allow ourselves the luxury of thinking, knowing that Brenda would not be returning to the Crisis Centre and safe in the knowledge that we would not again be confronted with the terrible reality of Brenda's internal world.

The striking contrast between Brenda's state of despair and the glimmers of insight the team were gaining, with the help of the clinical group, was very apparent at this time. At first we felt it was an indication that Brenda had given up on us. She made no attempt to contact us or engage with us, and no mention was made of the possibility of her returning to the house at a future date. We then began to realize that, in fact, it was the other way round, and that Brenda felt that we had given up on her – that by holding onto hope we had not understood her despair, and that we had not understood that she believed no-one could help her.

> 'What reinforcement we may gain from hope
> If not, what resolution from despair.' (John Milton)

We had failed to achieve a balance, leaving Brenda feeling alone with this unbearable knowledge, and her despair. This is a paradox common in psychotherapeutic situations: how to bear the patient's belief that no one can help, while still maintaining some hope that enables you to try. As I write this I am reminded of the words of a clinical supervisor as he reminds me not to try to help my patients but to analyse and provide insight and understanding. Bion talks of the need for the analyst to approach each analytic session without memory or desire. By this, he is referring to the need for the analyst/therapist to approach each therapeutic session without preconceived ideas or a desire that the patient will change.

Rosenfeld talks about being

> dubious about an attitude of detachment. It seems to me impossible to destroy our desire and intention without severely damaging the relationship with our patient... However, it is essential that we thoroughly analyse our attitudes and intentions. The desire or expectancy which interferes in analysis and which is felt to be disturbing by our patients is our narcissistic desire to do well or to have a patient who gives us satisfaction in our work and so indirectly increases our satisfaction with our therapeutic capacities. (1987, p.35)

Rosenfeld uses the words 'desire' and 'expectancy', which he considers interferes with the analytic work. Desire and expectancy combined is the definition of hope. Was it therefore our narcissistic hope that interfered with our work with Brenda?

The hope, when it did come, came from where it needed to come from: Brenda herself. Some three weeks after she had left the Crisis Centre she phoned to ask if she could come and see us. We were taken aback by this sudden change. When we spoke to the hospital ward staff, we were told that Brenda was up and about, talking to staff and other patients, and was giving thought to her future and wanted to know if she could come back to the Crisis Centre. We contacted Brenda to say that we were very pleased to hear from her, that we had been giving a lot of thought to what had happened and would welcome an opportunity to share those thoughts with her, and that we would need to think very carefully about future treatment plans.

'United thoughts and counsels, equal hope,
And hazard in the glorious enterprise.' (John Milton)

The situation was discussed at length in the clinical group, the team's ambivalent feelings being reflected by the different views in the group. We had gained a very important insight into Brenda's internal world, which would aid our work with her. However, we had also been left in no doubt as to the reaction and opposition to any perceived interference to her psychotic self. For many of the guests who come to stay at the Crisis Centre, early life experience has been one of not having their feelings contained. That is, they have not had anyone able to bear their primitive life and death feelings, to contain them and to reflect their feelings back to them in a form that they as infants could tolerate. This is the work of the Crisis Centre: to be able to bear and contain these unbearable feelings, help to make sense of them and feed them back in a tolerable form that promotes insight and understanding. As a team we had failed to provide this function for Brenda: we had failed to contain her despair that no-one could help her, and failed to let her know that we understood this. This situation left her only two options: to project this unbearable mental content out onto others, or other objects; or to inflict it on herself.

However, despite our failure there had been indications that this therapeutic work with Brenda was possible. We also knew only too well what the reaction to this work would be, and that she could be plunged into despair and self-destructive acts. To continue the work would involve inflaming her psychotic self, and unless we could identify and track this process, also enabling Brenda to understand what was happening, we would once again abandon her to her despair.

'I can endure my own despair
But not another's hope.' (William Walsh)

We saw Brenda again and talked with her about this. We said how we felt we had not understood her despair and her belief that no-one could help her. Brenda told us how bad she had felt knowing that we were trying to help, but not feeling anything had changed. The accusations inside her head had become louder, telling her that she was bad, useless, and undeserving of our efforts to help and our care and concern. The attempt to cut off her hand was, among other things, a punishment for her perceived inability to take the helping hand that was being offered her.

After much further discussion it was decided to offer Brenda a further stay. Anxiety levels were high in the team and in the house. Our previous experience had made us wary of feelings of hope, but our fear was that too much despair would undermine Brenda's and the team's efforts. The usual support network of the Crisis Centre was widened and strengthened. The situation was monitored weekly in the clinical group, a second team leader was made available to the team for their weekly supervision, and the team leader on call for the Centre was kept abreast of the day-to-day situation. In this way the anxiety was contained, and members of the team were enabled to find a 'fine balance' between hope and despair, that allowed the work to continue.

'He who has never hoped can never despair.' (George Bernard Shaw)

Some weeks after Brenda's return to the house she told the team that when she got worried at home, the response would be, 'Don't worry about it Brenda.' This I am sure was said to reassure her, but had the unfortunate consequence of leaving Brenda alone with her worry and despair. What we had learnt was that Brenda *needed us to worry* and to be able to contain that anxiety – the anxiety that no-one could help, and that things would never change. She needed us to be able to bear this knowledge without being overwhelmed by it.

How we were able to do this was with the help, support and understanding of the wider clinical group, as well as the help of the non-clinical staff. Brenda's despair was at times too much for the team to bear alone. At such times the clinical group would take on the role of the functioning ego, assessing the situation and providing insight and understanding that served to revitalize the thinking capacity of the team. At other times, when the team felt hopeful, the clinical group would sensitively remind the team of the despair that lurked within. I am reminded of the words of Margaret Fagan, a team leader at the Crisis Centre, who would say: 'This is someone who needs all of these people to contain them and their feelings.' This was certainly the case for Brenda, and is the work of the Arbours Crisis Centre.

I wish I could conclude this chapter with a happy ending, but, as is the reality of life as portrayed in Mistry's book, there is no 'and they all lived happily ever after' ending. Brenda successfully completed her stay at the Crisis Centre; there were further incidents during her stay that alerted us to the fact that we were out of balance, but none that necessitated such horrific, self-destructive action as before. By the end of her time at the Centre Brenda was acquiring an emotional vocabulary through which she was able to communicate her mental state, rather than being imprisoned within it or having to demonstrate it through actions. This was a significant change, but only the beginning for Brenda in a long and uphill journey to gain the necessary insight and understanding that will enable her to adapt and begin to build a life for herself.

It was time for Brenda to leave the Crisis Centre, but there was nowhere for her to go that could provide adequate support and facilitate the continuing development of the work that she had started. She returned to her local area where she was provided with hostel accommodation and support. She remained in contact with the Centre for some years until the last resident therapist that she had known left. At that time she was still trying to find the long-term help that she needed.

I would like to end this chapter by quoting part of a poem by Andrew Marvell, entitled 'The Definition of Love':

> My Love is of a birth as rare
> As 'tis for object strange and high:
> It was begotten by despair
> Upon impossibility.
> Magnanimous Despair alone
> Could show me so divine a thing,
> Where feeble Hope could ne'er have flown
> But vainly flapt its tinsel wing.

> (Andrew Marvell, Collected Poems, pp. 252–3)

References

Berke, J.H. (1987) 'Arriving, Settling-in, Settling-down, Leaving and Following-up: Stages of Stay at the Arbours Centre.' *British Journal of Medical Psychology, 60*, pp.181–188.

Franklin, B. (1758) 'Preface to Poor Richard's Almanack.' In J.M. and J. Cohen (eds) *The New Penguin Dictionary of Quotations.* Penguin, p.167.

Hinshelwood, R.D. (1987) *What Happens in Groups.* London: Free Association Books.

Milton, J. (1968) *Paradise Lost.* Penguin Classics.

Marvell, A. 'The Definition of Love.' In *The Metaphysical Poets.* (1957) Penguin Books.

Mistry, R. (1995) *A Fine Balance.* London: Faber and Faber.

Rosenfeld, H. (1987) *Impasse and Interpretation.* London: Routledge.

Selkirk, A. In R. Lonsdale (ed) (1984) *The New Oxford Book of Eighteenth Century Verse.* Oxford University Press, p.591.

Shaw, G.B. (1946) *Caesar and Cleopatra: Three Plays for Puritans.* Penguin Classics, p.232.

Walsh, W. (1704) 'Song.' In D.M. Smith (ed) (1926) *The Oxford Book of Eighteenth Century Verse.* Oxford University Press.

CHAPTER 13

Psychotic Interventions

Joseph H. Berke

'Psychotic interventions' is an ambiguous term. But I use it deliberately. It can refer to therapeutic interventions done on behalf of individuals who are suffering or have previously suffered psychotic breakdowns. And it can refer to the actions of people, often designated as 'patients', who are going through the process of breaking down. Equally relevant, the term can point out the reaction of a human environment, the family or milieu that was supposed to be of help, but couldn't be and wasn't. The latter is a container which can no longer contain because of terrible pain, confused thinking and angry outbursts. In other words I am considering the situation when the therapist or institution has collapsed, even if only for a temporary period. So this chapter is about psychotic breakdowns on the part of both parties – those needing help and those giving it. It is also about the means by which these same two sides are able to reconstitute themselves.

All this has happened at the Arbours Crisis Centre, where, as I have previously described in my chapter 'Conjoint Therapy' (in Section Two), there are three interacting therapeutic systems. The third of these systems, the milieu, is the Centre as an active therapeutic environment. Perhaps 'active interpersonal environment' is more correct, for this milieu can also be non-therapeutic or even anti-therapeutic, depending on, as we shall see, who is at the Centre, and what is going on.

In order to illustrate the various implications of psychotic interventions, I will focus on the role of the milieu as the healing or the damaging agent. Specifically, I will tell the story of 'Hamid', a large man in his early twenties, whose family originally came from the Middle East. Hamid had a good intellect and did well at school. But as he approached university age, he began to bully his parents and younger sister, and make rude sexual overtures to women both inside and outside his home.

Hamid was first admitted to hospital in his late teens because of severe aggressive outbursts. He seemed to seek out women who were weak and vulnerable in order to terrorize them. At his worst he appeared to be totally out of touch with reality and his behaviour was nearly uncontainable. Hamid was referred to the Centre because, after several bouts of hospitalization with the diagnosis of schizophrenia, he remained an incorrigible human being. But his family had heard of our approach and thought we might be able to help him.

Hamid came to the Centre for a three-month period – what we call a medium stay. At first he was wildly abusive, and very demanding. He soaked up huge amounts of food, especially milk and sugar, while refusing to sit for any meals. He delighted in making huge messes in the kitchen. Otherwise, he seemed to take on the role of over-bearing potentate, especially in the way that he bossed around females in the house. In return they hated him. But when confronted he would deny what he had done and shout venomously. Generally he was extremely negative about the Centre, and refused to go to house meetings. But he did attend his team meeting regularly.

As his stay progressed, Hamid began to calm down and become more sociable. He surprised everyone with a keen sense of humour and a capacity for clear thinking. People began to see him as a bad boy, rather than a mad boy. Certainly he tried everyone's patience to the limit – so much so that on a few occasions he was asked to go home for a day or two so the house could cool down.

Towards the end of his stay Hamid showed long periods of sadness; at the same time he could be intellectually impressive, engaging people in longish discussions about politics or philosophy. But increasingly these reflective periods would be interrupted by angry, impulsive, demanding outbursts. All his accomplishments while at the Centre seemed in danger of being lost. He had reverted back to being chaotic and unbearable. Both the resident therapists (RTs) and other guests were at their wits' end in outrage and despair. This was a turning point. Hamid had begun his 'leaving crisis'.

Everything seemed to blow up before his leaving date. Over the previous week he had become increasingly abusive, and tempers were almost at boiling point among the therapists and other guests. Then, mid-week, the house itself seemed to respond in kind because the sinks suddenly blocked up with a black, foul-smelling liquid. The same morning we had our semi-annual medical inspection. There was a frantic rush to get the sinks unblocked, accomplished just before the inspector, a very pleasant, elderly doctor, arrived. She had been to the Centre many times before and always enjoyed a quiet, relaxed visit. But as she entered the kitchen for a cup of tea, Hamid suddenly brushed past her, screaming: 'Get out of the way you fucking old bag.' Everyone was appalled and one of the guests, 'Katie', started to cry. But the doctor was not the least taken aback. While even the RTs were shaken, she calmly commented, 'You know, it sure is exciting to have a taste of real life!'

The inspection over, the RTs began to prepare for a reception in the evening. At that time the Arbours sponsored a bi-monthly public lecture. Afterwards the lecturer, invited guests, and therapists would return to the Centre for refreshments and further discussion. So, having set out the food and drink in the front room, the RTs specifically asked Hamid not to touch the stuff. Well, this was like a red flag to a bull. Upon getting back to the Centre after the lecture they found that he had not only eaten a lot of the food, but had been insulting the female guests as well.

Hamid saw the RTs and tried to be jolly: 'George, George, did you have a nice evening?' But the RTs were furious. For them gobbling up the food was the straw that broke the camel's back. Once again Hamid had broken all boundaries, and they were left in complete chaos, rage and despair. All they wanted was for him to go, immediately.

They called his team leader and told him what had happened – that Hamid had been warned and had to go. They feared that if they backed down and he didn't leave, they would lose face and appear like his father – waffling and indecisive. The team leader concurred and suggested they call the father to come and collect him.

While they were about to do this, they saw that I had just come back from the lecture and was about to sit down and talk to people. Before I could do so, they, literally, pounced on me and insisted that I withdraw with them to a rear consulting room to discuss 'him'. So I excused myself and joined a group of very angry RTs. At this point I myself felt quite menaced. I could see that they would not take no for an answer:

> 'Hamid's been on the rampage. He's eaten the food, hit another guest. He's been warned several times. He has to go.'

Nervously: 'I can see that you have tried and sentenced him. It seems that I'm to act as your executioner.'

In the meanwhile I realized no-one was able to think. The situation was crazy. The RTs had collectively reverted to concrete, or, as Wilfred Bion discerned, 'beta functioning'. Hamid had become their 'dreaded object' (Bion 1977). It seemed that their sanity, or at least peace of mind, depended on my getting rid of him.

While all this was happening, I recalled a similar incident that had occurred several years earlier. The Norwegian government had referred a young woman to the Centre with a long history – I would say reputation – of autism and schizophrenia. She was a huge person and very aggressive. If she had lived a thousand years previously, she could easily have been a Viking, raping and pillaging the North of England. In fact the referral was so unusual that we decided that a main point was to simply get her out of Norway. Anyway, 'Ingrid' had been at the Centre for several months and had just begun to form ties with people and settle down. One late afternoon I was called to the Centre by a nearly incoherent RT. 'Ingrid has thrown a chair at me for the last time. Either she goes or I go.'

In fact she had also been upset by someone's leaving; and for someone who couldn't tolerate sadness or depression, she responded in the one way she knew that would destroy the feeling: violence. Yet, what she did was not dissimilar to previous episodes. During her first weeks at the Centre I came into the house one afternoon only to be overwhelmed by an atypical silence. Then I opened the door to the kitchen. I saw Ingrid holding a huge knife at her neck. The RTs were there too, but speechless and beset by a paralytic immobility. Their hands were outstretched in order to grab her, but they remained fixed, motionless.

The moment Ingrid saw me, she began to scream, 'Joe, Joe, I'm going to do it. I'm going to kill myself. Yes, sir, right now.' My immediate response was total terror. But after a few seconds, which felt like an eternity, I felt an intense sadness. So I replied, 'Ingrid, I can't stop you from killing yourself, but if you do, I shall feel very sad, and I shall miss you.' Almost as soon as she heard this, Ingrid smiled, put down the knife and exclaimed, before walking into the garden, 'Oh Joe, I was just kidding.'

In retrospect I had allowed Ingrid to pervade me with her fear and despair following the departure of a guest towards whom she had formed a covert, if not overt, attachment. What she wanted to kill was not herself, but the upset – the fear and sadness – which she could not contain. But when I allowed myself to feel it, and express it, she felt relief, because, as far as she was concerned, these painful feelings were in me, and not in her. She had successfully filled me with them. (That is, her threats flooded me with rage and despair, the basic manoeuvre of projective identification.) Hence there was no longer any reason to kill herself. 'Joe' handled the feelings and did not threaten to put them back in her, as might have happened had the RTs tried to discharge their upset by rushing at her and grabbing the knife.

However, this time Ingrid had thrown a chair, and I was taken over not by Ingrid's feelings, but by those of the RT. I focused on the wrong person. I thought that once I came over and spoke with Ingrid, the crisis would blow over. But it didn't. The RT was adamant. Either she goes, or he goes. In desperation I called my colleague Morton Schatzman, a co-founder of the Arbours, to come over and help me out. He too argued with the RT, while Ingrid was storming around in the garden. All to no avail.

Several hours passed. The atmosphere was explosive. It seemed that neither gentle persuasion nor harsh facts would work. So we told the RT to stay and said we would take Ingrid to the Emergency Room of the Royal Free Hospital in Hampstead for a shot of Largactil (Phenothiazine), and, we hoped, a bed for the night. We didn't know what else to do. By then we were tired and desperate and Ingrid was still storming. Off we went to the Royal Free.

By the time we arrived, Ingrid had begun to calm down, but we were extremely anxious, so much so that I was prepared to do something I rarely do, revert to tranquillizers and hospitalization. By now it was one in the morning. We had to wait for a couple of hours. Ingrid demanded that we buy her endless cups of coffee and cigarettes. Anything to shut her up. I thought, 'This whole thing is crazy.'

Finally the duty psychiatrist came out. I pounced on her, yelled a potted history, and insisted that she did what I wanted her to do. She looked up calmly and reminded me that she was the doctor in charge and wouldn't decide anything till she had seen the patient.

Another half-hour passed. Morty and I felt our levels of agitation rise to new heights. Then the doctor came out. I was just beginning to feel relieved that we could go home when I heard the hideous news. 'This person can go home. She doesn't need any medication.' 'What!' I roared, 'You can't do that. Look how upset and violent she is!'

While this was going on Ingrid came out and calmly sat on a chair smoking a cigarette. The doctor pointed out that Ingrid was perfectly calm and didn't need treatment. I was dumbfounded. Suddenly a smile crossed my lips. The doctor and I had exchanged roles. I had called 'the patient' a dangerous schizophrenic. The doctor saw her as a tired if slightly confused young woman. I was arguing for drugs, she was arguing against drugs. I wanted hospitalization; she said it wasn't necessary. And not only had I changed roles with the doctor, I had exchanged roles with Ingrid. She was calm and quiet, while I was raging like a maniac. The irony was not lost on Morty or myself. With that we began to calm down. Morty said, 'Listen it's 2:30. I'll take Ingrid back to my house for the night. A good night's sleep will do us all good.' I readily concurred, and that's how the Crisis ended. In fact Ingrid never did go back to the Centre. She stayed as Morty's guest for a few days and then we found her a small flat of her own. She had never lived in her own flat before.

This whole episode flashed through my mind while I was trying to think how to handle Hamid and the RT. (One might say that this is what Bion meant by 'learning from experience'.) A decision came quickly. Whatever was going to happen, I did not intend to become the knight in shining armour, the omnipotent father who provided omnipotent solutions for his regressed children. But I also realized that far from being the omnipotent father, the RTs had allowed me little room to manoeuvre. They clearly wanted me to become the impotent father, who had to do their bidding. Surely this was their sadistic revenge for my having inflicted 'him' on them in the first place, and for having caused them so much psychic pain.

Angrily: 'Well, what are you going to do? We can't spend another night with Hamid in the state he's in.'

Again, I was taken aback by the extreme hostility, but now wanted to avoid appearing omnipotent or getting sucked in further.

'Well,' (hanging my head a bit for effect), 'I don't know. I really don't know what to do.'

By now I was trying to buy time so that we could all begin to think.

'Let me see. You know we do have other options. I know we can get rid of him. Indeed that's one option. Let's see if there are any others. I recall my friend Ross Speck, who is a very skilful family therapist living in Philadelphia. He used to work with large family groups or networks. They invariably contained some overtly disturbed members, whom he'd call "the designated patients". Could it be that's the case with "him"? Could Hamid be our designated patient, the carrier of all our craziness?'

Murmurs of annoyance.

'What Ross used to do when the large family group threatened to fragment, and expel a member, was to expand the group. Bring in more members – distant relatives, neighbours, even relative strangers. The point was to get people who could think to join the group. Maybe we can do that, by carrying the discussion to the reception. Let's ask our visitors what they could do. Let's ask the other people in the house too.'

More murmurs, but at least the proposal wasn't rejected out of hand.

'You know, we could also ask Hamid to join us too. Maybe he might come up with something himself.'

At that moment, as if on cue, Hamid came into the back room and looked at me somewhat plaintively.

I said, 'Hamid, I feel very sad and upset about the situation.' (I actually did feel that way, but I was also being deliberately vague.)

Hamid, who knew everyone in the house wanted him out, was shaking. Then he shot off to the kitchen to drink some milk, then back in the room; and before anyone could comment, he came up to me and said, 'Don't worry. I'll go to bed.'

With that he started up the stairs towards his room. It was now 10:30. Hamid had been quite disarming and I thought it safe to suggest that we re-join the reception. I said this would help us to compose our thoughts. The RTs agreed.

There were about 20 people there, our speaker, a few of his friends and colleagues, a few Arbours therapists, and the rest from the Crisis Centre. Everyone seemed to want to talk at once: 'What's happening? Why weren't you here? Where is Hamid?'

I explained what was going on, that we had a big problem (trying to avoid being too specific), and asked everyone for their suggestions.

A few of the guests at the Centre went on the attack. Hamid had to go. 'Look, he hit me today! Why should we put up with that?'

Our lecturer, 'Dr Thompson', inquired: 'Is he on drugs?'

Somewhat flippantly I retorted: 'Maybe we should all take some drugs. It could help us to calm down.'

The lecturer let a few guffaws pass and continued: 'You say you want him to leave. This is an unusual problem. Usually we try to get patients to stay, not to leave.' He was quickly accosted by Katie, a thin young woman who used to cut her arms and face in order to reduce the tensions in herself. 'How can you say that? Don't you know what I've been through?' Another resident interjected that she hadn't been able to sleep for days because of Hamid, while the RTs, still angry, concurred.

Dr Thompson commented: 'You know, we could all leave. Leave him in the house. But then, where would the RTs go?'

An animated discussion ensued. After a few more minutes I encouraged the doctor to add to his earlier remarks. First, he asked a few questions. Why had Hamid come to the Centre? How long for? Then he presented his views about schizophrenia and schizophrenics, as well as the treatments available, especially medication.

People weren't too interested, and I could see they were shocked by all the medical psychiatric terms he deployed. Then he decided to tell a story. This was a story prefaced by the quip, 'You know, it's often easier to start again, than to clean up a big mess.' The story went like this:

> In Ireland there was a Mother and two boys. The boys went out one day to play by a bog. One fell in and was quickly pulled under. The other boy ran home to get his mother. She ran back to the bog and saw that her son was about to go under the quicksand. She rushed over and pushed his head under. Her other son was horrified. 'Mother, why did you do that?' The mother replied: 'Well, since I couldn't save him, I thought I might as well get it over with quick. Then I could start again.'

A stunned silence prevailed. Thompson added: 'In putting the boy back into the *mud*, she was really putting him back into the *mad*, into madness. Perhaps there was nothing more she could do. After all, she didn't have any drugs.'

This seemed to break the mood. I took a glass of wine, and visitors, guests and therapists started to tuck into the food and drink. Everyone seemed to be talking at once. There was a jolly, almost ebullient atmosphere.

Midnight came. Dr Thompson and his friends said they had to go. While I escorted them to the door, a complete change of mood took place. The residents seemed to forget 'him' and focused instead on the doctor. He had become the hated object, the whipping boy. Katie got angry with him for advocating drugs. Another accused him of being a tool of the establishment. And so on.

Midnight came and went. I had to struggle with myself to return to the meeting. I was dead tired and wanted to go home, especially since the Hamid issue was not pressing. But it had not been settled and I decided to stay as long as necessary to resolve things. In his talk Thompson had spoken about guilt and forgiveness. I hoped that the anger and guilt that previously had pervaded the house might be replaced by a mellowing of mood and feeling of forgiveness. Back at the meeting, I sniffed the atmosphere. The frenzied pressure to oust 'him' had gone. People were more uncertain about what to do.

Katie spoke about him: how he had called her a whore and slag. She queried whether that was how Hamid saw himself. An animated discussion about Hamid and sex ensued. Was he really angry with his sister because she was good looking? Weren't his ideas about women all perverted? Somehow the idea of 'condom soup' slipped in. Condom soup?

Sue, a shy black girl who usually tried not to be noticed, piped up: 'At least some of the shit is out in the open. Anyway there were times when Hamid was OK with me.'

Another guest at the Centre, Ron, seemed to be falling asleep on a big pillow. But he was awake enough to remark that Hamid reminded him how nervous he was at times. In fact, usually he was extremely depressed.

Suddenly, I realized that no-one was angry with Hamid. People were chatting away about other things. I, however, chose to focus on him, asking, 'What do you think it feels like to be Hamid? What is it like to be so full of despair and fear and terror?' More talk. Again I brought the meeting back to Hamid.

By now it was 1:15 in the morning. 'I think our feelings about Hamid have softened a bit. But I don't think we should just let things hang. You know, when I came over tonight after the lecture, you seemed ready to throw him out. So, let's go over what we can do, what the options are.'

Almost as if I were reading from a prepared list of possibilities, I started: 'One...two...three...'

1. We can get rid of him immediately, for ever.

2. We can get rid of him in the morning after allowing him to stay overnight.

3. We can ask him to leave for the night and come back tomorrow, as we have done before.

4. We can let him stay, but set up a rota for people to stay up with him during the night.

5. We can all stay up and cancel meetings for the next day.

6. We can bring him back into the group, into the meeting, right then and there.

7. We can follow the doctor's advice and use medication. But who should take it and how much? Should Hamid take 100 mg of Largactil (Thorazine), or the whole group?

8. We can all have a double Scotch.

At this point I interjected that when patients become agitated they tend to be given Largactil, but when therapists get upset they turn to alcohol.

More lively exchanges ensued.

Katie exclaimed: 'I'm against the use of all drugs.'

'OK then. I suggest we all have a glass of warm milk and honey. Let's give one to Hamid too. Then go up and express love for Hamid and hug him. Anyway Hamid's biggest problem is expressing and receiving affection. Let's all give him some affection.'

Katie shouted, as if speaking for the whole group: 'Joe, you give it to him first.'

I replied: 'No problem. But before I do, let's all hold hands.'

In this way, I tried to open a delicate subject – the open expression of affection in and by members of the group as a whole. After all, how could we direct it to Hamid if affection remained blocked among everyone else?

Very slowly, very reluctantly, the remaining therapists and guests stood up and shuffled around, in order to form a circle and hold hands.

Suddenly Sonia, the RT, said: 'Let's all hug, holding hands is not enough.' Then she proceeded to hug everyone near her. I was amazed. Sonia is an affectionate but not very huggy woman.

Sue found this all very difficult and half-started to run away. Sensing that she was frightened, and because she was near me, I stopped her and gave her a mild hug. At the same time I could see that the whole group had begun to exchange hugs.

Meanwhile Will had left for the kitchen. Like someone green with envy, he started to complain: 'Why is Hamid getting so much attention?'

George had gone to the kitchen to prepare the milk and honey. This, by the way, is a brew which the guests usually take at night in place of sleeping pills. At my suggestion, and when it is not inappropriate, we may also add a tablespoon of fine brandy. The brandy is an important part of the ritual. Because they can see that an expensive, special brandy has been added, the guests feel special too. The ensuing drink has been good-heartedly called 'The Joe Berke Special'.

Anyway, George made a point of giving Will some of this brew.

Back in the front room, Katie volunteered to take a cup to Hamid. But I proposed we ask Hamid to join the meeting. After all, all the hugs and warmth began after we had focused on helping Hamid to receive and express affection. He had sort of 'got lost', Will's complaint notwithstanding, during all the recent exchanges of goodwill.

So Katie went up to invite him down. A few minutes later she returned to the meeting to let us know that he had gone to bed. It appeared that while we all very agitated, Hamid had calmed down and fallen asleep. Once again I was reminded of the story of Ingrid. While Morty and I were so wound up at the Royal Free, she had wound down.

Nevertheless, everyone asked me to take Hamid some milk and honey. I went upstairs and brought it to him. In fact he was not asleep, just lying quietly on his bed. Hamid took the drink and thanked me in a pleasant, respectful way. He wasn't agitated. He wasn't psychotic.

By now it was 2:30 in the morning and it seemed that the immediate crisis with Hamid had passed. Nobody was suggesting that he had to leave that night, in fact no-one was talking about his having to leave at all.

I was very tired and said good night. In turn I was thanked and allowed to leave without feeling anxious.

But, as I was later told, the evening in fact continued. After I had left, Hamid came downstairs and joined the group of his own accord.

Sonia, who previously couldn't bear to touch him, suggested that they all hug. Hamid demurred, but agreed to hold hands.

Will shook Hamid's hands. The group greeted him and made a place for him. All, including Hamid, helped to clean up. They continued to be huggy. Hamid sported a huge smile. He was amused by the group's affection for him, and said playfully: 'You lot are all mad and gay.'

This statement was not a challenge. Rather it recognized the calm and pleasant mood that pervaded the house. By the early morning everyone drifted off to bed.

It had been a good night. The group had reconstituted itself. The mad behaviour of Hamid as well as that of the therapists and other guests had ceased. Clearly, their psychotic anxieties, and thoughts, or rather lack of thinking, had receded too. All of the residents seemed much more able to regain and contain their own feelings, more or less.

A couple of days later Hamid had his leaving meal. This is a big event for the guest who is finishing his stay, as well as for the whole house. Extra food is prepared, wine is served. Candles are lit. It's a real occasion. The celebration reflects work well done, on everyone's part. There may be joy, but usually there is an air of sadness, too. And, indeed, the house may feel flat and empty for days afterwards.

Hamid's leaving meal was by no means a certainty. He had never previously stayed for dinner at any time at all during his stay. Yet, on the day after the lecture, when asked whether he wanted to forget the meal and leave early he replied, 'Not at all. I can't leave. It's my leaving meal tomorrow.' And indeed he helped plan the dinner and stayed almost to the end. When he did leave, it was uneventful.

Now with hindsight, let's try to consider what took place. As we have seen with Hamid and with Ingrid, psychotic regressions in thinking and behaviour can brew up very quickly when guests are threatened with sadness and depression. Or to put it another way, this can happen whenever guests are threatened by attachment – whether by making friends, or losing friends. Then their capacity to hold depressive tensions can be very poor, and primitive defences against these tensions quickly unfold. I have used the word 'tensions' rather than 'anxieties' for a reason. In reality we are talking about a tense state of mind. This is a mind touched by sadness, loss, frustration, and so on, but which is unable to contain these experiences. The ensuing chaos – should we say madness? – can not only engulf this person, but also others in their immediate social circle.

The consequence of Hamid's stay at the Centre was that he formed an intense attachment to the Centre – both to the therapists and the other guests and to the house itself. The actual process whereby this happened was painful and laborious. In retrospect many of his angry outbursts can be seen to have had to do with his trying to reject the relationships which, concurrently, he was also struggling to establish, or had already established. His final blow-up – the fury and reversion to a prior state of extremely provocative behaviour – occurred when his stay at the Centre was coming to an end. It was a time when he was devastated by feelings of loss. One could equally say that he was devastated by feelings of attachment.

Ingrid, on the other hand, was tormented by the nascent process of forming friendships. This was something that she had never previously been able to accomplish, except in terms of a primitive symbiotic relationship with her mother, or to care-givers in various institutions. After the visit to the Royal Free, however, she was able to carry on in a flat and live with a boy she had met. It was a major accomplishment, although it still required a lot of support from the Centre, and although it did eventually break down. But I think we underestimated the attachments that Ingrid did form at the Centre.

The massive affective outbursts from Hamid and Ingrid initially provoked similar responses on the part of the Centre. The resident therapists closest to them were overwhelmed by panic, rage and despair. These feelings were so powerful that the RTs could not continue to think or act like therapists. Like Hamid and Ingrid, they just wanted to get rid of the threat – that is, the presence of very disturbing guests, experienced as frightening monsters. The concrete experiences were the counterpart of the 'dreaded objects', of sadness and depression, which Hamid and Ingrid were unable to face. Thus, when the therapists at the Centre called for help, it was not to contain or resolve the problem but simply to execute the demons.

It would appear that we acted differently in these two instances. In the case of Hamid we were able to keep him at the Centre and I was able to 'keep my cool'. But in the case of Ingrid we could not manage this, and Morty and I felt obliged to get her out of the house. And subsequently, I felt suffused by panic, and could not think.

On closer examination, however, the reaction of the Centre (and by that I include myself) can be shown to have been similar. In both interventions we acted to expand the group. For Ingrid, this included Morty and the duty psychiatrists at the Royal Free Hospital. For Hamid, this included Dr Thompson, all the guests and all the visitors who accompanied the doctor to the reception. In Hamid's case we also played for time, hoping that this would have an ameliorative effect – which it did. Most significantly, in each of the two interventions we were able to shift the focus of 'bad object' from the person designated as patient to another person.

Certainly, for a brief period at least, the duty psychiatrist became my 'bad object', the one who refused to take my instructions and frustrated my needs. The visiting lecturer served the same function for Hamid, by becoming a focus of anger for people at the Centre. They then neglected to be upset with their primary 'bad boy'.

In fact Dr Thompson is a highly-skilled and very experienced dynamic practitioner, who is very sympathetic towards the work of the Centre. He also favours psychotherapy as a basic part of treating psychotic patients. Certainly it was unfair to embroil him in an emotional maelstrom. He had just come back for a quiet drink. Nonetheless, when the episode blew up, it was very important for us to involve him and for him to become part of the treatment milieu. The doctor, as also, in the hospital setting, the duty psychiatrist, served commendably in the role of surrogate ego – as well as surrogate demon. In so doing, they helped us all to come to our senses.

Both periods of disturbance were essentially ameliorated by a therapeutic milieu that initially had been overwhelmed by chaotic currents, but was later able to reconstitute itself. The result was a strictly limited breakdown, contained by the willingness of the therapists involved to suffer, and by their capacity to ask for help and regain their thinking processes. This enabled the therapists as well as Hamid, Ingrid, and all the guests to discover and recover their sanity and humanity.

Reference

Bion, W.R. (1977) *Learning from Experience.* In *Seven Severants: Four Works of Wilfred R. Bion.* New York: Jason Aronson.

CHAPTER 14

Stepping on the Cracks

Lizzi Payne

A group of excited children play hopscotch dodging the cracks on the pavement; some, footholds secure and directed, triumphantly remain in the game. Others, status at stake and feeling pressurized, lose balance, step on the cracks and are disqualified; outcast, they are on the sidelines, having lost the game. How does this marginalized child deal with disappointment and rejection within itself and its peer group?

In my view this children's game can reflect the unfolding of the individual's life and psychic development. The presence of 'cracks', or more specifically, psychic cracks, is inherent within the human condition. However, variable circumstances and situations, along with particular susceptibilities of the personality, can influence the extent and depth of mark these psychic cracks make on the individual. I refer to cracks in the psyche as splits or fractures within the individual's mind – fragmented yet not fully disintegrated. These psychic cracks may give rise to weakened psychological foundations, which are likely to have a bearing on the psychological, emotional and psychosocial development of the individual's life.

What do I mean by a 'crack'? The Chambers English Dictionary defines crack: 'To give way under strain, torture…To change tone or register suddenly…to boast…to break open, a flaw, a blow…a moment…a friendly chat…'

In this chapter, I would like to examine the metaphor of a crack, exploring its diverse meanings and idiomatic expressions.

However, at this point, I wish to make a distinction between my use of the word crack/split and splitting per se. The crack/split, in this sense, refers to a psychic cleavage or fault line, which appears during an ongoing developmental process. It is therefore not the same as the active process of 'splitting', which is a defensive manoeuvre – an attempt to cope with intense and unbearable ambivalent feelings by separating them and keeping them apart.

What is it that makes one individual step on the cracks while another avoids stepping on the cracks and remains in the game of life, relatively unscathed? Of course, there are the obvious contributing influences of educational and cultural background, familial history, and socio-economic factors, along with a pre-morbid disposition that appears to some degree to affect the possibility and likelihood of cracks being either avoided or stepped on. However, this is not an exhaustive list. I hope to illustrate in this chapter that the way in which psychic cracks are therapeutically worked with (or not, as the case may be) does have serious consequences for the healing capacity of the individual. The title, 'Stepping on the Cracks', refers primarily to an internal act to deepen further the psychic crack or fault line in a destructive way. I see this as an opposition, or an incapacity, to explore the cracks of the psyche: self-destructiveness, raging resentments, shattered senses, broken hopes and dreams – in essence, the fragmented self. 'Stepping on the Cracks' can also refer to inappropriate and counter-therapeutic external interventions, that can be equally damaging to the individual. Cracking down upon the individual may give rise to the formation of deeper crevices and cleavages, possibly causing further breakdown and the eruption of increased damage, destructiveness and psychological debris. Stepping on the cracks of the psyche may invalidate and alienate the individual as a whole within their psychosocial environment. It may even form the start of a psychiatric career. The individual can become stuck, often sinking deeper into a mire of disturbing feelings and self-destructive behaviour, and frequently cracked down upon by the very system that is attempting to offer support.

My aim is to illustrate the way in which psychic cracks are viewed and treated in a psychotherapeutic community using a psychodynamic approach. I will also consider the social and psychological treatment of these cracks within a setting based on a medical model. I will contrast these two very different settings and approaches using a range of clinical vignettes from my therapeutic work within both settings. While both environments have different roles and objectives for the psycho-social treatment of the individual, the distress and disturbance of the individual remains the same regardless of the setting, with both institutions working with people whose cracks have been stepped on in one form or another.

I lived and worked at the Arbours Crisis Centre for three years as a resident therapist (RT) with individuals in extreme states of emotional distress and psychological disturbance. I currently work at the Crisis Centre as a nurse therapist. I also work as a psychodynamically-informed group therapist, on a twenty-one bed acute ward within a psychiatric clinic. The clinic welcomes psychotherapeutic group work within what is predominantly a medical model culture. The patients experience both milieux within the same setting – the generalized psychiatric environment and the more specific group therapy ethos. Participants of group therapy are exposed to the possibility that psychic cracks can be explored meaningfully in addition to being medicated. The struggle to relate to such different disciplines, co-existing within the context of a single ward-environment, does not just belong to the patient. We, too, struggle to find a common language and understanding within our multi-disciplinary staff group. However, in the absence of a group supervisory forum, or personal psychotherapy for doctors and nurses, the value of countertransference information (used as a working tool for the group therapist) can be unconsciously avoided, denied and projected out. The patient may at times be left to carry the sickness of the institution in addition to his or her own illness.

I will begin my illustration with an institutional dynamic, which I will describe as 'Cracking Down'. In the psychiatric clinic I am expected to carry a personal alarm while working with patients in the group setting. If I become too alarmed by a patient to be able to think and respond adequately and/or I feel physically unsafe, I can initiate immediate concrete action and be rescued from such disturbance by a team of 'control and restraint' nurses. The patient is cracked down upon in a very literal way. 'Controlled' (through injected medication) and 'restrained' (through being jumped upon and held down at all angles), 'the disturbance' is removed – all in a matter of seconds. Denied any choice, the patient is taken out of sight, though not out of my mind. By means of injected medication the patient is taken out of his or her own mind, with the crack filled in by tranquillization; there is no opportunity for exploration or expression.

In my view this invasive ritual functions as a social defence against an anxiety about madness. It offers little or no thinking space for assessment of the situation but rather brutally cracks down upon the patient's humanity by violating the psycho-social, interpersonal and emotional aspects of the whole person. Such action can be defended in terms of safety maintenance, yet this profoundly unthinking, mechanistic response of cracking down on the individual's body, mind and spirit has huge repercussions on the psyches of patient and staff alike. This cracking down may also echo the patient's own internal control, restraint and attack, as is evident in self-harming and other similar destructive acts. The internal cracking down can also be reflected externally in attacks against staff and the therapeutic environment, with the violence being projected outwards.

There are occasions, however, when appropriate and considered cracking down can be of immense therapeutic benefit – when it is done in the service of boundary setting and containment of chaos and disorder. There was an occasion at the Crisis Centre when, late at night, the use of a personal alarm would have been welcome in order to preserve everyone's physical safety. 'Damion' was playing his music at midnight in a loud and obtrusive manner. For months he had refused to turn the volume down or turn off the music late at night and continued to avoid engaging in any discussion about this. Eventually, in the absence of any co-operation from him, I did crack down: I took away the electrical lead of his stereo unit. This alarmed him and provoked a furious and terrorizing reaction. He became physically and verbally threatening, he followed us and eventually grabbed the lead back from me. Was I insensitive? And did I take too much of a 'lead', or did a considered and therapeutic crack down lead to the house being more contained? With no medication to sedate him with, no control and restraint rescue team, the only hope was that the terrified group, including Damion, could come together and think about the meaning of their experience. This was in fact what happened. Rather than raise alarm bells, expel the real or perceived threat and the carrier of the disturbance, the group was able to offer a space to reflect and listen to the alarms that could not be sounded but only experienced.

On other occasions, however, considered therapeutic crack down is ineffective; we are not able to contain and manage a guest at the Crisis Centre and, regretfully, we ask the guest to leave. It is important that we recognize our limitations and are prepared to implement the decision for the guest's benefit as well as the Centre's. And we are then left with a plethora of institutional and personal cracks to review in order to understand the reasons for a therapeutic stay's breaking down. On still other occasions we are unable to contain a guest and have to send them to hospital for a short time. We are not omnipotent, and, when necessary, we have to crack down on our therapeutic zeal and ambition, and recognize that hospital can be an important and necessary container that secures life. In reality, it has kept some of our deeply disturbed guests from killing themselves.

In the hospital setting a different kind of cracking down exists, which can impact adversely on the depth and quality of the staff–patient relationship. A quick turnover ensures minimal opportunity for the development of therapeutic relationships which hold and contain, with staff inadvertently stepping on the cracks of their patients' psyches. These cracks may be papered over, however, and the reduction of symptoms can give the appearance of psychological work having been achieved. The inadequacies of an under-resourced system, and the lack of skilled supervision and appropriate training, can produce a defensive structure that guards against, controls, pathologizes and, at times, even punishes what are thought to be unacceptable phantasies and associated behaviour. This produces a distancing from unbearable exposure to the patients' suffering. Treating symptoms only in an over-crowded ward can evoke a sense of disillusionment and reinforce a disabling institutional despair. Within this environment subjective experience can be devalued or invalidated, with experiential suffering being treated solely as illness, and the meaning of depression and psychosis being lost for staff and patient alike. In addition, there can be tremendous persuasion from the patient's own harsh super-ego, as well as from the very structure of the institution itself, to crack down and step on these human experiences. The psychic equilibrium of the staff group can be profoundly disturbed by the anxiety that exposure to and management of psychoses presents. For anxieties in hospital can equally be dealt with by a structure, embedded in concrete defence and avoidance. The nursing office door, often shut, is one such defence, shutting down on the enmaddened world of both patient and staff, and shielding each from the other. The firmly closed door precludes the acknowledgement of intense anxieties, projections and disturbance.

Faced with similar problems, the Crisis Centre uses different rituals of cracking down as a way of dealing with intolerable anxiety. Isabel Menzies (1970, p.78) suggests: 'The success and viability of a social institution are intimately connected with the techniques it uses to contain anxiety.' The Centre attempts to contain anxiety through the provision of skilled group and individual supervision. In addition every RT is required to be in intensive psychoanalytic psychotherapy to help the anxiety to be processed through reflection and understanding. However, while attempting to contain anxiety through understanding and exploration, the Centre is also capable of inadvertently shutting the door on disturbance and anxieties. We may not spend hours writing copious clinical notes as may be required in the traditional psychiatric setting. However, we do take note of the transference, projection and splitting mechanisms in a multitude of supervisory meetings; and exceptionally, situations do arise where 'talking about' (our guests) can become more important than 'being with'. This can be used as an organizational defence and may indicate our difficulty with containing our own anxieties adequately. And yet, there may be fears of and resistance to both 'being with' and 'thinking about' our guests, without the one having to compromise or conflict with the other. Effective change requires analysis of the common anxieties and unconscious collusions underlying our defences, which can be challenging. It can give rise to primitive anxieties, which lead us consciously, and unconsciously, to crack down through projection and avoidance of our own anxieties.

The presence of psychic cracks may, however, be used as an impetus for change and healing through the provision of sensitive exploration and understanding. I refer to this process as *'Cracking Open'*. However suffering is viewed, as pathological or as an opportunity to gently crack open the meaning of experience, it poses a challenge.

Cracks in the psyche are not solely confined to our guests. Being in the position of offering a sanctuary for those in extreme states of anguish does not necessarily provide immunity from the opening of one's own psychic cracks. For the RT, living at close quarters with seriously disturbed individuals, entering and exploring the deep crevices of his or her own psychic cracks in personal psychotherapy is vital and deserved. Indeed, it is considered an essential component of life at the Centre.

There were times, especially at the beginning of my experience as a RT, when I would long for a set of rules and regulations, therapeutic policies and procedures to contain my own anxiety. I recall how on the morning on my first day I locked myself out of my bedroom in my dressing gown. Was I 'allowed' to go downstairs in such attire?, I asked myself. I would have, in my own home, but how could the Crisis Centre be my home? A curious ambiguity and confusion lay between my professional therapeutic role and my being there as an ordinary human being. I had some concept of a shared community life and how to live in a house and some experience of working with people therapeutically. Yet, I did not know how to live with and be alongside people in such extreme distress in a formal residential therapeutic setting, where I shared the same living space. This was the struggle for me as an RT; concealing one's cracks for long was impossible and, yet, to crack open one's defences and vulnerabilities in a premature or a forceful way could be counter-therapeutic. In my view, and as I was challenged to begin to discover that day, to hold the balance and be an authentic therapeutic presence means extending beyond role – beyond formulaic responses and set therapeutic procedures or protocol. It is bringing one's entire self, 'cracks and all', to the therapeutic setting and the relationships within it.

In contrast to most psychiatric clinics, overall emphasis is placed upon the therapeutic nature of the relationships. The RTs are encouraged to think symbolically, using their countertransference to inform and aid their understanding of the guests. In addition to assisting the individual in finding a firmer psychological foundation, we also make use of the group's ego strength and capacity to contain and heal, providing as it often does a much-needed emotional scaffolding while psychological excavation into the cracks is in progress.

Sometimes *going crackers* and becoming *the crackpot* may not be confined to the guests. The RT endeavours to provide a consistent therapeutic presence, coping with and working through the transference and countertransference implications of living and working with extremely disturbed people. However, the RT also has to bear anxiety and attacks on thinking and linking in the service of containing the guests' thoughts and feelings. The object of intense projections, the RT can at times find it hard to distinguish who is more crackers – the guest or himself (herself). The guests equally tolerate and make use of the idiosyncrasies of the RT, expertly homing in on the RT's personal cracks with skilful precision for the purpose of projective identification.

I recall one of my guest's persecutory and punishing attitude to me – demanding she be given a different RT, furiously complaining to the Centre director about me, insisting it was outrageous of me to go away on holiday. She would terrorize me when I came out of supervision, provocatively pouncing on me, demanding to know how I should be using supervision more effectively in my work with her. (This was my question as well as hers…!) This guest spent many of her team meetings making accusations about me, taunting me and humiliating me in quite brutal ways, while the team leader remained idealized in her mind. It was hard to withstand this persistent and consistent barrage of attacks. At times, I was unable to do this, giving way to tears of hopelessness and inadequacy after the team meetings. Oblivious to the cracks in her own psyche, she was unable to experience any anger, self-blame, loss, despair and sense of hopelessness for herself. She could not but disown her own state of psychotic disturbance by projecting it into me and persecuting me. I had to become the crackpot, the mad one. Mirroring her psychotic mind, my thinking would at times become concrete, and rather than explore her cracks I felt tempted, reactively, to step over and on not just her psychotic cracks but her entire self. I regard this as a state of mutual projective identification in which both of us became locked, both assuming the role of crackpot.

Another guest, 'Annie', had been sexually abused by both her parents. She arrived with a plethora of severe self-harming rituals in a desperate attempt to avoid feeling and thinking, preferring instead to act and react. She was intelligent, good looking, powerful and seductive.

On one occasion, early on in my experience as a RT, Annie awoke me at 3 a.m. feeling suicidal. We sat together, myself half-asleep, wishing for a 'daytime head' to think with. I longed for the protection of an institution, where I could hide behind a professional mask. She had written a suicide letter. She told me of the string of past illicit love affairs with unavailable heterosexual women, one of whom was a therapist, then stated she had fallen in love with me at our first meeting. I felt disturbed and uneasy. It was the dead of night, and I was alone with a woman who wanted me to seduce her and initiate sexual contact. Externally calm and thoughtful, internally struggling with feelings of terror and shock, I wanted to push her away. However, I felt there was a 'her' who was longing for a different kind of intercourse – an emotional intercourse, that would be characterized by psychological holding and sensitive understanding.

Annie's nightmarish disclosures shed new light on our work in the team. It seemed she was desperate to negate the terrifying reality of a therapeutic relationship with me, preferring an all-too-familiar eroticized one. To a part of her, therapeutic holding and care was experienced as abusive. That night she wanted to test me out with the seduction routine so familiar to her: would I perpetuate the abuse she was so terrified of and yet so familiar with? At other times she acknowledged phantasies of being the perpetrator, locking me up in a cage, raping me and bringing in a group of men to abuse me. She was simultaneously contemptuous and desirous of me. On other occasions she wanted to be carried in my womb as a developing foetus, wholly dependent and reliant on my provision of a lifeline.

Given her traumatic history as victim and perpetrator, it seemed she had had to disown her own genitalia and project out this part object – unwanted, contemptuously attacked and abused – into me. These psychotic phantasies, although indicative of a state of mind in which she appeared to be cracking up, were successfully held and contained within the therapeutic team meetings. In time, gradually and voluntarily, Annie began to exchange the props of her life – the razor blades, tablets and alcohol – for a bounded therapeutic relationship, which could often be frustrating and disappointing but which was one that became good enough.

Needless to say, however, the impact of these phantasies did spill into the life of the house. She became jealous of my lifeline, my friends, who would come and visit me. On occasions, she cut her wrist when I was about to go out, angrily demonstrating that even if she couldn't control me, she could at least cut out her envious feelings instead. I felt invaded and caught up with her. Enmeshed, I wanted to escape from her powerful presence inside me, for fear she would engulf me with her needs.

Living with this level of psychotic projection was a struggle. I had a fundamental liking for Annie and, almost inspite of herself, she was prepared to explore her tortuous cracks. In addition, therapy and supervision aided my understanding and strengthened the survival of my psychic backbone. From being the crackpot, Annie was able to integrate disowned parts of herself that had been got rid of through projection. She was not medicated, and neither was I kept away from her ('taken off her case') a familiar and often preferred approach within traditional psychiatric settings. Sharing daily life, living under the same roof together, and witnessing one another in all psychological weathers did challenge her phantasy life and add considerable authenticity and realism to the cultivation of a therapeutic relationship.

One Christmas, when 'Cracking Up', or going mad, was not the sole domain of the individual, we were indeed able to witness this process ripping into the group psyche. Most team leaders were away; I felt depressed, exhausted and resentful, wondering why I was a RT at all. There was an all-pervasive aggressive and potentially violent atmosphere in the house. The RT group was fragmented; we were hostile towards one another. One guest had badly cut herself with a razor blade, while another guest appeared drowsy and confused. An empty box of 24 paracetamol tablets lay hidden under her bed. It was getting late, with our anxiety increasing with our tiredness. We found ourselves placed in an impossible position, the guest whom we assumed to have taken the overdose refusing to attend the casualty department. Despite an impromptu house meeting to mobilize the group's available ego strength, we were still left not understanding the reason for these events. Christmas and New Year was laden with meaning and not experienced as a time of good will. In fact, it was a time of ill will – to one and all.

My guest 'Debbie' called me a 'fucking bitch' and stormed upstairs, letting me hear from within the midst of her hurled abuse the words: 'What do I fucking have to do to get your attention?' Much discussion about meaning and management ensued. It was three o'clock in the morning before I finally retired to my bedroom exhausted. Unusually for me, I locked the bedroom door in order to draw a boundary and re-define my own space. My foot felt something cold and wet in my bed. Horrified, I found red paint smeared all over my sheets. This felt like a deadly violation; a murderous rape. I was shocked and traumatized. I wanted to punish my guest, take revenge. My personal space had been violated as well as my internal world. I hated my guest, the Crisis Centre and myself for being in this abusive position. Perhaps the provocation was Christmas – the time I had with the other guests. Certainly, her forceful and invasive Christmas present had succeeded in getting my attention now. She was determined to penetrate my nights if not my days – my personal space if not the group time. That night the Crisis Centre felt untherapeutic and uncontaining. Even my own bed was not safe.

Cracking up and becoming the enraged crackpot over night, I did not want to understand how Debbie had been feeling. I wanted to react, retaliate and punish her with my aggression and sadism. Debbie initially denied responsibility and was pleased I was suffering. She hoped I would suffer more and accused me of being false and uncaring with the eyes of the devil. She spoke of her jealousy of the other guests and wanted to get inside me in one way or another.

The following day my fellow RT helped me change the stained red sheets and turn over the mattress. It was more than the mattress that turned over. This savage attack marked a new beginning; something remarkable had been given birth to and delivered to our group. The birth of a deeper understanding extending beyond what was a violation.

I came to see the attack as an opportunity to learn about my own denied aggression and of the RT group as a whole. It was not just Debbie's murderous rage but the group's disowned cracking up that she carried. It was important she did not assume the role of scapegoat. She found my depressed feelings intolerable and wanted to kill them off, which echoed my own wish to expel and avoid them. We, the RTs, were unable to deal with our aggressive and hostile feelings for one another; the guest group held it for us – encased, as we were, in a house full of suicidal persuasions and cutting attempts within an all-pervasive hostile atmosphere. Once we were able to make the necessary conscious connection to own this unwanted aggression rather than project it into the group receptacle, it was no longer necessary for the guest group to hold it for us.

Debbie and I both survived and came to a greater liking for one another. She left when her stay was completed without saying goodbye. It was too painful for her. However, she did return to say goodbye some months later with a gift in her hand, a photo diary of trees. Perhaps this did symbolize her own psychological unfurling and growth – the laying down of some tentative roots.

Psychic cracks may also function as openings which provide the individual with meaning and new opportunities for change. I wish to use the metaphor of the *Crack of Dawn* to describe such an unfolding process. I will consider a contrasting approach to the clinical handling of an erotic transference that occurred in relation to a patient at the psychiatric clinic.

Susie was adopted, subsequently abandoned by her adoptive mother, and brought up by her biological uncle and his second wife. Sexually abused by him and unable to make sense of her experience, she became heavily dependent on cocktails of illicit drugs, made numerous suicide attempts and bodily mutilations. She had also had a string of affairs, including one with a therapist whom she had met in a professional capacity. She was homosexual in her sexual orientation.

We noted in the early days of her attendance of groups that there was a marked correlation between my availability and her presence in the sessions. Soon, she began to hint to the clinic staff that there was someone she especially liked. It was difficult for us, a multi-disciplinary group, amid amusement and intrigue, really to consider what this might actually mean for our patient as these hints were being taken by us at face value. Her comments were viewed only as flirtatious and titillating. Susie began to use my group therapist colleague like her adoptive mother, disclosing her desire for the primary object that she wanted to merge with and be held by. Similarly to the dynamics with her real mother, she was unable to let me know about her desire. Setting up and clearing the rooms with me, she became like mother's little helper. One day, as I was leaving the ward, she thrusted a letter into my hand, hoping I might be 'allowed' to take it but worried that I would refuse her. I was placed in an impossible position. Not to take the letter would reinforce Susie's sensitivity to rejection and abandonment, yet, equally, to take it (at face value), outside of the group setting, where one could not work with it, felt untherapeutic and even collusive. I was in a double bind that surely echoed her own experience. I took the letter. It spoke of her warm and loving feelings, her wish to talk more, and a fear that I would be repulsed and not speak to her again.

It was five days before I would next be on the ward. Susie had ensured we could not work with it directly but would rather be obliged to deal with it through the safety of her 'adopted' mother therapist, to whom she was attached. I spoke with the nursing team. Unfortunately, her letter was cracked down upon and viewed as 'inappropriate', 'unacceptable' and 'had to be put a stop to'. She was, however, able to be held and contained by her 'adoptive mother', who took care of her and held the thinking space with her.

It was crucial that her seduction was not acted upon but equally that she was not rejected by me. In the following week's group session, group members spoke in terms of the struggle to communicate with one another, wondering among them how feelings get conveyed. There were several questions on my mind: was I to hold the family secret with my being privy to something the rest of the group was unaware of? Was that part of the test and seduction? Would I expose her out of my own needs and inability to contain them within myself? To Susie's credit, in the women's group she was able to speak at length about the letter, separating out her issues and underlying motivations. She cried about the loss of her real mother.

When Susie finally left the ward, she was able to say a meaningful goodbye and later wrote a postcard of gratitude to the ward. She had not returned to drugs, had made contact with her primary family, and was developing good relations with her mother. Amid the backdrop of troubled skies, a new crack of dawn had broken through, brightening the horizon and symbolizing a new beginning.

While this experience was containing enough for Susie, it did highlight the difference between the approach of the ward staff and that of the group therapists. It gave rise to the realization of the necessity for further work within the multi-disciplinary staff team in order to appreciate and understand our contrasting approaches. This is a challenging process for us all and poses many questions that remain unanswered.

Expressing creativity and spontaneity is essentially healthy and thera-peutic. Exploring psychic cracks in this way is a vital ingredient in the healing process. Guest and resident therapist 'Share the Crack' through the use of humour, laughter and play. The benefits of the intensive psychother-apy tend to manifest and bear fruit within the informal context. Glimpses of guests being spontaneous, playing, being creative, and, most impor-tantly, healing their cracks with laughter, abound. Living at the Crisis Centre holds some beautiful moments that can inspire and renew the spirit. A severely depressed guest may burst into peals of spontaneous laughter; a fragmented hostile and destructive group may muster their creative juices and, almost inspite of themselves, play charades with hilarity and sponta-neity. I recall times when we have all impersonated one another, highlight-ing well-known idiosyncrasies! Interacting socially through the creative medium of play is essentially therapeutic and necessary in the art of becoming a human being.

On one occasion I recall receiving some personal news and becoming upset in front of the guest group. A guest, who rarely thinks to extend any consideration to another human being, was able to extend a gesture of con-solation by putting her arm around me in a warm and affectionate way. Witnessing my distress harnessed concern and care that was rare for her. For many guests this kind of experience affords an opportunity to be moved enough to reach out to another human being.

A shared intention to work with, and understand, the powerful com-munications of our guests at the Crisis Centre lies at the heart of our work of *Healing the Cracks*. However, living together for guest and RT can never-theless be simultaneously heaven and hell, touching and infuriating, tender and hostile. The psychic survival of RTs relies upon the understand-ing and holding of the team leader group. Yet team leaders are not them-selves immune to the disturbance of the house, nor to the projective processes of splitting and psychotic thinking, and the resultant maddening behaviour. At times, when the wider group is locked in crisis or individual guest teams are caught up in transference enactments and projective identi-fications, we struggle with one another to unpick some of the processes. During these times, the guest group may unconsciously carry the burden of our own struggles, similarly to the dynamics in hospital.

Without the stable and supportive presence of the team leader group, and art and movement therapists, it would become virtually impossible for the RT group to maintain its capacity to reside with the guests therapeutically. It would undoubtedly crack up – fall down deep crevices into defence and reaction, concrete thinking, regression and, sometimes, destructive acting out. All of these processes can occur now and then, even when we are functioning as a good enough group. Effective teamwork, at all levels, is an imperative. There are times when we struggle with interpersonal dynamics in the wider staff group, cracking down on one another through competitiveness, envious attacks and unspoken rivalries. It can be difficult for us to explore the Centre's institutional cracks, despite our valiant attempts.

This said, however, we are committed to doing our best to support and contain one another in order to maximize our capacity to help our guests go beyond the madness. With a commonly shared intention, and while fostering hope and perseverance, our group continues to survive, against a clinical backdrop of extreme disturbance. We struggle, and persevere in adversity, with an underlying conviction to be of assistance in the healing of our guests' cracks, and we do this ultimately through offering what is essential to us, namely our humanity.

To conclude, I have used the title of this chapter, 'Stepping on the Cracks', to refer to an internal opposition to exploring or an incapacity to explore the cracks of the psyche which appear during an ongoing developmental process. As I have shown, this internal state can be reinforced by counter-therapeutic interventions. I have used various detailed clinical vignettes to illustrate these issues. Using the metaphor of a crack in its diverse meanings, I have highlighted the way in which psychic cracks are viewed and treated at the Crisis Centre. I have compared and contrasted the social and psychological treatment of these cracks within a medical model setting. From the clinical material presented I can conclude that the type of medical, psychological and socio-therapeutic interventions made does have major implications for individuals' capacities for healing and further integration. The presence of psychic cracks, for us all, can act as an impetus for change and healing with the provision of sensitive exploration and understanding, as, indeed, we attempt to provide at the Crisis Centre. This exploratory process can lead beyond the madness, to new opportunities for life enhancement, creative change and the development of meaningful relationships.

Reference

Menzies, I. (1970) *Containing Anxiety in Institutions.* London: Free Association Books.

CHAPTER 15

Doors at the Crisis Centre, Doors in the Mind

Kate Hardwicke

In his book *The Lion, the Witch and the Wardrobe* (1950) C.S. Lewis creates a separate, transitional world discovered by children stepping through a door in a wardrobe. He brings to my mind how the experience of loss through separation from parents draws on an imagined and enriched picture in the minds of the child-evacuees. In the story, Narnia represents an internal fantasy world, free from the 'real world' half of this separation. The worlds are separated by the door of the wardrobe, which helps to describe an attempt to integrate these two worlds, conveyed by how the children begin to reconcile themselves with their loss.

Lewis understood that this Narnia world was both magical in its beautiful, brilliant whiteness and deadly in its cold, unfeeling empire, devoid of relationships. What he illustrates through his metaphor is how the traumatized mind can split. One part takes refuge in an unreachable place, free of the devastating impact of trauma by the turning of phantasy into concreteness; while another part struggles with its psychosocial reality. In this way, Lewis could be describing a psychotic world. The richness of this metaphor drew me to what doors represent: a functional shutting in and shutting out, also demonstrating in another way, perhaps, an internal splitting in the mind.

I worked for two-and-a-half years as a resident therapist (RT) at the Arbours Crisis Centre. For the guests the Crisis Centre is a new world, where embarking on a journey towards pulling together split-off and lost parts of themselves is an experience that it is hoped can be had. Now, I see the transitional aspect of Lewis' story as in some way analogous to my experience of living at the Crisis Centre. The textures of the realness of fur coats inside the wardrobe that bury Lucy as she makes her way through them, bewildered by the space that has no back to it. She is both retreating into the comfort of the softness of motherliness, soothing herself as she imagines she is close to her mother's smell, and she is struggling ahead, searching for the parameters of the wardrobe until she feels the crunching of something soft but alien beneath her feet. She is making her way through and out of a contained space of sensual familiarity while being drawn further into a world of conflict, cold reality and intrigue.

Confusion and irritation in relation to the multitude of doors, and how to negotiate them, may exasperate new arrivals at the Crisis Centre. Rules are uncertain and not made immediately clear. The lack of rigidity about which rooms, through which doors, access is permissible can leave new guests feeling as if they are navigating an obstacle course. Sometimes they feel left to flounder: 'What are the bloody house rules?' This is a somewhat contrasting experience to that of a hospital setting, from which many have come. Hospital rules tend to be clear. Patients know where they are and what to expect from the system. The living-in nature of the Crisis Centre and its smallness allow for something considerably more intimate to evolve between staff and guest and for things to function in a very different way. The fact that there is no shift system and that it is a small residential setting does mean that time between people can be extensive, initiating something both exposing and baffling to those whose previous experience is that the divide between staff and themselves is clear. The Crisis Centre is neither a family home nor a hospital.

The house contains thirty-five doors in all. Beyond the practical necessity for doors, their symbolic function creates scope for thinking about what separates and what draws together aspects of what we might want to avoid and what we might want to hold on to. Even if we take a few obvious ideas about what doors provide – private space, division, exclusion, access, rites of passage – what is conjured up in my mind is a parallel internal fabric of compartments that both store and get rid of unprocessed feelings. If we can store away what feels unbearable then we would seem to have a solution to our difficulties. An even better option would be to store them so far away in our minds that we don't even know that this is what we've done with them. In Lewis' story Lucy, I think, was taking us on a journey in her mind. We follow her through the wardrobe as she fumbles through the furs in the dark, and as she is reminded of her mother. It is almost as if at the moment of this painful reminder we are led out and beyond the ordinariness of this pain and transported into a phantasy place that wipes out the real quality of a sense of loss and replaces it with an adventure in a new landscape, ruled by a heartless white witch (the bad mother). This is evidence, perhaps, of the fact that to the internal view the reality of feelings of separation, if left unprocessed, is a reality to be avoided; separation under these circumstances can all too easily become equated with death. Relationships are understandably jettisoned as a result since they are cluttered with obstacles of rejection that require expert navigation, and the internal urge is to avoid them.

Perhaps in a more direct and less pathological way, doors can be a useful way of communicating feelings that are difficult to address and put into words. This is perhaps what guests are battling with. An internal world of compartments may reflect ways in which aspects of experience are split and kept separate, or locked up. For many who come to the Crisis Centre, compartmentalizing is a way of managing an internal world – a system that protects them from feelings that they fear will be overwhelming. Arriving at a house where few doors are locked can feel threatening to the psychotic part that wants to keep the mind rigidly compartmentalized for fear of being taken over. This is perhaps reflected inside the house, in the way guests position themselves and use the space. Hiding away in a room for long periods might be a way of managing a fear of bad thoughts getting acted upon in the house; it might also communicate the fear of being forgotten about.

Doors help to negotiate space in the house. To find one's own safe space, or to take all the space where there are no demarcations, or to endanger space by leaving the front door open, are on some level very basic ways of communicating one's needs. Whether or not these needs can be explored in a less concrete way is perhaps dependent on whether the relationships in the house and the struggles within them can be recognized as a resource – something different from and less fearful than the damaging experience of the past.

In concrete terms the character of doors at the Centre is as follows. While most doors at the Centre do not have locks, there is a locked office protecting confidential material (and a locked cellar storing historical files, also used to keep non-perishable food and other domestic necessities). Only the RTs have access to this cellar, which can exasperate guests, who may see it as the store of good things not to be had immediately or by them but reserved for the immediate gratification of the RTs. The medication cabinet is locked and out of the way inside a cupboard in a consulting room with soundproofed double doors! A registration rule ensures that medication is locked up and that no-one shall store medication in individual rooms. Guests are expected to ask for their medication. Therapists' supervision meetings exclude guests, while the guest group may exclude therapists. Although guests' doors do not have locks, bedrooms can only be entered without permission when there is serious cause for concern.

Doors often divide groups or draw them together in contained spaces. The different spaces which define the social aspect of the household makes provision for structure, house meetings, team meetings, art and movement therapies, clinical meetings and weekly domestic meetings, in which the group works out timetables for shopping and cooking.

Through the wardrobe door into Narnia the reader enters the enchanted world of frozen beauty and stillness. This powerful, shimmering white landscape draws the children in the story to an illusion of safety. In the psychotic mind doors may be closed partially or altogether. This might be to keep the psychotic part safe and intact, for fear of being either engulfed or annihilated. Or it might be to keep the sane part safe from the threat of being taken over. Such fears of engulfment and annihilation often pass to and from guest and therapist. By allowing something to evolve between them, however, and between individual members of the guest group, doors can open up new understandings for a self that fears an ordinary experience of relating.

A transitional experience is particularly hard on guests who come to the house directly from hospital. The hope is that the professionals involved can help form a bridge between hospital and the Centre. However, it may be that this process doesn't run smoothly and exacerbates difficulties the individual has in tackling this transitional move. It may be that a form of 'sectarian defensiveness' divides the settings, like separating parents who tussle over the children. If communication breaks down between the Centre and the referring agency, a culture of blame emerges which tends to bind the professionals in their respective approaches. Acknowledging the different systems of treatment and being open to dialogue between different approaches ought to create a pathway to a joint way of working and of the containing of extremely disturbing behaviour. But this shared aim sometimes gets lost in a struggle to be the only rightful resource. It is like the psychotic state of mind in which omnipotent control is used to safeguard and defend against any experience of relating, for fear that the person will be overwhelmed by his or her need for the other.

Why is joint working difficult to achieve? One view of the psychiatric model is that it attempts to confine the symptomatic behaviour, diagnosing a pathology that is dangerous and unwanted. This reflects the power of the destructiveness of the psychotic part of the mind, which is subsequently reacted to and subdued, alleviating the anxiety of the professionals involved and confirming in the mind of their patient their own terrifying omnipotence. In this sense the psychotic part is validated as an all-annihilating and palpable force that requires immediate restraint.

At the Crisis Centre there is an attempt to open a door to an encounter with the psychosis. It is an attempt to make sense of it, demystify it and, as it is hoped, integrate it with the guest's other, non-psychotic states of mind. But this sounds rather too ideal, and I think it is important to make clear that for the most part an RT's experience is like being in the dark. Hope and optimism can get lost in a stew of powerful feelings of despair and anxiety. In my experience it was above all in these times of despair that I would feel part of a troubled process a guest might be sharing with me. While the hope of connecting together split feelings could be held onto by the group as a whole, sometimes at the Centre, there could be the danger of assuming a position of professional omnipotence, where thinking about and acknowledging limitations gets lost.

Hospitals can provide a physical holding. This might mean a physically secured admission, according to policies under the Mental Health Act. Guests are invited to the Crisis Centre, however, to find out whether a transition into a more symbolic holding experience is possible, and whether they can begin to use psychoanalytic psychotherapy. This arrival is often frightening and a critical time for the whole group.

In the Lewis story, the white witch possesses the magical allure of power and beauty, in which the children appear to wish to be cocooned. The disappointment when this fails to materialize propels them into a crisis, as each child deals with this new enchanted world in a different way; but eventually, enlisting each other's help, they discover in their encounters their own capacities to process the elements of their struggle.

Holding meetings with the guests in order to open a dialogue generated by the living experience in the house arouses feelings often connected with past troubles and new feelings of attachment. Although, as

I have indicated, the Crisis Centre is not a place without doors, where anything goes, new guests are not quite sure what to make of the process of negotiating boundaries for themselves. Compared to hospital, the Centre can feel like a neglectful or even cruel place because on some level each guest wants to work and be part of the house. This means owning a wish to take responsibility and to choose to remain in a more or less open house. All guests possess a key to the front door. Doors can lead you to other people who are there essentially because they are prepared to listen, talk, think and make an emotional connection with you.

Although some guests might feel that hospital has ensnared them in order to keep them alive, the Crisis Centre can become for them an equally negative place – a place that allows them to die by not keeping them shut in. This is why guests often express the wish that RTs would respond like nurses who can provide medication and take away the bad feelings. This wish might also be communicated through cutting, where the immediate and first response is a nurse's response: to ensure that the cut is assessed and appropriately dealt with. But beyond addressing the practicalities in contact of this kind the next consideration would be the exploration of why contact could only be made in this way – through what seems to be the cutting-off of feelings to do with needing emotional contact. Hospital, with its secure setting, is seen as a good parent, keeping the guest physically safe. The Crisis Centre, on the other hand, is denigrated by the psychotic part of the guest, threatened by the thought of emotional holding through relationships and by talking about what is happening within.

From this perspective it is understandable that arriving at the Crisis Centre should be an inflammatory experience to the psychotic mind. As therapists, we are often invited by the guests not to think but to bear and act from anxiety. A guest arrives clinging to a familiar and particular way of dealing with internal splits. For those who communicate through acting out or projective identification, talking and exploring these splits makes little sense when the idea of contact, internally and externally, is the very thing that generates anxiety and that is to be avoided.

I should like to illustrate these points with three clinical vignettes. The first describes my experience of a guest whom I felt needed to show me concretely her wish to 'get inside'. My second illustrates how a guest communicated his distress by sabotaging his life and 'throwing himself out'.

The third describes something of the struggle to 'arrive, stay and move on' – in this case, to one of the Arbours' Communities.

'Java', an Asian woman in her late thirties, came to the Centre for a three-month stay. She had come from living in a shared hostel, following a long period of hospitalization. She had been readmitted to hospital because of the extent of cutting to her legs. Self-cutting had been Java's coping strategy for some years. Her recent cutting was, she said, precipitated by an argument with a female member of staff at the hostel. This revealed something of her difficulty in negotiating intimacy and distance in relationships. When we first met her for a consultation at the Centre, she told us in a frank and measured way that her mother had sexually abused her. She and her mother had shared a room until she was sixteen, which is when she managed to leave home. Her ready disclosure of this experience suggested to us a testing both of our capacity to bear this knowledge and also of that of another abuser inside her, and raised the question of whether it was possible for intimacy to become a different experience.

Java would wake me nightly by coming into my room, standing by my bed, and shouting my name. Although I did manage to encourage her to knock on the door, her nightly visits, her demands, and my involuntary acceptance of them came to be a focus of dread. I felt abused by her. This just seemed to reinforce the view that doors did not exist in her mind, and their existence in the house was experienced by her only as an experience of exclusion, of getting shut out. She was being shut out, in her mind, by me. She wanted to live in my room with me. Boundaries did not make sense except as excluding barriers which needed to be removed. At the same time Java seemed to be making sure that I would eject her from my space. It was as if her way of getting inside me, by entering my room at night, was the only way she could feel alive but abused. These nightly intrusions became fraught with issues of how to make sense to her whose space was whose, without simply resorting to keeping the door concretely locked.

With the help of the other RTs, I worked out a system of calling on them for support in the night when I was called on by Java. Together we were able to open the door to thinking about what was happening, rather than resorting to my solitary attempts to keep the door shut. This certainly helped to relieve my fear and anxiety, and it seemed to relieve Java of her own fear and anxiety of having the capacity to do me damage and turn me into an unthinking and unyielding parental figure.

It was as if my room, phantasized by her as the parental room, had become a concrete representation of her need to be in the mother. At the same time, getting inside was a way of turning me into the zombie it seemed she had become through her experience of abuse. Her opening my door was, in a very concrete way, her way of showing me what it was like to feel like her: invaded and intruded upon. This was an essential means of communicating to me the level of her abusive experience. In this sense, by my experiencing something of her projections, she was engaging me in a dynamic which could either turn into a further abusive experience, where I became the abused and abuser and close the door on thinking, or could open the way to a more symbolic communication, in which we might experience the need to begin to understand her need for help, in a thoughtful way.

Although Java completed her stay, and wanted to return for a second stay, funding could not be raised for her. She was re-admitted to hospital.

'Colin' came to the Crisis Centre for a four-week assessment. He had had many hospital admissions for severe self-harming and suicide attempts. He experienced terrifying nightmares that hospital staff had had to awaken him from. When Colin was very young, his cousin reported an experience of sexual abuse to the police, but was not believed. Later, this cousin became very ill and died. Colin felt guilty for not having backed up his cousin's statement to the police.

Colin was a fifty-five-year-old father. He seemed to relive the horrible abusive events of his childhood through nightmares. The nightmares turned into literal experiences. His relationships with others, including his children, were extremely destructive. His children were also witnesses to his vicious and brutal attacks on himself. As an RT, living with him became a nightmare. It was difficult for both of us to distinguish what was a dream and what was waking life. There was no door between his reality and his phantasy world.

It became as if the therapist's part was to participate in Russian roulette. On the one hand, Colin was afraid that if we RTs were not a constant physical presence, we were not guarding him from himself. On the other, to be a psychical presence was felt to be an intrusion and a threat. Encouraging thinking was for him further evidence of neglect and passive participation in his deadly world. He became enraged at not being physically restrained or prevented from leaving the Centre, and for not being woken from his fitful nightmares. He tried to insist on a carte-blanche invitation to walk into his room and wake him whenever we heard him shouting in the night. But to think about this ambivalent message – his need to be held and abused at the same time – was, for him, apparently impossible. Thinking about this ambivalent need inflamed the psychotic him into preferring death to such humiliation. We were left with the task of containing for him his wish to leave and his wish to stay at the Centre.

Although we have had other guests with similar patterns of behaviour, Colin's internal condition was a dire one. His dilemma was either that he did not speak out and was left with the nightmare of terrible abuse and the sadistic indifference of people watching without doing anything, or that he attempted to take care of himself by putting himself in the hands of a 'terrible nurse', who one minute smiles and the next minute gives him a lethal overdose. This murderous internalized nurse was in competition with the professionals who were treating him, trying always to prove them wrong. Any attachment was considered lethal and further measures taken to stop it. In phantasy, the problem was dealt with by the murderous nurse killing the patient.

When Colin withdrew into a dissociated frame of mind, shouting out to himself, we would try to speak to him. One time he ran for the front door. One of the RTs tried to barricade the door to stop him from leaving. Eventually he returned to the room but quickly fell back into a dissociated state and repeated his attempt to leave. As we responded physically again we also realized the madness in our actions. What were we trying to do? Something was going on where we were pulled into a re-enactment of forcing him to stay and at the same time responding to what could be his need to be forced to stay.

The dilemma within Colin was also reflected by whether he could allow himself to stay and have a relationship with us: how could he do this without the attachment turning into an abusive experience? What the psychotic part of Colin was proposing was that the only way to keep him safe was by imposing restraint, a wish that would have to come from the outside. This would mean our responding to him in a preventative way or leaving him completely – in the murderer's hands, as it were. Both were equally collusive and abusive responses but responses that the RTs felt a pull to act upon. The realization of this dynamic was a turning point both for those involved in Colin's care and also for Colin himself.

It may indeed have been this realization that led to Colin's stay ending prematurely. The part of him who wanted 'out' could not let us 'in' to help him. We were not able to keep him safe from the murderer inside. Colin returned to hospital.

'Sharon', a young West Indian woman, arrived at the Centre for a long stay. She came with suicidal wishes and a complex early history that included sexual abuse, over-involvement with her mother, and a secretive and violent family. Early in her stay, she attempted to kill herself. This was her only suicide attempt at the Centre and served to communicate, in the only way she knew, the seriousness of her distress and capacity to harm herself. Sharon demonstrated how terrifying it was to be in a house where she would not be under the continuous watchful eye of hospital staff. It was also interesting that hospital was all bad in her mind, as the Crisis Centre eventually turned into something all good. This splitting was projected onto the RTs and divided her team; and this was how we came to understand something of Sharon's fragmented internal world.

Any kind of separation was experienced by her as devastating, as if this was evidence of her own self-hatred and her view that she was evil. Throughout her stay people's breaks away from the Centre were very provoking experiences for her and became an important focus for the teamwork.

During one of her team leader's breaks Sharon barricaded herself in the living room. She shouted that I, her RT, was neglectful and hostile. Aggressively isolating herself in a communal space seemed to be her way of communicating her need to find her own resourcefulness. It was perhaps also her denial of a need for me and the Centre itself. But, at the same time, she was clearly letting me know how frightened, alienated and threatened she felt: contact could only be tolerated with the door between us, as if opening the door would mean either violence or violation.

I often felt saturated and consumed by Sharon. She seemed to need to merge with me. Sometimes she would wear clothes that imitated my own. Often she would say she believed I had the same thoughts, or at least knew her thoughts. At times it was as if she would experience me as someone who was attacking her from the inside; and this was indeed often how I felt. I did not know how to keep a door open to her without getting filled up with feelings of denigration and hopelessness.

While Sharon desperately wanted to get inside, she seemed set to destroy the inside that reminded her of the abuse and her confused yearning for intimacy. In her time at the Centre she struggled with her relationships and I struggled in my relationship with her. I would feel consumed with hatred for her and in need of a lot of help from the rest of the group to stay in touch with some empathy toward her. What I learned from her was how undifferentiated her experience of love and hate was. Often, I would feel as if I was the only person in the group who experienced Sharon as intrusive and vengeful. This was when I needed a lot of help to make sense of the countertransference and projective identification process. I had become the over-involved mother, who was rejecting as well as being profoundly impacted by her rage and hurt and overwhelming need. But these transferential feelings seemed only to be arising in me.

Others did not share these same experiences of her. This meant that in some way I was experiencing something of what she had experienced when she felt alone and disbelieved during and after her sexually abusive relationship with a friend of the family. Through these periods of sensed isolation I came to understand what it was like to be governed by split feelings. It was hard for Sharon to hold onto the relationship and the work, without at the same time holding onto the view that she was being shut out for ever and would have to shut us out. It felt as if she wanted to turn the Crisis Centre into a place inside which she could be for ever. The anxiety of being separate seemed to overwhelm her, and at the same time she seemed to feel destructive towards the object of her need and towards the part of her that sought that object. Sharon worked extremely hard with the team and within the house to understand something of how obliterating her envy was of what was on offer. She eventually become an integral part of the house. Her struggle to stay and her struggle with leaving and moving on, and the growth of her capacity to hold onto something good, were, I think, remarkable feats on her part, supported by the other guests during her stay and by the team. Sharon has not returned to hospital and continues to have psychoanalytic psychotherapy.

How do we at the Crisis Centre think about and work through the experience of the internal and external threat of an open house? For most people coming to the Centre the experience of safety is an unknown. People arrive in a state of mind in which symbolic thinking is not possible: human contact means physical contact, and safety means physical security. It is as if the experience of being interned is the only one that comes close to keeping the psychotic part intact.

I have attempted to show in these vignettes how guests have organized a mind-structure made up of compartments. The psychotic part is preserved, safe in a walled-up room, protected from the possibility of a door or window slipping open into an adjoining chamber of thoughts and feelings. These guests project out these mental compartments into concrete experiences in the milieu. Some guests might stand rigid at a door, unable to go in or out, and will stay in-between rooms, reflecting an internal conflict. Some might feel unable to enter certain rooms, or feel terrified of being in a room and will keep themselves out and excluded, becoming increasingly isolated and set apart.

The separateness or the splitting can become reflected in the RT group, where a guest may engage with each RT in a different way and can stir up conflicting sets of feelings in those around them. The fragmented internal world in its projection makes sure that the parental figures have to keep these parts in mind and are, as it were, pushed into thinking together about the guest. As relationships evolve, this can also mean that the psychotic part is in danger of being exposed and further threatened by a humiliating defeat. This may arouse an annihilating defensive structure in preparation for a fight to the death.

In the C.S. Lewis story the developmental process of the children, like that of the guests at the Crisis Centre, starts from a position of defence against loss but moves to a more stable depressive position, where loss is acknowledged and borne. To achieve this, the characters in Narnia have to overcome their fear of the dominating white witch. She forbids the warmth of relationships, which would melt her kingdom. Some may come to the Crisis Centre expecting a Narnia, hoping for magical Turkish delight to gorge on to help push down the feelings, as Edmund does in the story. The disappointment of this not happening is the start of a new and perhaps different experience of allowing something of a door to be opened, a door through which the warmth and struggle of human relationships can be experienced.

Reference

Lewis, C.S. (1950) The Lion, the Witch and the Wardrobe. London: Geoffrey Bles.

CHAPTER 16

Then and Now

Laura Forti

The Arbours Crisis Centre was founded in 1973 by a small group of psychotherapists who offered their services virtually for free. Twenty-eight years later it is functioning from its own much larger premises, with many more guests (patients) and psychotherapists. It is now registered by the Local Authorities, funded by many Social Services and Health Authorities, and recognized for its unique work.

I intend to look at the evolution of the Crisis Centre in these twenty-eight years and in particular to discuss how our principles and clinical practices have changed. As I have been involved with the Crisis Centre throughout this time, first as resident therapist and now as team leader, I have seen its philosophy and its way of working consolidating and evolving.

When the Crisis Centre first started to operate in the early 1970s, alongside the Arbours Therapeutic Communities, one of its main functions was to provide an alternative to the traditional psychiatric institutions, seen as repressive and damaging. This involved a rejection of the traditional psychiatric model, which considered mental illness as a psychological or physical state isolated from its social context and from its treatment. The latter was seen as more or less violent, aiming at repressing physical symptoms, sometimes at the expense of the mental functioning of the patient. Over the years the Crisis Centre has drawn from different psychotherapeutic models, from existentialism to psychoanalysis, to family therapy, group therapy, communication theory and therapeutic community work, to develop its own unique style.

229

At present, with most of the oldest mental hospitals closed down and replaced by smaller structures which often are trying to integrate a psychotherapeutic approach into their traditional practices, the Crisis Centre offers not so much an alternative as a specialized service based on the therapeutic community model enriched by intensive analytic psychotherapy.

The Crisis Centre aims to make comprehensible, and therefore less frightening, disturbing states of mind: depression, confusion, anger, suicidal thoughts, self-harm, psychosis. It is in the context of a relationship that they can be understood and changes can take place. Twenty-eight years ago the Centre could accommodate entire families: parents with young babies, couples, mothers and children. Within the secure holding of the Crisis Centre, complex family dynamics as well as individual states of mind could be understood, and old and new patterns could be made sense of.

I will begin by presenting two clinical examples from our work at the Crisis Centre twenty-eight years ago and will review them in the light of our present clinical approach.

When Mike arrived at the Crisis Centre he had just been discharged from psychiatric hospital and he was on a heavy dosage of psychotropic medication. Before going into hospital he had started to gradually lose contact with reality, to isolate himself from his wife, Jane, and his friends, and to become suspicious. He spent the whole day in bed staring; he heard voices; he behaved in strange ways; and he tried to cut off one of his fingers with a knife. At that point his wife asked for help and Mike was admitted to hospital. There Mike was not offered any chance of talking about what was happening; instead he was given electro-shock treatment and high dosages of oral and depot antipsychotic medication.

When discharged, Mike was warned that if he interrupted the pharmacological treatment, he would have a relapse and a new hospital admission would be inevitable. His wife, who had given birth to their first baby daughter while Mike was in hospital, had been warned always to check on her husband, especially when he was holding the baby. All this was creating in Mike and in his relationship with his wife an unbearable tension, on the verge of precipitating a new crisis. It is at this point that Mike and Jane got in touch with the Crisis Centre. Rather than considering Mike's crisis in isolation, and thus further separating him from his wife, as had happened previously when he was in hospital, we accepted him at the Crisis Centre together with his family.

When they arrived, after a long journey, they looked very young and lost, Jane clutching her baby and Mike holding a small bag with their possessions. They seemed relieved to be in the security of the Crisis Centre and settled in quickly. Mike was quiet and withdrawn, while Jane was happy and cheerful and established easy relationships with the other people at the Crisis Centre. She was the one who mostly took care of the baby, but he took care of her too, in a very detached way, as if she was an object. During their stay we had four meetings a week: with the three of them, with Mike and Jane without the baby, and with Mike and Jane individually. We also spent long hours in the kitchen talking more informally about their lives.

Mike and Jane were both twenty-three and had been married for four years. They both came from middle-class families and had grown up in big cities. During the past three years they had abandoned their urban life and had withdrawn to a remote place in the countryside. They lived in rough conditions, in a derelict farm they had fixed up themselves, with neither water nor electricity, and grew their own food. The nearest town was sixty miles away; they went there to do the shopping once a month. Besides working on the land, they read and spun their own wool.

It became clear that Mike's crisis was strictly connected with his wife's pregnancy, and that he had started to isolate himself from Jane and the outside world as the pregnancy progressed. The arrival of a child would have completely changed their relationship, which was almost symbiotic. From a practical point of view Jane would have been forced to stay at home and look after the child, and Mike would have had to work in the fields on his own. A similar crisis, though not so dramatic, had started three years earlier, when Jane became pregnant for the first time; but this was spontaneously resolved when she had a miscarriage. While Jane seemed to live her new maternal role with joy and spontaneity, Mike found his paternal role difficult; he looked awkward, almost sad. In our culture the birth of a child represents the final transition to adulthood with all its responsibilities. Probably Mike did not feel ready for this; he had only accepted his wife's wish to have a child, without sharing it. Perhaps he did not even believe that he could generate a child, and this could explain the extreme jealousy he had developed towards his wife while she was pregnant. In fact he had started to doubt that the child she was carrying was his own and was continuously accusing Jane of having relationships with other men. Furthermore, the birth of their daughter had evoked in Mike feelings that went back to his childhood, when the birth of his brother had ended his exclusive relationship with his mother.

His final desperate gesture, trying to cut off his finger, could be seen as containing all these feelings. This attempted amputation seemed to express his anger, pain and rejection. Through trying to cut his finger Mike was showing how cut off he felt from his wife and the baby she was carrying in her womb. He was also turning against himself the anger that would have been too dangerous to express towards his wife, and at the same time demonstrating in a concrete way the pain that he felt inside. It could have been also a desperate strategy to get back the attention of Jane, so absorbed by the pregnancy and by the forthcoming birth. By attacking his very ability to work in the fields he was also making sure that he would not be left on his own to contend with an unyielding land and the rough forces of nature. Finally, his gesture could be seen as a form of self-castration, as an expression of his lack of potency and of his feeling incapable of carrying out an adult sexual relationship.

For her part Jane seemed to encourage her husband's feelings of exclusion and lack of power. She was totally absorbed with the baby, from which Mike was cut off. She held her the whole time during the day and kept her in their bed at night. It was almost as if she had replaced Mike with the baby. As the whole family was at the Crisis Centre, we could observe their relationship, explore with them its implications, and help them to develop ways of communication that by now had ceased (as for example between Mike and Jane, who had become isolated from each other from the beginning of the pregnancy) or other channels that had never been open (as between Mike and his daughter). Furthermore, feeling contained and protected by the security of the structure of the Crisis Centre, Mike and Jane could start to overcome the constant threat of a relapse and experience family life together. They were at the Crisis Centre only for two weeks as they were keen to go back to their croft as soon as possible. We made it clear to them that we would continue to be available should they need more support.

Our intervention mainly addressed the immediate crisis and the present dynamics of their relationship. More generally, rather than let Mike be transformed into a long-term hospital case, we tried to make sense of what appeared mad and therefore unbearable. As the frightening thoughts and feelings could be named and understood, the crisis became more contained.

My second example concerns Alexandre, a young man in his early twenties, who was overcome by an acute psychotic episode.

Alexandre's mother, Corinne, rang us from Paris to ask for help for her son, who was in a full delusional state: she wanted to come to London, to the Crisis Centre, with him. When we asked her whether Alexandre was willing to come, the mother answered that Alexandre did not want to come, at a conscious level, but, as she was in analysis, she knew from his dreams that unconsciously he wanted to come. We told her that at the Centre we could only accept those who consciously wanted to come. If Corinne felt that she could not cope any more she could come for a few days for her own benefit. We have found that helping relatives is often a way of helping the person in crisis. In any case, whether it was only herself or both of them, they had to wait five days, as the Crisis Centre was full. After a couple of days we received a very confused telephone call from the son, who was asking for help. We decided that they should both come to London and that on the day of their arrival we would have a meeting with them to decide how best to intervene. The meeting was organized for Monday evening. On Monday morning, the mother, already in London with her son, rang to ask whether the meeting could take place earlier in the day; she was insistent and found it difficult to accept that we could not see them more urgently.

They arrived one hour early. Corinne was exhausted from having spent the day trying to contain her son's madness in an unknown city. We were told that when they were in a car on their way here, Alexandre had removed some of the more visible elements of his Parisian delusion – pendants, crosses, necklaces, that he had borrowed from the people around him. Corinne was dressed simply and looked very tired. The son introduced himself as one of the Apostles: he blessed us, preached humility, criticized the vanity of this world, asked to have a Bible, praised the Lord, and spoke to the animals as if he were Saint Francis of Assisi. To punish himself, wishing to suffer, he hit the wall with his head several times. Then Alexandre said that he needed to regress. He started trembling and shaking and eventually fell down in a state of exhaustion, curled up in a foetal position.

When eventually Joseph Berke, the director of the Centre, arrived, the atmosphere was very solemn. Alexandre performed a ceremony in which he both blessed Joe and adored him as God. Alexandre appeared like an Apostle who had come to London to found a religious community, as Christ's messenger. Slowly, however, he was able to acknowledge that he had come because he needed help. At the same time he could not decide whether he wanted to stay in London or go back to Paris. This doubt, with its different meanings, continued to be present throughout his stay at the Centre. Going back to Paris meant going back to his delusional world; staying in London meant deciding to face it and try to understand it. Going back to Paris also meant running away from the mother who was there with him and whom he said he hated. But Alexandre had mixed feelings about it. At times it seemed he wanted to remain at the Centre only if the mother left, and at other times he wanted her to stay and himself to go. At other times he wanted to come to a decision together with her, whether it was to leave or to stay.

Alexandre was in a manic state: he paced up and down; he was extremely anxious; he was excited; he talked all the time. Corinne, who was initially silent and withdrawn, confessed that the heart of the matter was the fact that Alexandre had three mothers. Two more women had participated with her, the 'real' mother, in bringing him up. One of the mothers, Marguerite, was in London, too; and Alexandre would have liked to have reached her. In his delusional state he had projected onto Marguerite the image of the good loving mother, and onto Corinne, the biological mother, all his hate and anger.

At the end of this meeting we had not reached any decision. Alexandre and Corinne would spend the night at the Crisis Centre and the next day we would face the problem again. Alexandre was quite agitated during the night and spent part of it in bed with his mother. A few days later Corinne would claim that their proximity did not have any sexual connotation; on the contrary, it was similar to the closeness that they had both experienced when he was a newborn baby, and sometimes he used to sleep beside her with his head against her breast.

At the Crisis Centre Alexandre appeared to be extremely generous, offering presents to everyone. The next morning his kindness reached manic levels. He had set up a sort of a shop with a notice that said: 'Help yourself.' But after a few hours this generosity was replaced by anxiety, restlessness and rage that became more and more explosive. One could speculate that Alexandre was raging partly at his mother for 'helping herself with him' and partly at us, as we knew what was happening but did not intervene to keep her away from seducing him. Perhaps he was saying that he needed to help himself, as we were not going to set up limits for him or his mother, nor tell him what to do. Indeed, we could only help him to find possible meanings of his recent crisis.

We decided not to stop him when he announced that he was going back to Paris. Corinne, on the other hand, declared that she was going to stay. This was an important point for her, as she acknowledged that she had come not only to accompany her son but also to look for help for herself. At the same time she thought that Alexandre was not able to look after himself, and even if she pretended that he was free to leave, in reality she was refusing to give him the money for the train ticket. The problem of financial dependency had important implications for the family. Alexandre became more and more agitated and ambivalent about the journey. He made an attempt to ring Marguerite, who was ready to leave the next morning, in order to go with her, but never managed to dial the telephone number. He tormented Corinne in order to get from her the money for his ticket, and, after her refusal, decided to hitch-hike back to Paris. He went to the door and asked which way was South in order to know in which direction he should get a lift. After saying some dramatic goodbyes and asking everyone to pray for him, he was off, only to be back after half-an-hour, like a poor sinner who repents and asks for refuge.

Nevertheless it was important for Alexandre that he had been allowed to leave and to come back on his own accord. When he came back he seemed to be more settled and ready to work. In fact, despite still being in a delusional state, he was also able to try to understand the origins of his delusion. Later in the afternoon, by then exhausted from the hectic day, Alexandre went over the recent events, identifying what seemed to him to be his first delusional thought. He remembered that he was talking with a friend when suddenly he had thought that the friend was the Pope! It seemed that at a certain point what was only 'peut-etre', 'maybe', had become real. Alexandre managed to remember the fleeting second when his fantasy, his impressions, his wishes had taken over the reality. In his mind, the thought that this friend deserved being the Pope, and in some aspects was similar to the Pope, had become directly, 'this friend is the Pope'. What was important was the word 'maybe', that expresses only a possibility but that in Alexandre's mind had become a reality. That afternoon Alexandre discovered another important piece of language, 'comme si', 'as if', that distinguishes phantasy from reality. So Alexandre stopped saying that he was Jesus Christ and started saying that he suffered like Jesus Christ. What was quite extraordinary was Alexandre's lucidity in going back in his delusion to find where it began.

Alexandre's understanding of his delusions seemed to fit with Silvano Arieti's (1955) elaboration of the schizophrenic's thought. 'His thought is not illogical or senseless but follows a different system of logic, which leads to deductions different from those usually reached by the healthy person' (Arieti 1955, p.156). According to Arieti this different faculty of conception is the same as that which is followed in dreams, in forms of autistic thinking, and in the thinking of people living in prehistorical times. Therefore, he refers to it as 'paleologic', to distinguish it from our usual logic, which is generally referred to as Aristotelian. The schizophrenic adopts this primitive logic in order to escape the anxiety provoked by the unbearable truth of the reality interpreted by means of Aristotelian logic. Crucially, this new logic will permit him to see reality as he wants to. The paleologic way of thinking is to a great extent based on Von Domarus' (1944) principle. According to this principle, while the normal person accepts identity only on the basis of identical subjects, the paleologician accepts identity based upon identical predicates. Arieti quotes the thought process of a patient: 'The Virgin Mary was a virgin; I am a virgin; therefore, I am the Virgin Mary' (Arieti 1955, p.195). As Alexandre felt contained by the safety of the Crisis Centre he was able to let go of the paleologic – the logic of the schizophrenic and of children – and to go back to the more acceptable Aristotelian logic.

That night Alexandre's mother put him to bed, giving him some hot milk, which represented her relationship with him – still in her eyes as needy as a child, though now more able to separate from her. Thus also, in the safe environment of the Crisis Centre, the mother–son relationship appeared to progress from a position of fusion towards a progressive separation. The next morning we had a meeting with Marguerite, ready to go back to Paris, as if her mission, to take Alexandre and Corinne to London, to safety, had come to an end. Until now she had represented the good mother; in leaving she allowed Corinne, too, to become a good mother. Alexandre was now very different from the young man who had arrived at the Crisis Centre only two days previously. He was aware that he had been in a delusional state and, even if he missed Paris, wanted to remain a few more days to make some sense of what had happened. Corinne and Marguerite were very moved by Alexandre's 'miraculous' change. Marguerite hugged him and held his hands tightly; the mother, more contained, was smiling.

In the following days we got to know Alexandre and Corinne better – both their histories and the more recent events – and we developed a close relationship with them. In this process different things started to connect, with an emerging sense of meaning. Here I will only touch upon some of them. Alexandre's mother came from a very religious Catholic family. Her own mother, who had devoted all her energies to her family, had not developed her own profession and, regretting this, had strongly encouraged her daughter to think about her career. Corinne, who from a very young age had wanted to become a doctor, became absorbed in her studies and gave no time to relationships. As a student, she went through a deep religious crisis, following which, she said, she would have liked to reveal her faith to everyone, but she felt shy and kept it all to herself. While at the Crisis Centre Corinne said that Alexandre, through his religious delusion, was living out her own religious experience in a very open and explosive way, as she would have wanted to live it out herself when she was young.

Corinne was thirty when she met a man who was already married and had children; they fell in love and for a few months they lived in a state of natural and instinctive happiness. When after some time Corinne became pregnant, Alexandre's father went back to his wife and family. Corinne enjoyed the pregnancy and Alexandre's birth, and felt happy to look after him. At the same time, however, Alexandre represented her guilt and shame. This was apparent throughout Alexandre's childhood, with his mother alternating in her loving and rejecting roles. Corinne left Alexandre in the countryside in the care of a country woman (a fourth mother?). During that time she worked in Paris and went to visit him at weekends. The theme of shame came up several times at the Crisis Centre. Alexandre said that he was his mother's shame as she gave birth to him without a husband, and that he also represented his father's shame as his father had gone back to his previous family and severed all links with him. Perhaps, also, Alexandre was also ashamed of having 'married' the mother, ashamed of the symbiotic link that tied him to her, and which he did not know how to interrupt without having to go mad.

Alexandre's mother, perhaps because she was missing a family, welcomed two women who joined in and shared her maternal role towards Alexandre. One was Marguerite, whom we have already mentioned, and whom Alexandre saw every day. The other was his god-mother, to whom he was now no longer close. When Alexandre was four, Corinne married a violinist and they had two children, a boy and a girl. This relationship greatly upset the closeness between Alexandre and his mother. During his delusion Alexandre used to go to his mother's study pretending to play the violin, and she would simply respond: 'I know that you have suffered a lot because of a violinist.' Was Alexandre, for his part, trying to seduce the mother? Or did he feel that he had to replace the missing husband? And was the mother commenting on Alexandre's suffering, or on her own pain and abandonment caused by the violin player? When the marriage had come to an end the mother, again on her own, had had to play a paternal and maternal role towards her children. Corinne's relationship towards Alexandre was close and intimate, but at the same time it had never been complete, not even during his childhood. Therefore we felt it was important that Alexandre and his mother could be at the Crisis Centre together, as this would allow us to explore their relationship with a view to helping them to separate and live more independently.

Religion was something they both had in common. Corinne had recently joined a new Catholic group, where young people got together, 'miracles' happened, and some of them spoke through 'divine inspiration'. Soon after, Alexandre had also joined this group and devoted his whole life to it: he prayed obsessively and he walked the streets preaching. This religious bond between Alexandre and his mother was very important for an understanding of his mystic delusions, as his delusional language could be seen as a way of communicating with his mother. At the same time his search for God was his search for the father he never had.

Alexandre and his mother were at the Crisis Centre for only five days, during which time he underwent a radical transformation. It is difficult to conceive of such a dramatic, almost cathartic change in such a short period of time. We tried to think what had made this possible. Was it something inherent in the structure of the Crisis Centre, or in the nature of our work, or in their own explosive crisis? Was it possible that mother and son experienced us as god-like healers, performing miracles? Their presence together at the Centre certainly helped us to understand what was happening and how to intervene in their relationship. Away from Paris, the city of his delusions, Alexandre was able to create a thinking space. The explosive madness was contained in an environment that was safe, tolerant, understanding, and therapeutic. I might also add that this was not the end of our contact with Alexandre. After returning to Paris with his mother, it became clear that he needed a longer stay at the Crisis Centre. Perhaps due to this initial stay, he was able to come back for a longer period, this time by himself, so as to work in more depth on his own difficulties.

The interventions described here illustrate our work at the Crisis Centre of containing and understanding, through the physical setting of the Centre and through our presence and thinking, two situations involving psychotic breakdown. Both Alexandre and his mother, and Mike and Jane were lost and confused, taken over by madness. Freud wrote about mental patients: 'They have turned away from external reality, but for that very reason they know more about internal, psychical reality and can reveal a number of things to us that would be otherwise inaccessible to us' (Freud 1933, p.59). The Centre gave them the space to explore their inner realities, and the safety to make some sense of what was happening and to remove some of their fear.

The Crisis Centre's function is thus comparable to that of the mother who, according to Bion (1967), is able to contain the baby's frustration and in so doing enhances the conditions for the development of his thinking. 'A capacity for tolerating frustration thus enables the psyche to develop thought as a means by which the frustration that is tolerated is itself made more tolerable' (Bion 1967, p.112). The Crisis Centre provides a calm and reflective space where frustration, pain and horror have the op-portunity of being transformed into something bearable and meaningful. Looking at it from this point of view, we could say that those who come to the Crisis Centre have experienced failures in the nature of the relationship between the container and the contained; they are in need of the kind of containment which the Crisis Centre can provide. This containing function has remained unchanged over the past twenty-eight years, even if the Centre's structure has changed. While the external pressures have increased, the Centre has expanded its 'thinking space' so as to continue bearing the unbearable.

If Alexandre were to get in touch with the Crisis Centre now, he would probably not be able to come in as quickly as he was able then. Precious time would be lost dealing with bureaucracy and applying for funding. In all likelihood he would end up in hospital before arriving, or he would arrive already heavily medicated. Mike would not be able to come with his wife and baby, as the Crisis Centre, now registered as a Nursing Home, is not allowed to accept babies, children or young adults under the age of eighteen. Some meaning would be lost. Arguably, the Crisis Centre in the

past had a more flexible structure rendering more immediate crisis intervention work possible. Rather than inviting Alexandre together with his
mother, or Mike accompanied by his wife, we would probably offer each
of them, individually, stays of a few weeks or few months. The therapeutic
team working with them would concentrate on intensive individual
analytic work. These days most of the thinking is done in team meetings
rather than around the kitchen table. Special attention is devoted to the
transference and countertransference as ways of understanding the
intricate mechanisms of the individual in crisis and of producing therapeutic change. As the daily structure of the Crisis Centre offers more analytic
space, each guest's stay is more clearly structured in terms of space and
time, and different stages are more clearly discernible, with a deeper
clinical understanding of the different phases of arrival, settling-in,
settling-down, leaving and following-up (Berke 1987). Even if the
structure that we offer each guest gets richer, the small size of our
container, the Crisis Centre, has remained constant throughout the years
(Fagan 2000). Nonetheless the Crisis Centre has seen some slow changes
in its size and in the differentiation of roles. I will mention some of them.

When we first started, we could accept a maximum of three or four
guests and now we have six. At the beginning we had two resident therapists, who would inevitably become a parental couple for the guests. Now
we have three resident therapists, onto whom a variety of feelings and
phantasies get projected and to whom the guests relate in different ways.
When the Crisis Centre was smaller, the resident therapists would be responsible for tasks that are now performed by separate workers such as a
Clinical Assistant, who liaises with the outside agencies; a Finance Officer,
who deals with finances and funding; a Nurse Manager, who deals with
specific nursing issues. The Director is now helped by the Associate
Director. More attention is given to different levels of supervision. In the
early days the differentiation of roles was less clear. Even nowadays,
however, while the resident therapist works with the team leader as
co-therapist, he or she also prepares the dinner, giving to the Crisis Centre
that unique situation where clinical treatment and daily life blend together.

In more recent years, rather than working with young individuals
affected by their first breakdown, as we had originally envisaged, we work
more with people who have been in trouble for many years; the Crisis
Centre becomes for them their last resort rather than their first place of
help. Guests stay at the Centre for three months, six months, or one year,

re-creating in their daily life here some of the original conflicts and inter-actions which are explored at a group level as well as in their individual psychotherapy sessions. As they have been battling with their distress for many years, their original knots have tightened, and their links with their families have loosened. The therapeutic team, with more long-term and painful work, explores some of these original knots and relationships and tries to come to grips with them in a more symbolic way.

I have explored what have been some of the continuities and changes in our approach at the Arbours Centre in the past twenty-eight years in terms of our structural and clinical development. This is not to suggest that different perspectives could not have been used to follow its advancement. For, indeed, this very notion is characteristic of the Crisis Centre itself, as a container that has maintained its flexibility throughout the years.

References

Arieti, S. (1955) *Interpretation of Schizophrenia*. New York: Brunner.

Berke, J. (1987) 'Arriving, Settling-in, Settling-down, Leaving and Following-up: Stages of Stay at the Arbours Centre.' *British Journal of Medical Psychology 60*, 181–188.

Bion, W.R. (1967) *Second Thoughts: Selected Papers on Psychoanalysis*. New York: Aronson.

Fagan, M. (2000) 'Small is Beautiful.' *British Journal of Psychotherapy 17*, 2, 217–219.

Freud, S. (1933) *New Introductory Lectures on Psycho-Analysis. Vol 22: The Standard Edition of the Complete Psychological Works of Sigmund Freud*. London: Hogarth Press.

Von Domarus, E. (1944) 'The Specific Laws of Logic in Schizophrenia.' In J.S. Kasanin (ed) *Language and Thought in Schizophrenia: Collected Papers*. Berkeley, CA: University of California Press.

Section Four

Authority and Money

Introduction

Joseph H. Berke, Margaret Fagan, George Mak-Pearce
and Stella Pierides-Müller

In the eyes of society and the law psychosis renders the person incapable – non compos mentis – and leads to his or her social disempowerment. Paradoxically, persons suffering from psychosis were, and still are, perceived as extremely powerful, with unusual physical strength and seductive or manipulative powers. Money and 'authority' are believed to be the most important adjuncts of such power, providing the all-powerful means to overcome feelings of powerlessness. From the ancient 'Midas touch' to the power that Mephistopheles bestows on Faust, the omnipotent connection between authority (mis-conceived power) and money permeates minds, societies and cultures. Furthermore, as Freud (1908) pointed out, noting the ancient Babylonian doctrine according to which gold is described as 'the faeces of Hell', there is a most intimate connection between money and dirt which is found in archaic, mythical modes of thought. While a number of projective and counter-projective processes are at work here, it is clear that conflicts over money, authority, control and power are central to psychosis and psychotic thinking. For instance, at the Arbours Centre we have found that when the parents of guests are paying for stays privately, they often use money as a means of control over the behaviour and experience of their offspring.

In a hospital situation, money, authority and power are more easily hidden from view. These issues seem rarely thought about or openly discussed in the modern-day mental health world. Individuals in the throes of psychotic breakdown may be offered, in a reactive manner, any treatment, whatever its cost, in the private or the public sector, without a

clinical assessment of their need or suitability for a psychodynamic intervention having taken place. Alternatively, they may be offered the cheapest
bed available. In a cash-strapped Health Service, a hierarchy of options
may be set up, where the cheapest, least thoughtful, least staff- and
space-demanding options become the first resort.

Edith David's and George Mak-Pearce's chapter considers money and
helps clarify the real cost effectiveness of psychosocial interventions. The
authors point out that, in a climate of cost awareness, lasting improvements
in the patient's psychological and social situation beyond the period of
treatment must be demonstrated. They discuss cost effectiveness, taking
into account the whole picture of the particular intervention, not just
itemized meals, beds and consultations, or short-term benefits. Using the
Arbours Crisis Centre as the basis for their costing of psychosocial interventions, they portray a picture where financial prudence underscores and
mixes with charitable acts, thoughtfulness and generosity.

Significantly, because of its links with power, the concept of authority
often suffers misconceptions. While there are various types of creative
authority, such as parental or moral authority, the word is most often used
to mean 'authoritarian', implying the use of undue or imposed control,
limit-setting and power. That is, authority easily comes to mean the abuse
of authority. Thus, while there may be appreciation of knowledge, wisdom
or position, as in parental authority, or the circle of the elders, negative
characteristics, such as 'the oppressive', 'the controlling', and 'the tyrannical', may be unconsciously inserted to confuse the term.

As a consequence, the real authority of the doctor or therapist struggling to understand an extremely difficult situation is undermined by his,
as well as his patient's, excessive beliefs in his power. Stanley Schneider
and Rena Bina point out that in the hierarchical model of authority the
view often becomes one of the patient being the passive recipient of
treatment at the hands of an all-knowing, all-giving and all-controlling
doctor. Milieu therapy, these authors say, provides an alternative medium,
in which that relationship can be looked into more openly, and the issues
of authority, power, control, and money be worked through. Milieu
therapy, it can be argued, allows for everything to be questioned and
thought through, not only what the person on the next hierarchical step
allows to be discussed.

While development of the ability to bear frustration through
piecemeal learning from the experience of living-in is centrally involved –

the guest becoming increasingly able to risk waiting or showing a wish or a need – Schneider and Bina point out another factor. Risk, for them, is also associated with the controlled use of the death instinct: to achieve an aim one bears pain in the service of gain. For the hierarchically or pyramidally organized staff, this may lead to the ability to allow a 'flattening of the pyramid', which allows for a more humane and effective form of treatment. Schneider and Bina's argument is that the flattened pyramidal structure is less likely to revert to authoritarian ways of being, and more able to use the resources of all of its members to the full.

Reference

Freud, S. (1908) 'Character and Anal Erotism.' *Vol 9: The Standard Edition of the Complete Psychological Works of Sigmund Freud.* London: Hogarth Press.

CHAPTER 17

Is the Arbours Crisis Centre Cost Effective?

Edith David and George Mak-Pearce

> To most people the concept of making a profit or having a surplus arising from sick people is distasteful. Yet almost everyone accepts that the only way to provide better treatment for patients out of finite sums available is to improve the use of those resources. The problem is how to combine caring for health and life, which is beyond price, with the practical fact that if the cost per effectively treated patient is reduced, more patients can be treated. (CIMA 1992)

The 'practical fact' mentioned in the extract above takes us straight to the heart of an important question. Is the PsychoSocial treatment offered by the Arbours Crisis Centre more or less cost effective than other forms of treatment? And, in particular, how does it compare with more traditional psychiatric treatments, such as hospitals employing drugs and ECT? Is it an expensive luxury? Or is it an approach that could be used to effectively treat more people because it actually costs less?

The Conservative government of Margaret Thatcher (1979–1990), in its bid to streamline British public sector services, make them more accountable, and move them away from what Lady Thatcher termed 'the Nanny State', introduced a variety of financial management initiatives in 1982. The aim was to make each department accountable for its activities by appraising three financial measures: the economy, the efficiency and the effectiveness of their services. The 'New Labour' government has pursued essentially the same ideology with an increased performance monitoring of public sector services that now requires each department to ensure that services are provided at what is called 'best value'.

Following the attempt to create an 'internal market' within the National Health Service, many operational roles were contracted-out to independent providers, such as charities and profit-making businesses. The strategic role remains with Health Authorities, who are responsible for purchasing care on behalf of their local populations. Hence a consultant psychiatrist referring a patient to a provider's services would first need to know that funding will be available for the placement via what is known as an Extra Contractual Referral (ECR). The Health Authority in turn needs to be assured that the proposed placement meets its own best-value assessment. Therefore, the Crisis Centre has to satisfy specific best-value criteria in order to ensure that referrals can be made to it. Yet there are few other services comparable to the Centre in the UK. The Henderson and Cassel Hospitals both offer in-patient psychotherapy, and are probably the closest alternatives within the NHS, but their funding structures are completely different.

The nature of the charity sector makes it particularly important to achieve a monitored best-value accounting system. Friedman (1980) classifies spending under four headings depending on whether you are spending your own money or someone else's, and whether you are spending for your own benefit or for the benefit of somebody else. If you are spending your own money on yourself you are concerned with economy, efficiency and effectiveness. If you are spending your own money on somebody else, as when buying a present, you are concerned with economy but less with efficiency (as the useless presents one often receives eloquently testify). If you are spending someone else's money on yourself, as with an expense account lunch, you do not worry too much about economy but you do ensure effectiveness and attempt to get your money's worth. If you are spending someone else's money on someone else, you have no direct motivation to seek economy, efficiency or effectiveness. Hospital financial administrators (both in the private sector and the NHS) occupy the latter position. So does the Crisis Centre administration. However, there is an important difference. The Centre, by virtue of its size, can be affected quite quickly when finances go wrong. There is a direct link between monies coming in and the Centre's spending – a link that provides a motivation to enhance economy, efficiency and effectiveness. Consequently, the Centre aims to reflect and justify the full cost of providing a particular service. The contribution of volunteers and charitable funds can be identified separately under the heading of 'added value'.

There is no simple way to compare costs, particularly when one attempts to compare an NHS psychiatric bed to a Crisis Centre room (all guests at the Centre have their own private room). This is largely because of the problem of trying to determine which of the myriad costs within the elaborate NHS accounting structure are pertinent to the comparison. In addition there are other highly relevant but more subtle factors that need to be taken into account. For example, regarding the level of disturbance of patients we need to ensure we compare like with like. We need to be conscious of the goals of the treatment as well. The NHS has statutory obligations under the Mental Health Act that include sectioning. The Crisis Centre, being a Registered Nursing Home, has a very different set of obligations. Often a psychiatric ward functions in a broader way for Social Services and Police as a safety net for those with multiple problems such as addictions, criminality, learning difficulties, money and other social problems. The Crisis Centre being a six-bed unit does not even start to function in this way.

Perhaps most importantly, the cost of treatment must also take into account outcome and follow-on costs. The so-called 'revolving door' syndrome needs to be factored-in. A treatment that results in a high level of re-admittance is an expensive treatment. A treatment that results in the individual returning home and going back to work is, from a societal point of view, an highly cost-effective one. Not only is this person no longer a drain on health resources but they may stop claiming benefits and, of course, make a positive contribution through starting work and providing tax revenue. In comparing cost effectiveness, one has to keep an eye on the larger picture, on what we shall refer to as 'indirect costs'.

The direct costs of psychiatric treatments outside the NHS are easier to compare. In the year 2001 most private psychiatric hospitals charge in excess of £350 per day. In addition to this base rate all charge a variety of fees for such services as admission (averaging £145), consultancy (averaging £175), medication (about £12 per day), as well as sessional fees for specific therapies (which can often include individual or group psychotherapy). Other charges pertain as you would expect for ECT (£220), EEG (£230), ECG (£70), and so on. Thus each patient's total costs will vary but will certainly be well in excess of the basic £2500 per week.

The Crisis Centre charges a fixed amount per week that is an all-inclusive figure for accommodation and food as well as treatment. A discount is offered for those at the Centre funded by Social Services or the NHS. The fees for 2001 are £1500 per week for privately paying guests, and the discounted rate is £1400. Thus as far as private psychiatric hospitals go, the Crisis Centre is considerably less expensive. In fact at £200 a day it is about the cost of a medium-priced hotel room in Central London without meals! The prices are set primarily at a break-even level and designed at most to make a margin of 10 per cent surplus. One crucial measure of efficiency in our planning is the occupancy level, which is regularly monitored. At full occupancy four days per week the Centre will break even; that is to say, it will cover its costs for the week with no surplus.

How can the Centre maintain such low direct costs? The Centre benefits from its charitable status. It receives a lot of good will from those who work there. The Centre tends to attract staff who, by and large, are not primarily motivated by earning potential but by being able to gain experience in the work in which they believe. Moreover, the Centre has been the beneficiary of a charitable fund, the Planned Environment Therapy Trust, which has given various capital sums towards building projects and has also sponsored a number of guests with financial difficulties. Likewise, Project Arbours, a group of North London business people, raised the funds that allowed the original building to be purchased with the help of a mortgage. Volunteers are an integral part of the activities of the Centre. Students come from many different training institutions in the UK and abroad, with various clinical and academic backgrounds. They may be trainee psychiatrists, psychotherapists, social workers or nurses. They are intensively supervised and add a rich diversity to the input available to the guests. The Crisis Centre is also actively involved with the Middlesex University Nursing School, which offers training placements to their students.

Now let us think about indirect costs. The Centre gets its main income from providing services that are purchased by the NHS, Social Services or by private individuals. The mix of these three sources of income seems to be showing a gradual trend over the last ten years. The amount of NHS funding has been increasing, as has the number of guests arriving with funding provided jointly by a NHS Trust and by Social Services. The total amount of funding from Social Services has been gradually falling, and the private guest numbers have remained more or less constant. At the moment (2001) the NHS funding accounts for approximately 50 per cent of income; Social Services about 30 per cent; and the remainder is from private individuals. This trend towards an increase in NHS funding is probably a reflection of the political changes over the last two decades and the greater acceptance to contract-out treatment. The result is that, on average, one half of the guests at the Centre arrive following a psychiatric in-patient treatment (often long-term). This development may also be the result of better relations between the Centre and the psychiatric services. The Centre's PsychoSocial interventions have demonstrated over many years now that they can provide a successful alternative to hospital. Inevitably stays break down from time to time, and it is important that the Centre can refer the guest back to hospital temporarily and without delay. A good functioning relationship between the Centre, the guest and the referring consultant reduces splitting and is a powerful framework in which to contain projective processes. However, the net result is that the Centre receives progressively more chronic psychiatric patients. These are the patients that potentially incur the greatest indirect costs to society, through needing long-term financial and health support.

Is there any way to assess how the Centre has performed in the face of this gradual shift in the guest population? Remarkably our follow-up studies have shown that only 4 per cent of guests return to psychiatric hospital within a month of leaving the Centre. Unfortunately we do not yet have statistics for a longer follow-up period. Nevertheless, there are good grounds for confidence on this front. The Centre sponsors a Support Programme for prospective and former guests. It offers a twice-weekly session in art and group therapy. Long-stay guests who have been funded by the NHS are additionally funded to attend the Support Programme for a year following the end of their stay. Therefore, for these guests, we have good follow-up information, and the re-admission rate is very low. We likewise know what happens to those guests who leave the Centre and move to an Arbours long-stay community. Additionally, all guests are sent follow-up questionnaires at three months and a year, the return rate being about two-thirds. Consequently, we do have a good empirical basis to be confident in our outcomes, although the data obviously need to be collated and analysed statistically so that more detailed and significant results can be demonstrated.

A most significant fact is that over the past thirty years no-one has ever committed suicide while a guest at the Centre. Given the level of distur-bance of many of those who come for stays we feel that this alone validates the approach of the Centre. In this way the Centre has made huge savings for individuals, the family and the community at large.

An interesting cost–benefit analysis of in-patient treatment in America of schizophrenic patients using psychotherapy has been reported by Karon and Vandenbos (1981). They conclude from a study undertaken in the Detroit Psychiatric Institute that 'even a cursory scrutiny reveals that 75 per cent of the patients treated by medication alone received welfare benefits in the first 20 months of treatment as compared to 33 per cent of their randomly assigned comparisons who received psychotherapy' (Karon and Vandenbos 1981, pp.443–446). They also found that, after leaving treatment, those patients that were not receiving psychotherapy were subsequently hospitalized almost twice as much as those patients receiving psychotherapy. Further, they also found that the treatment costs of using experienced therapists were considerably lower than those using trainee therapists, if one assessed outcome over a longer period of 44 months and factored-in the cost of subsequent hospitalization.

To compare the direct costs of the Centre with the basic costs of a single acute psychiatric bed in the NHS is, as we said before, more difficult. Many variables influence the figure. However, if one looks at a range of estimates (Lelliot 1999) there seems to be a general convergence of opinion that the cost of one acute psychiatric bed is in the region of £50,000–£70,000 a year. Let us take the cost to be the mid-point of £60,000, which is £164 per day. While this figure is somewhat less than the Centre's fee of £200 a day, it places the Centre much closer to the NHS than to the private psychiatric hospitals. Moreover, we believe for the reasons already given that the savings on the indirect costs make the Centre highly effective as a treatment option, and in the longer term, cost-wise, make it highly competitive.

In the climate of cost awareness that now dominates the NHS, the onus is clearly on services to effect lasting improvement in their patients' psychological condition beyond the period of actual treatment, and to evaluate such treatment in financial terms. People suffering with psychotic or borderline disorders place a high demand on health, as well as on social and criminal justice services, all of which tend to get 'sucked in' in a reactive and unproductive way. The antisocial and destructive behaviour of such individuals often leads them to be considered as less deserving of health care provision. This view may be especially prevalent when budgets are limited and the use of resources has to be closely monitored and rationalized. But refusing to fund treatment is a false economy even if viewed solely in financial terms, as the untreated will continue to be a burden to family and society. In the words popularly attributed to John Ruskin: If you pay too much you may lose some money; if you pay too little you may lose everything. Losing everything in this context can mean suicide and death.

Above all the Crisis Centre cares about people – their humanity and self-respect. It is to be hoped that guests who leave the Centre feel 'richer' in different, often intangible ways. To this end the Centre offers diverse activities involving art, movement and drama. There are regular excursions as well as more adventurous trips, when resident therapists and guests alike have visited other centres abroad. Holiday times are special, and former guests are always welcome to return and join in the festivities. When a guest leaves the Centre there are a number of leaving rituals, including a meal into which a great deal of effort is put. None of this is seen as an 'extra'; rather it is viewed as an entitlement.

Similarly, 24-hour cover is achieved not through regimented work practices and complex shift rosters but through an ethos whereby the resident therapists treat the house as their home. The true value of our work is this attempt to humanize the essential contact between people. This is something we treasure but which can never be priced.

References

CIMA (Chartered Institute of Management Accountancy) (1992) *Foreword to the CIMA Management Accountancy Guides for the NHS: Return to the Capital Employed Techniques in the NHS.* CIMA.

Friedman, M. (1980) *Free to Choose.* London: Penguin.

Karon, B.P. and Vandenbos, G.R. (1981) *The Psychotherapy of Schizophrenia.* New York: Jason Aronson.

Lelliot, P. (1999) Letter from the Director, Royal College of Psychiatrist's Research Unit, London, *British Medical Journal*, Oct.

CHAPTER 18

The Hierarchical Authority Pyramid in a Therapeutic Milieu

Stanley Schneider and Rena Bina

In any group, large or small, one finds a built-in hierarchical structure that sets apart the staff from the group members. Needless to say, this dichotomy also exists in organizations, where there is a clear distinction between the directorate and subordinates. And, in fact, there are parallels between groups and organizational structures, including therapeutic milieux.

We want to conclude this book by exploring whether it is possible, or even desirable, to flatten the hierarchical authority pyramidal structure. One can take the position that clearly defined hierarchical roles are necessary in order to maximize efficient group behaviour. On the other hand, one can take the opposite position, such as at the Arbours Centre, that rigidity in structure and boundaries imposes a feeling of alienation, poor motivation for therapeutic work, and unwillingness to take responsibility for oneself; moreover, that it engenders feelings of guilt and inferiority. In order to understand the 'argument' here we will need to understand the unconscious processes that lurk within us.

We need to bear in mind that psychotic thinking – in those suffering from the psychoses as well as in others who are in unclear and unfamiliar situations – can leave the person with feelings of overwhelming power or powerlessness; an intense need to control or be controlled; impotence; or omnipotence. The collapsing of the hierarchical authority pyramid has implications for that psychotic part within all of us. It allows us to view the border between madness and normality; dictatorship and strong leadership; and breakdown of organizational authority and flexibility in the service of organization. To do this, we will look at some common elements found in 'groups', and 'milieux': hierarchical structure, boundaries, power, and authority. Our focus will be on therapeutic groups and the therapeutic milieu.

The treatment of persons with emotional disorders had always been situated in the domain of the medical profession. Since most hospitals followed the medical model, it has been very hard to break out of the dyad of doctor–patient; this can be seen in Freud's 'Papers on Technique' (Freud 1911–1915). This ideological framework of casting the patient in the guise of the passive recipient of the medical treatment at the hands of the all-knowing, all-giving and all-controlling doctor was questioned by some brave souls who fought for the humanity of the patient and the need to involve the patient in the treatment process.

In 1792 the local Quaker community in York, England, opened the York Retreat, where a treatment philosophy was developed that had a profound effect on the patients by investing in the power of the patients to control their disorders (*see further* Kennard 1983). Over the next 150 years there were some isolated efforts made to try to give patients some autonomy in engaging in their treatment. August Aichhorn (1925) made use of a manipulation of the environment in his work with wayward and institutionalized youth in Vienna. Among others, Bettelheim and Sylvester (1948) and Redl (1959) in the United States further developed Aichhorn's methods and psychoanalytic philosophy.

However, it was not until the writings of Tom Main (1946) and Maxwell Jones (1956) began to appear in professional forums that a philosophical and ideological approach was formulated. Main wanted to curb the anarchical rights of the doctor, and Jones wanted more patient involvement. Main was influenced by the pioneering group work of Bion (1948–1951) and Foulkes (1948). Jones was influenced by the American desire for democracy and humanism. The therapeutic institution (Main) or therapeutic community (Jones) was created!

In the late 1950s and early 1960s social scientists were starting to challenge existing treatment philosophies. As we have seen with work done at the Arbours and in other therapeutic milieu programmes, the therapeutic community model refers to a method of organizing the social structure of a treatment setting in order to engender and take advantage of natural social relationships and use them to enhance the therapeutic growth process. In therapeutic milieux the patients – or synonymous concepts such as 'clients', 'persons', 'group members', 'residents', or 'guests' – have

> now become active agents in the treatment process. Staff members make great efforts to flatten the traditional authority pyramid. There is an effort to develop a community cohesion by frequent community meetings, and the deployment of a patient government. In addition, there is more open communication between staff and patients and constant re-evaluation of roles and patterns of functioning. (Schneider 1978, p.4)

However, while philosophically and ideologically there are areas of overlap, therapeutic communities differ in their interpretation of how this democracy and shared treatment process is to be effectuated. There are some that are very liberal and allow the patient and doctor equal status in the decision-making process. There are others that are more judicious in their apportioning out of duties and responsibilities.

The uniqueness of the Arbours Centre as a therapeutic milieu is to be found in the special relationship that develops between resident therapists and patients or guests. At the centre of this relationship is the concept of hospitality, and through it the hardened role-relationships which may have been learned in previous treatments are avoided. It is this that creates the therapeutic process. 'Since 1970, Arbours has meant sanctuary, asylum and refuge for a large variety of people' (Berke, Masoliver and Ryan 1995, p.xiv). This chapter will explore how staff and clients, or guests, interact in the therapeutic process.

The 'activity' and/or 'passivity' of the players in this therapeutic encounter varies according to the philosophical orientation of the therapeutic milieu. We need to remember that 'milieu' comes from archaic roots meaning 'an alternative medium' (medius + lieu). This means that there may be many types of treatment for those in need of assistance. The therapeutic milieu offers an alternative medium in order to further the therapeutic work that needs to be done.

In order to arrive at a clearer analysis of the workings of therapeutic communities and milieux, we need to explore the collapsing of the hierarchical authority pyramidal structure. This includes looking at the relationships not only between patients and staff but also between the upper echelon administrative/clinical staff and the on-line staff. Technical neutrality is an interesting clinical concept in psychotherapy, implying that the treatment staff members need to distance themselves from the patients. How does this apply in a therapeutic community? Can staff be 'friendly' with patients or is there a hierarchical 'pecking-order'? Close friendships between staff and patients may hasten the therapeutic process, or, conversely, close friendships can contaminate the therapeutic process, interfering with transference dynamics. This needs to be addressed in the light of concepts of authority, power and hierarchy.

Authority is the right to assert control, and power is the possession of such control over others. Hierarchy, on the other hand, is the ranking of persons (or things), one above the other. In therapeutic milieux, all of these operate. Theoreticians in the fields of marital and family therapy have searched for ways of shifting the power distribution within their client groups in order to realign the unbalanced homeostasis. What is clear is that whoever holds the key to power is the one who is invested with some type of legitimate authority. In groups, therapeutic milieux and organizational structures it is understood that the one who controls – in the area of admissions and discharges; diagnoses and medication; and hiring and firing, for example – is the person of authority, who wields the wand of power. As Otto Kernberg states, 'authority is defined as the functional exercise of power within an institutional setting' (Kernberg 1998, p.127).

Many of the famous studies of psychiatric institutions in the 1960s and 1970s focused on how psychiatry can be abused both by conscious as well as unconscious processes. David Clark (1964) wrote a pioneering book in which he discussed the role of the medical doctor in the therapeutic community. He made the point that open communication was needed in order to change the traditional hospital attitude toward repressed communication, which had ultimate authority invested only in the ward doctor, who stood at the apex of the authority pyramid. He called this flattening of the authority pyramid. Change involved a risk of sorts. But, without the risk, the dangers of institutionalization with patients refusing (or being afraid) to take on any responsibility for their lives would foster regression, acting-out and negative therapeutic work. Those in the upper positions of authority on the authority pyramid needed to be reassured that the change towards democratization was not a 'putsch'.

In a therapeutic milieu staff members are invested with authority that places an onus of responsibility upon them for moving the treatment forward. Yet, this should not diminish the responsibility that is upon each individual member of the community or milieu. While authority may be delegated, it should not be imposed forcefully, and ways should be found to integrate both poles of the authority pyramid.

Otto Kernberg (1996) adds an important ingredient to the authority issue. He looks at the concept of 'technical neutrality', which is the way the analyst relates to the patient. (He discusses this concept not as a total blank screen and not as an anonymous entity, but as the position of the trained therapist who chooses what, when and how to reflect back or interpret to the patient.) Kernberg is a strong believer in 'functional authority': the analyst is the one in the position of authority placed there by the patient. The analyst needs to make decisions which are part of the delegated role. In groups and in therapeutic milieux, the concept of 'technical neutrality' takes on a more complex position because of the group matrix and the multiple transference figures that predominate. It is inevitable that the therapist's personality will play a role in the treatment process and will impact on the group members. However, 'the noncommunication of the analyst's own value system and life experience best protects the patient's freedom to arrive at his or her own conclusions through the understanding and resolution of unconscious conflicts' (Kernberg 1996, p.156).

What gives power to a group or organization is the decision-making capability. In groups and milieux the group conductor or staff members may be involved in a greater number of decision-making duties (i.e. responsibilities). If the clients have a large say in the decision-making process, that means that the staff have relinquished some of their decision-making control. In order for this to succeed, both staff and clients need to be accepting of the limits of power and control of both themselves as well as the other. What hinders collaborative efforts is the internal ego struggle that a person faces in trying to do what he or she thinks is best. The decision-making process centres more around narcissistic needs and what is best for the individual rather than around what is best for the 'collective'.

In re-designing hierarchical structures, the ultimate purpose is: to increase the milieu's ability to implement strategies and decisions. The issue of hierarchy ties in with the concept of boundaries. Boundary derives from the Anglo-French and Middle English *bounde*, which means something that indicates bounds or limits. However, the Semitic language root gives a richer, and more meaningful, definition. The word for boundary in Hebrew is *gevul*. This derives from the generic Semitic root word in Arabic, *jebel*, which means 'mountain'. For over two millennia land boundaries were defined by fixed physical terrain – mountains and rivers; that is, immovable objects. Interestingly, in both Hebrew and French the word for real estate is 'immovable property'. From here we derive our modern definition for boundary: up to a certain point and no further. We do not compromise with boundaries or limits: 'There is the need to set clear and understandable external boundaries and limits so that the person's internal boundaries and limits can resonate with the external ones' (Schneider and Cohen 1998, p.82).

Boundaries serve a very valuable function in separating spatially and emotionally. While group and milieu members may struggle to take on the conductor or staff members role, there is a strong feeling of safety in knowing that there are limitations. Only after experiencing external boundaries can internal ones be formed; hence the need to have clear and consistent limits. Following Kernberg's concept of 'technical neutrality', as discussed above, the fact that group members do not know personal details of staff members' lives allows them to introject and project onto and into the image that the staff member evokes for them in the transference.

In the therapeutic milieu we are constantly faced with the conflict concerning how much staff should allow patients or residents to be part of the therapeutic process. Needless to say this is bound up with feelings of self-esteem and self-worth, as well as with issues of control. At the Arbours Centre resident therapists need to gauge when to allow residents certain kinds of freedom without thereby empowering them to be 'junior therapists'. The residents need the feeling of security and containment. Yet within that 'holding' there is enough leeway for growth and risk-taking on both sides. Therapeutic work within a milieu requires consistent and understandable boundaries. Often the negotiation of boundaries between therapeutic staff and residents may be a necessary part of the therapeutic process. This negotiating posture allows both parties the mutual respect to be able to decide upon an appropriate boundary – one that both can live with. Further, it allows residents who have experienced inappropriate boundary setting in their lives (generally extremes of too much or too little) the important opportunity of experiencing boundaries that can be respected and adhered to. Negotiation in the treatment process is a key element in the resident therapist's ability to effect successful change in a client's more rigid self-perceptions and patterns of relationship formed in the past.

We think that, as Larry Hirschhorn has written, 'when people face uncertainty and feel at risk, they set up psychological boundaries that violate pragmatic boundaries based on tasks simply to reduce anxiety' (Hirschhorn 1995, p.32). While boundaries (and hierarchies) can be reassuring by allowing identification, and then internalization, there are downsides to them. Hirschhorn states:

> A boundary can create anxiety in three ways. First, when inappropriately drawn, it creates destabilizing tendencies so that people are unable to accomplish their tasks. Second, when appropriately drawn, the boundary may highlight the risks people face in trying to accomplish their tasks... Third, when appropriately drawn, the boundary may stimulate the feared consequences of one's own aggression or aggression from others. (Hirschhorn ibid., p.37)

So much for the pros and cons of hierarchical lines.

In groups as well as organizations we encounter the concept of 'risk'. People need to risk in order to grow, otherwise they face stagnation. To risk means putting oneself in a position of vulnerability; one is never sure how this will develop. One places oneself in such a situation because of being prompted by internal feelings and cues. This, of course, arouses anxiety, which in turn may mobilize aggression. In any flattening of the hierarchical authority pyramid, one needs to take risks which arouse anxiety. This raises questions as to whether flattening is the answer. Fears, anxiety and resistance intermingle.

Nowhere is this better seen than in Freud's concept of the death instinct. While this term has evoked considerable controversy, our intention is to suggest an understanding of the concept as a 'risking' of oneself in order to further grow emotionally. This growth is a complex network involving the patient, the staff, and the institutional organization. For, in therapeutic milieux, 'risks' – such as a striving for personal autonomy versus the potential for suicide or aggressive actions – need to be taken, and very often where one positions oneself on the scale of risk-taking reflects one's anxiety level and capacity for 'holding' and/or 'being held'. Staff members are willing to take risks on behalf of the guests' autonomy and personal growth, in spite of the great anxiety that is felt by them – especially residential therapists and team leaders. And although guests may exhibit severe disturbance, it is clear that they still feel the powerful containment and holding that the Arbours Centre provides.

This, in part, may contribute to the fact that in the 28 years that the Arbours Centre has been in operation, there has not been a single suicide.

J.C. Flugel (1953) begins his voluminous essay on the death instinct with the following 'disclaimer': 'There is little doubt that of all Freud's concepts, that of the death instinct has proved the most provocative and embarrassing both to its own disciples and to psychologists at large' (Flugel 1953, p.43). Part of the problem may possibly lie in Freud's poor choice of terms. When one sees the concept of death attached to an instinct, it raises the spectre of our being subject to the elements and Fate. It's as if we have no control over our destiny; we are being driven to suicidal, self-mutilating, masochistic, sadistic and destructive tendencies.

Historically, the Bible sets the stage for Freud's conceptualization by itself suggesting the existence of a life instinct and a death instinct. In the Book of Deuteronomy we find:

> Today I have set before you [a free choice] between life and good [on one side] and death and evil [on the other]... Before you I have placed life and death, the blessing and the curse. You must choose life, so that you and your descendants will survive. (30: 15,19)

While the Bible doesn't talk of instincts, there is the element of free choice that enables us as a species to choose either life or death. It is clear: there are two choices – and death is one of those choices.

The concept of the death instinct can help us understand the flattening of the hierarchical authority pyramid. In order to move the therapeutic group along better, the staff member needs to allow himself or herself to relate empathetically to the group members. In some way this means to lower his or her role as the *Übermensch* (in Freud's terms) but not totally to become part of the *Untermensch*. In a previous paper, Stanley Schneider noted that this risk involves resistance, fear and anxiety. Paternalistic feelings and attitudes may also play a role here. In trying to bridge the gaps between group members and staff, there is the risk that the group member may perceive the staff member as paternalistic and this may lead to a negative therapeutic reaction (Schneider 1999). The death instinct allows us another way of understanding how this potential risk can provoke the arousal of an internal drive or struggle to risk and potentially hurt oneself.

Regarding risk, in the sense of opening oneself up to exposure, scrutiny and criticism, Franz Alexander (1929) offers us an interesting metaphor:

If we want to enjoy anything, it means a sacrifice, and this sacrifice consists always of pain. If the tourist wants to enjoy the fine view from a summit, he must first toil up perspiringly, and moreover he has to pack his knapsack full if he does not want to freeze on the top, nor to have to enjoy his view in a hungry state. And in the same way every enjoyment on this planet of ours is tied up to a heavily-loaded knapsack. (Alexander 1929, p.259)

This sounds vaguely familiar to the American adage 'no pain, no gain', relating to the inevitable difficulty one has in exercising. Alexander's nice example makes eminent sense. However, with regard to the collapse of the hierarchical authority pyramid, one does not generally expect to enjoy more intense interactions with less structured boundaries and rigidity. Nonetheless, the fact that one needs to work hard in order to achieve something important and purposeful is a reality. So intensive interaction in a less stratified environment can be seen as a necessary pain in order to gain.

We need to address what appears to be a self-destructive drive on the part of those who choose the direction of flattening the hierarchical authority pyramid. If pain is necessary in order to grow and move forward, does this not border on a masochistic tendency that may have potential pathological attributes? Freud (1924) introduced the term 'moral masochism', where out of unconscious guilt one desires the position of victim, 'the suffering itself is what matters' (Freud 1924, p.165). On one hand 'the suffering' may be helpful in moving forward. However, this is fraught with the danger in that 'it originates from the death instinct' (Freud ibid., p.170).

Franz Alexander (1929) also noted: 'The psychic apparatus only takes upon itself the precise amount of self-restriction and suffering that is necessary, just as much as is absolutely essential for the attainment of instinctual gratification' (Alexander 1929, p.264). This would seem to imply that even while risk-taking and exposing oneself, one unconsciously has an innate ability to know the limits of how far to go. Even if the anxiety level is raised, one 'knows' how far one can be pushed.

No doubt, there are some who feel overwhelmed by the process and have difficulty to be able to think clearly, without feeling stuck. Stanley Schneider has referred to this as a reversion back to inflexible or constricted thinking (Schneider 1987). The emotional moment has such a forceful impact that the anxiety overloads the psychic evaluative mechanism, and may force one into a feeling of unreality mode. The resultant can go in either of two directions: one may feel blocked, unproductive and, therefore, guilty. Or, one can feel the need to push oneself forward in a sort of self-destructive pattern. Flugel (1953) observed: 'The death instinct, through its destructiveness when directed outwards, is thus ultimately responsible for anxiety' (Flugel 1953, p.54).

In our paradigm, if one feels too much distance in the relationship and process, one may feel isolated and alone. Feelings of persecutory anxiety take hold, and anger and feelings of retaliation are on the ascent. Similarly Melanie Klein (1948) writes of 'the relation between aggression and anxiety' (Klein 1948, p.290). Thus, a more libidinal relationship may still have anxiety as a component, but it will be more of the depressive anxiety kind. Klein's thinking continues (1932): 'The vicious circle dominated by the death-instinct, in which aggression gives rise to anxiety and anxiety reinforces aggression, can be broken by the libidinal forces when these have gained in strength' (Klein 1932, p.150).

In our understanding of the therapeutic milieu this would mean that a flattening of the authority pyramid would work if the libidinal expression in the relationship between resident therapist and guest is one of mutual respect and reciprocity. That is, it would be necessary for there to be a close interactive relationship based on clear and consistent boundaries, with judicious use of parameters. In order to monitor the relationship so that the empathic qualities needed for maintenance of the relationship and the growth that should occur in the therapeutic process are appropriately governed, there is a requirement for ongoing supervision and self-reflective introspection. In particular, this will help to gauge the countertransference and levels of projective identification.

Let us now provide some examples of how the flattening of the authority pyramid works:

1. The collapsing of the authority pyramid can have very positive ramifications for the guests. When staff members are closer to the guests, guests feel that they are part of the decision-making process that concerns their daily living activities, and they feel more independent. On the other hand, when there is a clear and rigid authority on the part of the professional staff, guests may feel they are in an inferior position, and may feel like institutionalized patients. In a half-way house, or any other type of rehabilitation facility, one of the goals is to bring the

guests to the point where they begin to feel independent and able to take control over their own lives. This can be done only when the authority is not rigid and the staff not distant from the guests.

When half-way houses first opened there was a clear pyramid of authority. For example, the staff decided what food will be eaten, and when, and who will prepare the food. After a while staff members realized that they were getting into too many arguments with the guests in relation to the food. This brought them to the decision to let the guests decide on their own what they would like to do about these issues. After a number of group discussions the guests decided on meal hours as well as arranging a rota for preparing the meals. From that point onwards there were no more arguments regarding meals.

2. The collapsing of the authority pyramid can be a problem when a staff member has low self-esteem, or is bombarded with feelings of projective identification on the part of the guest. In a case of this sort the professional staff member will have difficulty in placing boundaries for the guests, whenever they are needed. When staff and guests are on a more equal footing, there are less structured boundaries, and more reliance on guests' co-operation. In cases where a guest has difficulty co-operating, the staff member has to set clear and consistent boundaries. However, when a staff member is suffering from low self-esteem he or she will tend to be too pre-occupied with the threat perceived to be coming from the guest to be able to detach himself or herself with any ease from the situation and to put these boundaries in place for the guest. This will lead the staff member to become over-involved in the guest's inner world, rather than confronting the guest with reality.

Molly is a House Mother in a half-way rehabilitation home for emotionally disturbed women in Israel. She is 60 years old, and the ages of the women guests range from 20 to 55. Rachel is a 20-year-old woman who lives in the half-way house. It was Rachel's turn to prepare supper one evening with Molly's assistance. However, Rachel did not want to prepare supper, and Molly's persuasions did not help. Rachel began yelling that she didn't like Molly and her food and that's why she wouldn't prepare supper. Molly was very hurt and told Rachel that she would punish her because of her attitude. Molly's countertransference only made things worse, and she and Rachel got into a protracted argument.

In analysing this incident, we can note that Molly knew that Rachel constantly gets into arguments with her mother, with whom she does not get along. However, instead of detaching herself from the situation, and taking account of her feelings of countertransference, Molly felt personally very hurt, due to her low self-esteem and her thinking poorly of herself. Molly didn't realize that Rachel was projecting her feelings about her mother onto her. Molly's emotional turmoil couldn't allow her to deal with Rachel in a way that wouldn't make Rachel more upset, and Molly wasn't able to place rational, consistent boundaries for Rachel.

This example points to the important interface between the professional staff and the patients who are entrusted to their care. If the attitude of the professional staff is one of 'eliteness', then we feel that the empathic bond, that is so important for allowing treatment to foster and grow, will be adversely affected. The PsychoSocial model of rehabilitation that is part of the Arbours philosophy (as well as other quality rehabilitation programmes) requires that the empathic bond be the tool that allows movement and growth to occur. In effect, both the therapeutic staff as well as the patients (guests) gain from this intensive interaction. This model, in our opinion, is necessary for effective, humane treatment. Otherwise, we revert back to the old medical model of hierarchical power structures. This model has received reinforcement by the theoretical framework and underpinnings of the object relations and intersubjective schools of thought.

We see from the above that the strength of the relationship and the empathic feelings that are generated enable a mixture of the death and life instincts to come into being. The death instinct is necessary in order to propel one forward and enable one to risk and thereby grow emotionally and professionally. The life instinct is important as it allows one to find purpose in the therapeutic experience. Flugel (1953) commented: 'Pleasure accompanies successful striving while unpleasure results when striving is frustrated' (Flugel 1953, p.65). Reality governs the admixture of both pleasure and unpleasure, of both success and failure.

The above view relates to the philosophy of the Arbours Centre which has been reflected in this book. The treatment should be a 'treat' and not an excuse for deploying harm. Joy, smiles, laughter and lightness of heart in the context of an attentive and sympathetic relationship can lead the most despairing persons to reach 'beyond medication' or other invasive treatments. The ultimate aim is for them to regain a renewed sense of self and of life, and to live as far as possible 'beyond madness'.

References

Aichhorn, A. (1925) *Verwahrloste Jugend.* Leipzig: Internationaler Psychoanalytischer Verlag.

Alexander, F. (1929) 'The need for punishment and the Death-Instinct.' *International Journal of Psycho-Analysis 10*, 256–269.

Berke, J.H., Masoliver, C. and Ryan, T.J. (eds) (1995) *Sanctuary: The Arbours Experience of Alternative Community Care.* London: Process Press.

Bettelheim, B. and Sylvester, E. (1948) 'A Therapeutic Milieu.' *American Journal of Orthopsychiatry 18*, 191–206.

Bion, W.R. (1948–1951) 'Experiences in Groups.' *Human Relations, Vols I–IV*; repr. in W.R. Bion, *Experiences in Groups and Other Papers.* London: Tavistock.

Clark, D. (1964) *Administrative Therapy.* London: Tavistock.

Flugel, J.C. (1953) 'The Death Instinct, Homeostasis and Allied Concepts.' *International Journal of Psycho-Analysis 34* (Supplement), 43–73.

Foulkes, S. (1948) *Introduction to Group-Analytic Psychotherapy: Studies in the Social Integration of Individuals and Groups.* London: Heinemann.

Freud, S. (1911–1915) 'Papers on Technique.' *Vol 12: The Standard Edition of the Complete Psychological Works of Sigmund Freud.* London: Hogarth Press, 1981.

Freud, S. (1924) 'The Economic Problem of Masochism.' *Vol 19 The Standard Edition of the Complete Psychological Works of Sigmund Freud.* London: Hogarth Press, 1981.

Hirschhorn, L. (1995) *The Workplace Within: Psychodynamics of Organizational Life.* Cambridge, MA: MIT Press.

Jones, M. (1956) 'The Concept of a Therapeutic Community.' *American Journal of Psychiatry 112*, 647–650.

Kennard, D. (1983) *An Introduction to Therapeutic Communities.* London: Routledge and Kegan Paul.

Kernberg, O. (1996) 'The Analyst's Authority in the Psychoanalytic Situation.' *Psychoanalytic Quarterly 65*, 137–157.

Kernberg, O. (1998) *Ideology, Conflict, and Leadership in Groups and Organizations.* New Haven: Yale University Press.

Klein, M. (1932) *The Psycho-Analysis of Children.* New York: Delta, 1975.

Klein, M. (1948) 'On the Theory of Anxiety and Guilt.' In M. Klein, P. Heimann, S. Isaacs and J. Riviere, *Developments in Psychoanalysis.* London: Karnac, 1989.

Main, T. (1946) 'The Hospital as a Therapeutic Community.' *Bulletin of the Menninger Clinic 10*, 66–70.

Redl, F. (1959) 'The Concept of a Therapeutic Milieu.' *American Journal of Orthopsychiatry 39*, pp.721–734.

Schneider, S. (1978) 'A Model for an Alternative Educational/Treatment Program for Adolescents.' *Israel Annals of Psychiatry 16*, 1–20.

Schneider, S. (1987) 'Psychotherapy and Social Work Training: Individual Differences.' *Jewish Social Work Forum 23*, 38–48.

Schneider, S. (1999) 'Resistance, Empathy and Interpretation with Psychotic Patients.' In: V.L. Schermer and M. Pines (eds) *Group Psychotherapy of the Psychoses.* London: Jessica Kingsley Publishers.

Schneider, S. and Cohen, Y. (1998) 'Potential space in Milieu Therapy with Children and Adolescents.' *Therapeutic Communities 19*, 81–88.

CHAPTER 19

Conclusion

*Joseph H. Berke, Margaret Fagan, George Mak-Pearce
and Stella Pierides-Müller*

We believe that the work of the Crisis Centre and associated facilities over a period of almost thirty years demonstrates that the PsychoSocial approach to psychosis is clinically and cost effective. Perhaps more importantly, most guests leave the Centre with their dignity and self-respect intact, and with a greater degree of empowerment in their lives.

The Centre makes considerable efforts to follow up the men and women who have been at the Centre. Former guests receive an extensive questionnaire three months after they have left the Centre which gives them the opportunity to reflect on their stay and reply both qualitatively and quantitatively. There is also a brief follow-up questionnaire sent out after nine months.

One former guest wrote:

> Knowing someone was there to talk or comfort me at any hour if I needed, was a great comfort in itself. I was treated with kindness, gentle understanding and respect, and at no time did I feel like a patient. I responded quickly to the relaxed, calm atmosphere and found answers to questions that had kept me on edge for years. (Unpublished)

Another person simply stated that the Centre was a place where he 'didn't have to go mad'.

The Centre has carried out several major reviews over the years and is currently in the middle of a ten-year retrospective study of the work that took place during the 1990s. Preliminary results are consistent with earlier reviews, which show that most guests return home after being at the

Centre, and a smaller number go to an Arbours long-stay community or other community. On average about 4 per cent of residents require hospitalization. For years we felt a failure when this happened. But we discovered that some guests seemed to need a respite by returning to hospital, before becoming engaged with people at the Centre. This has happened enough times for us to recognize the countertransference currents of failure and worthlessness that hospitalizations engender.

We also recognize that the Centre's work needs a more focused and consistent degree of follow-up research, and that more time and effort needs to be put into this work in order to confirm the validity of our interventions. But there does exist a large body of very sophisticated research which demonstrates the effectiveness of PsychoSocial therapies. This is the work of Dr Loren Mosher and his colleagues, who initiated and developed the Soteria Project in the San Francisco Bay area of California in the 1970s and early 1980s. Initially they had been impressed by R.D. Laing's Kingsley Hall community in the late 1960s, and wanted to pioneer a kindred effort in the United States.

With the financial backing of the US National Institute of Mental Health, Mosher established a number of residential households where people who had entered a psychotic state could live and go through their psychotic experiences without receiving neuroleptic treatment. In many ways similar to the Arbours Centre, the Soteria Project differs, however, in that there are few direct psychodynamic interventions, and that the staff are mostly non-professionals who have been chosen for their ability to tune into the states of mind and being of the residents. Also the staff members rotate every few days, rather than using the houses as their home. A brief extract from a Soteria brochure illustrates the similarity of approach:

> It is believed that by allowing and helping the resident to gradually work with and through his crisis in living, or schizophrenia, he will be better able to understand himself, and his fears. So rather than ignoring, or quelling, this altered state, he will explore it, understand it, and finally learn from it. (Quoted in Berke 1979, p.167)

In the ensuing years Mosher and his colleagues have published over forty papers documenting the effectiveness of their 'unconventional' interventions, and challenging the prevalent wisdom of pharmacological and hospital-dominated treatments.

Most importantly, they were able to cross-correlate their results with a comparable cohort of patients in a nearby mental hospital. Thus, in one of their many reports they concluded:

> Specially designed, replicable milieus were able to reduce acute psychotic symptomatology within six weeks, usually without antipsychotic drugs, as effectively as usual hospital ward treatment that included routine neuroleptic drug use. (Mosher, Vallone and Menn 1995, p.157)

Sadly, Mosher points out that his studies have not been welcomed with open arms by the American mental health community. In fact his work has been generally ignored in the States, for it seems that no amount of methodologically rigorous research can have an impact when it runs against the 'prevailing biological zeitgeist' (Mosher and Bola 2000, p.68).

However, the Centre's work and Mosher's research are being confirmed by a slowly increasing stream of studies. Stanley Schneider has shown promising results at the Summit Institute in Jerusalem, Israel, which he directed for twenty-five years (Schneider 1978). Meanwhile more studies have been published showing the effectiveness of 'therapeutic community treatment' at the Henderson Hospital in Sutton, Surrey, and the Cassel Hospital in Richmond, Surrey, the progenitors of the therapeutic communities (Dolan, Warren and Norton 1997; Griffiths 1997). In addition Luke Chiampi has published a study of a Soteria-type project in Berne, Switzerland (Chiampi et al. 1992), and a five-year review has just been completed of the work at Varpen, Sweden, which Mats Mogren discussed in a early chapter in this book. This latest work was published by the Department of Psychology, Umeå University. It shows that residents of Varpen had 'remarkably large improvements in psychotic symptoms', with attendant major increases in self-esteem and social relations (Armelius et al. 2000).

These studies, which range over several decades and at least three continents, point to the validity and humanity of the PsychoSocial approach. They encourage the Centre in the aims which we articulated at the beginning of our project, and which we have managed to achieve, if not with all the guests who have stayed at the Centre at least with many of them:

> We intend that the Centre should be a place where people may encounter selves long distorted and forgotten, where they can contain and regain their experiences, and achieve a sense of integrity and autonomy. In

other words our task is to enable them to perceive and apperceive reality and to dream the dreams which are truly their own. (Berke *et al.* 1995, p.xviii)

References

Armelius, B. *et al.* (2000) *A 5-Year Study of Patients and Staff at Varpen Therapeutic Community, 1993–1998.* Umeå, Sweden: The Department of Psychology, Umeå University.

Berke, J. (1979) 'I Haven't Had to Go Mad Here.' Harmondsworth: Pelican Books.

Berke, J., Masoliver, C. and Ryan, T. (1995) *Sanctuary: The Arbours Experience of Alternative Community Care.* London: Process Press.

Chiampi, L. *et al.* (1992) 'The Pilot project: "Soteria Berne": Clinical Experiences and Results.' *British Journal of Psychiatry, 161* (suppl. 18), 145–153.

Dolan, B., Warren, F. and Norton, K. (1997) 'Change in Borderline Symptoms One Year After Therapeutic Community Treatment for Severe Personality Disorder.' *British Journal of Psychiatry 171,* 274–279.

Griffiths, P. (1997) *Psychosocial Practice within a Residential Setting.* London: Karnac Books.

Mosher, L. and Bola, J. (2000) 'The Soteria Project: Twenty Five Years of Swimming Upriver.' *Complexity and Change 9,* 1, 68–74.

Mosher, L., Vallone, R. and Menn, A. (1995) 'The Treatment of Acute Psychosis without Neuroleptics: Six-Week Psychopathology Outcome Data from the Soteria Project.' *International Journal of Social Psychiatry 41,* 3, 157–173.

Schneider, S. (1978) 'A Model for an Alternative Educational/Treatment Program for Adolescents.' *Israel Annals of Psychiatry 16,* 1, 1–20.

Epilogue

Brian Martindale

Retaining or even attaining meaningful emotional contact with persons suffering from psychosis or borderline psychosis requires a great struggle with opposing forces that come from many sources. Some of the most important hurdles are those within all of us human beings, but it is important not to minimize the problems of our contemporary cultural climate, in which there are relentless pressures to view persons with psychosis as victims of only genetic and chemical disturbances.

The work of the Crisis Centre stands out proudly as a beacon pointing in a very different direction. The provision of an ordinary house setting for both living and understanding, independent of the health service, is an approach that has continued to develop considerably over nearly three decades. This is no mean achievement in view of the many opposing forces.

Fortunately the cultural tide and even that of the mental health field seem to be just beginning to turn and to be more favourable. This is partly a result of the fact that families and persons who have suffered from psychosis are now beginning to find healthy voices of protest at their experience of 'treatment'. Before the advent of neuroleptics in the 1960s, there seems to have been a reasonably widespread network of professionals (especially in the United States) who were able to use psychoanalytic insights to try to stay in emotional contact with persons with psychotic problems. Nowadays an international network – the ISPS (International Society for the Psychological Treatments of Schizophrenia) – is gathering momentum. (See http://www.isps.org for more information.)

However, during these decades of the brain – which have been such dark times for psychological approaches to psychosis – it is salutary to note that there is good evidence that the prognosis for schizophrenia has often been better in developing countries than that of developed countries (Jablensky *et al.* 1992). This is in spite of the advent of neuroleptics! This disturbing fact can probably be explained by a greater acceptance of these persons as persons in the developing countries, with the greater likelihood that they will be given a positive role in the community in contrast to Western attitudes that currently are only likely to compound their alienation.

There are now quite large numbers of studies trying to evaluate some of the newer psychotherapeutic interventions (such as cognitive behavioural treatment) for psychotic problems, and some have compared the intervention not only with 'treatment as usual' but also with some sort of 'non-specific befriending' or 'supportive intervention'. Overall, the statistical conclusion is that it is hard to find significant differences between an intervention such as CBT and those classed as supportive interventions, though both tend to be clearly better than 'treatment as usual' (Sensky *et al.* 2000; Tarrier *et al.* 1998). This tells us that the treatment relationship aspect of 'treatment as usual' is really very poor and lacks even basic empathic contact on a regular basis.

If even basic unsophisticated empathic human contact improves the psychotic condition – how much more do people benefit from the intensive interest, concern and constant attempts to understand that are the central planks of the Arbours approach, combined with all that goes with the 'close to normal' living environment of the Crisis Centre?

The strengths of this book are the detailed descriptions of those intense human encounters that take place within the Centre and the accounts of the careful use of containing structures of human relationships with staff and fellow residents that have evolved to enhance reflective capacities. Though the Centre, like many therapeutic communities, had a particularly gifted pioneer and founder, its continuing achievements must surely be due to the profoundly useful insights into psychotic and borderline psychotic functioning that stem from contemporary psychoanalysis. It is this theoretical underpinning, its evolution, and of course its practical application that should be of great assistance in ensuring the Centre's longevity.

With both its solid theoretical identity and clear practical framework for its application, it is going to be vital that the Crisis Centre continues to develop pertinent educational and other means that demonstrate to a wide audience the importance of its work and its relevance to other mental health settings. This book will play a most important part in that educative role. As stated at the beginning of this epilogue, there are tremendous hurdles to be overcome at all levels of our contemporary Western societies if those vulnerable to psychotic retreats are to have the optimum chances to find a meaningful life within those societies.

Although the Crisis Centre itself is in many ways unique, a number of centres around the world have now been established with not too dissimilar treatment philosophies. The further development of relationships between these centres will be very helpful in expanding the opportunities to inform and educate both the wider public and interested professionals as to ways in which our mental health services can be greatly improved by PsychoSocial interventions and rendered therapeutic for this group of fellow human beings.

References

Jablensky, A., Sartorius, N., Ernberg, G., *et al.* (1992) *Schizophrenia: Manifestation, Incidence and Course in Different Cultures.* Psychological Medicine Monographs, *Suppl. 20.* Cambridge: Cambridge University Press.

Sensky, T., *et al.* (2000) 'A Randomised Controlled Trial of Cognitive-Behavioural Therapy for Persistent Symptoms in Schizophrenia Resistant to Medication.' *Archives of General Psychiatry 57*, 2, 165–172.

Tarrier, N. *et al.* (1998) 'Randomised Controlled Trial of Intensive Cognitive Behaviour Therapy for Patients with Chronic Schizophrenia.' *British Medical Journal 317*, 303–307.

Subject Index

Note: 'Arbours Crisis Centre' is abbreviated to 'Centre', apart from the main entry where it is named in full.

Author Index